The Friendly Enemy

Adult Reference Book

Lorraine Fast

Content Editor: Dr. Jamie C. Lee, DNP, APRN-BC

Dr. Lee is a licensed, board-certified Child and Adolescent Psychiatric Clinical Nurse Specialist. She holds a Doctor of Nursing Practice degree, a Master of Science in Psychiatric Nursing and an Associate of Science in Nursing. She is a lecturer and teacher in the School of Nursing at Kennesaw State University.

Technical Advisor: Jessie Richards, MSW

Ms. Richards is retired, with over thirty years experience from the Department of Juvenile Justice for the State of Georgia. She holds a Masters of Social Work degree, is a Criminal Justice Specialist, a Certified Forensic counselor and a Human Services provider. Jessie co-authored The Friendly Enemy Adolescent Workbook and helped develop the programs and seminar presentation materials.

Literary Editor: Lynn B. Pugh

Lynn Pugh has over fifteen years experience integrating information into publishing formats. She serves writers, organizations, and publishers throughout the United States and offers a wide variety of editing, writing, coaching, and publishing services. Lynn's brand, Mrs. Wordswork says ... I can help your words work for you. www.MrsWordswork.com

Published by Yawn's Publishing
210 East Main Street
Canton, GA 30114
www.yawnsbooks.com

ISBN: 978-0-9834910-2-6

Printed in the United States

1983 First Edition
2003 Second Edition
2011 Third Edition

DEDICATION

I dedicate this workbook to my husband Joel, who stands by me, encourages me, and together with me gives all the glory to God; to my sons, Ray, David and Daniel and my grandchildren, James, Paul, Joshua and Jordan who motivate me and bless my socks off. Special thanks to my dear friend Vicki, the first person who read this book and found her way back from her own personal hell as a victim of incest; and for all of the wonderful, brave, and unselfish people, both young and grown, who have shared their stories with us so that others can find the same courage—to come out of the murky shadows of sexual abuse and exploitation and take steps toward forgiveness, healing, and productivity—you make this work possible.
I could not have done this without you.

Thanks!

Lorraine

God help those who still struggle with the demons of abuse.

NOTE FROM THE AUTHOR

My life-long work is to create a resource for the general population to learn how to protect children from becoming victims of one of the most degrading crimes against the human race; and for the scores of professionals who work for the healing, health, and welfare of youth and adult victims of childhood sexual abuse and exploitation.

This informative book is factual, yet easy to read. Each chapter covers a different aspect of sexual abuse. The information can be accessed according to the reader's specific concerns.

In addition to *The Friendly Enemy Adult Workbook*, we have created workbooks for children as well as adolescents. Our goal is to make it possible for people around the world to be aware of this serious problem and to prevent child sexual abuse and exploitation.

It takes all of us to make a difference.

Lorraine M. Fast

ACKNOWLEDGEMENTS

I wish to acknowledge Dr. Jamie Lee and Jessie Richards, MSW for their many years of encouragement, professional guidance, and undying loyalty and support.

Thanks to Clint Beckett and Lauretta Hannon for their persistent cheerleading and for knowing when I needed it the most.

For those who give so much—many thanks to: my sister Joan, for never allowing me to give up; Jan Dalton for all the prayers; Sandy Cwach for the technical support in production; Rhonda Durham for her amazing prophesy about *The Friendly Enemy;* Lynn Pugh for her professional editing assistance; and to the multitude of people who attend our training seminars and go forth empowered and ready to fight the good fight.

You're The Best!

Lorraine

TABLE OF CONTENTS

FORWARD

INTRODUCTION

FORWARD

Children... the very word brings to our hearts and minds feelings and thoughts of great intensity. Love, beyond our own understanding or reason. Joy, so close to perfection it inspires thoughts of Heaven. Like a mother lion protecting her young, our love is so intense, we would give up our own lives to insure that no harm comes to our children.

If you ask a parent to what measure they would go to protect his or her child, the answers obtained would vary greatly and perhaps tilt toward socially unacceptable behavior, even illegal acts. Some may be able to name what type of dangers would provoke such consequences, and this is justifiable, righteous anger. Yet, sad to say, a malignant enemy we rarely think of as comfortably imbedded into our day-to-day lives and this ever-present and unimaginable danger is stalking our children.

There are secret threats our children fall prey to, through no fault of their own. Unsuspecting enemies, whose actions have declared they will do grave harm to our young, are causing damaging life-long effects to body, mind, and soul.

This enemy we are speaking of is friendly, completely acceptable in everyday society, and may even be an established leader in the community where we live. Some are professionals in which we place our trust for physical care or spiritual growth, members of every profession, socio-economic class, education level, neighborhood, color, creed, and belief system. Some live in our own homes. They are often intelligent, extremely charming, and have an excellent rapport with children. Some are positioned as pillars of the community and by all outward appearances, pleasant and helpful to everyone they know.

Regrettably, these friendly enemies are not thought of as a threat. They often inflict their crimes without hindrance because we fail to notice changes in a child's behavior. We need to listen to that "still small voice," and that "gut feeling" when something does not seem quite right.

Pedophiles are in our communities. We pass them on the street, or meet them as we go about our daily activities. Their deeds are unknown to us, yet they smile, converse, and weave their webs of deceit with ease, knowing their evil acts will change our children's lives forever.

Masters of manipulation, they are secretive and select their victims in advance of the molestation, watching and planning, they fantasize their future acts with the intended target. Some have the patience of Job; others are bold as a burglar entering a fully occupied home in bright daylight. Usually the crime has been committed; the damage done—an evil perpetration of a child—long before parents or caretakers notice the subtle changes indicative of the problem that the child is facing. It can happen suddenly.

A normally gentle, loving, and snuggly child of yesterday is transformed into an angry, hostile, raging, out of control, weepy, clinging, or fearful child.

Far too many parents will never know the cause of this sudden change in their "babies." This is due to the child's fear of telling, their innocence or inability to understand what is happening. They simply are not mature enough, nor equipped to explain the acts forced upon them; therefore, unable to verbalize a concept for which they have no reference point. If the victim is older, they may feel shame or embarrassment thinking they did something wrong. This can lead to a form of self-hatred that is so deeply rooted it has the ability to destroy their health or hope for a happy future.

Loving your children is simply not enough. As with everything today, we must be aware, educated, and armed with the newest information. In America, and around the world, we see an ever-changing world of technology, constant financial tensions, and drastic changes in our children's education. All of which affects our communities. We have many decisions to make. This means we must use our intellect, common sense, and courage and be sensitive to hear when our inner voice is trying to tell us something. Pay attention and use the tools the Good Lord gave us; heed the warning symptoms of impending, very real, very close danger to our precious children.

As a survivor of some of the horrific things you will read of, I bring you this workbook designed to give hope that with the help of God, you can know you did all you could to protect your children and there is a brighter tomorrow ahead.

The Friendly Enemy Adult Workbook will educate you through facts, not rumor, and lead you to an enlightened and improved safety in your lives and in the lives of those you love.

May God bless you as you read further. Please stay in prayer; you may find occasions in which you will need it when delving into the heinous world of this enemy.

Vicki Lynn

This book is uncluttered and insightful. I was relieved to find that it didn't include testimonials or grotesque details of the actual act of pedophilia, since this is unnecessary.

I was further gladdened that I did not have to relive any unbearable childhood memory in order to get to the meat of this book. At one point, it actually enlightened me about where my emotional maturity was initially crippled.

I found hope as I became more knowledgeable about this friendly enemy, exposed as a spirit that creeps through generations, hiding itself in secrets and acts of darkness.

My biggest fear is that one of my children would fall prey to this evil. In order to deal with this enemy, we must expose him. Lord, help me to do this. I believe this book is effective and grateful that the author is compassionate and delivers a clear message from beginning to end. Lorraine Fast defends our most treasured ones, and not without love for the enemy. In this way, she certainly heaps many coals upon his head.

A Victim

The truth about our childhood is stored up in our body and although we repress it, we can never alter it. Our intellect can be deceived, our feelings manipulated, our perceptions confused, and our body tricked with medication. But someday the body will present its bill, for it is as incorruptible as a child who, still whole in spirit, will accept no compromises or excuses, and it will not stop tormenting us until we stop evading the truth.

Miller, 1986

INTRODUCTION

As a homemaker and stay-at-home mom, I found friends and relatives consistently came to me with a request—to talk to their children about some things many parents have difficulty discussing: puberty, self-esteem issues, peer pressures, and of course, the subject of sex. Somehow, I was able to convey the right words without stumbling too clumsily, and thankfully, the message came out—loud and clear.

In 1982, I decided to write a series of small books on how to effectively talk to children about these sensitive, but necessary issues. I began my research on the topic of sexuality, knowing this was a hot topic with the kids. When I came across a word I was unfamiliar with, "pedophilia," I looked it up in my dictionary and became physically ill at the thought of what this word implied. Disgusted, I tried to push it out of my mind. But I found that ignoring it was like trying to ignore being in the path of a ravaging tornado.

I engaged in intensive research and located a support group, **Societies League Against Molestation** (SLAM). My life has not been the same since I began interviewing child victims of sexual abuse, adults who were sexually abused as children, family members of the child sexual abuse cases, and many professionals who work to help these brave individuals. I witnessed many survivors climb out of the pit they had been cast into by pedophilia (child sexual abuse). Once I realized the enormity of this problem, I continued working with local police departments as well as county, state, and federal agencies fighting this heinous crime.

A year into my crusade, I was able to sit down long enough to write the first edition of *The Friendly Enemy*. Upon sharing my manuscript with one of my dearest friends, I experienced first-hand the terrible, sick feeling that comes when you find out someone you love is a victim of child sexual abuse. Vicki Lynn read only a few pages, then burst into tears and ran from the room. Surprised, and a little frightened by her reaction, I quickly followed and found her huddled in a corner. I knew right away, and my heart sunk as I realized her pain—she had experienced the things described in my book. I made up my mind at that very moment. I would do everything possible to make this information available to everyone and committed to this life-long work to stop this insane nightmare.

I shared the first edition of *The Friendly Enemy* with friends, neighbors, my children's teachers, and with practically anyone who would listen. Some parents of victims begged me to get this information out there, for everyone to know. Copies of the book went to support groups, battered women's shelters, and parents who recognized this dangerous problem does exist.

Today, news and media sources expose child sexual abuse and exploitation, which has resulted in greater public awareness of this horrific danger to children. In 2004, I took a giant step and promoted my extensive research and work in this field. Our message was now met with more acceptances and I began teaching The Friendly Enemy Workshops and Seminars.

A few years later, I began updating the original 86-page book to include more of the pertinent information the public needs to know. The guide you hold today contains nearly 300 pages of valuable information, awareness, and prevention tips for child sexual abuse and exploitation.

We were pleased when the seminars and books gained success and received encouraging reviews. But in my heart, I knew that this information—a massive compilation of material from every corner of the globe—needed to be put into the hands of all people who care about our children.

Millions of children and families are suffering unspeakable torment and pain; pain that will not go away until we are all educated and armed with how to recognize, treat, and hopefully prevent child sexual abuse. Every two minutes there is a victim of child sexual abuse. You may be shocked to learn this statistic includes sexual acts on newborn infants.

This revised edition of The Friendly Enemy is dedicated to children throughout the world. Our hope and prayer is that this work will prove to be a light in the darkness for those who have suffered and that we may find a way to prevent children from ever experiencing the nightmare of pedophilia.

Chapter One

CHILD SEXUAL ABUSE—HOW SERIOUS IS IT?

Who Is The Friendly Enemy?

Vicki was only three years old when her mother married the man who would become her biggest nightmare. As was his plan, her new father began grooming her as his "little princess." Throughout the early years, this clever pedophile inflicted tremendous emotional pain and stress upon his fragile wife. Eventually, he was able to commit Vicki's mother to a mental institution and he initiated the devious deeds he had planned for so long. In the darkness, on the most dreaded night of her life, thirteen-year-old Vicki felt her father embrace her in a way that made her blood run cold. She tried to fight him off, crying loudly with alarm, "Daddy, you're supposed to love me. Why are you doing this to me?" He forced her to cooperate with him with threats to institutionalize her mother for the rest of her life. She was just a child and believed whatever he told her. Off and on, for years to come, he re-committed Vicki's mother to mental institutions as he continued to have his way with his little princess.

The following statement was made by a nepiophile (sexually attracted to toddlers and infants) on a website where like-minded deviants express themselves freely:
I would like to say that I am happy being a pedophile, as well as a "nepi," and think that there is nothing wrong with our love and fantasies towards children—just as long as we never act on it without the child's say or consent and sometimes not even then. I just love being who I am and I love that there are places like this website where I can come and tell my story.
Sexual assault continues to represent the most rapidly growing, violent crime in America, claiming a victim every four seconds. (1)

Reported cases of child sexual abuse reached epidemic proportions, with a 322% increase from 1980 to 1990. (2)

The National Center for Child Abuse and Neglect (NCCAN) receives greater than 300,000 reports of sexual abuse against children each year. This is in addition to over 1,700,000 reports involving other forms of child abuse and neglect. An estimated 89,000 cases of child sexual abuse were substantiated in 2000. (3)

There are an estimated sixty million survivors of childhood sexual abuse in America today. (1)

The Department of Justice estimates approximately 450,000 convicted pedophiles currently reside in the United States, averaging one per square mile. (4)

A typical sex offender molests an average of 117 children. Most of these children do not report the offense to anyone. (5)

Legal Definition Of Child Sexual Abuse:

In most states, the legal definition of child sexual abuse is: an act of a person, adult, or child, which forces, coerces, or threatens a child to have any form of sexual contact or to engage in any type of sexual activity at the perpetrator's demand. (6)

Definitions Of Sexual Offenders:

The different terms we use to define a child sexual offender depends on the age of the child and the characteristics of the offender. For instance, a person who exclusively prefers children as sex partners are called a pedophile; whereas, a person who has no age preference and will molest a child or an adult is legally referred to as a child sexual molester.

Pedophile:

Taken from the Latin translation—pedo, meaning child, and phile, meaning lover of, or one having a strong preference for. The word pedophile is used for a lover of children. The pedophile has developed a sexual interest in children that ranges from fondling to mutilation and murder. (7)

Pedophilia:

Psychosexual disorder in which there is a preference for sexual activity with prepubescent children. (8)

Lolita Complex:

A term sometimes used to refer to an adult male attracted to adolescent females, as in the 1955 novel by Vladimir Nabokov about a gifted and seductive adolescent girl. (9)

Nepiophilia:

Or infantophilia, is the sexual attraction to toddlers and infants (usually ages 0–3). Some researchers suggest there is a distinction between pedophilia and nepiophilia, especially for same-sex pedophilia, as it is unusual for pedophiles to prefer toddlers. (10)

The US Dept. of Justice, Bureau of Justice reports statistics on child sexual abuse. (11)

- One in four girls and one in six boys will be sexually abused
- 10–20% of all boys are sexually abused in some way
- 67% of victims of sexual assault are juveniles
- 34% of sexual assault victims are under age twelve
- One in seven victims of sexual assault is under age six
- 40% of offenders who victimize children under age six are juveniles under the age of nineteen
- 1 in 4 adult women were sexually abused in their childhood. This crime is under-reported and the statistic is likely much higher. In the highest percentage of the reported cases, the perpetrator is a male adult. (11)
- The average age for reported abuse is 9.9 for boys and 9.6 for girls. Victimization occurred before age 8 for 22% of the boys and 23% of the girls. The majority of abuse (both boys and girls) came from offenders 10 or more years older than their victims. Girls were more likely than boys to disclose the abuse. (12)

The Act of Child Sexual Abuse:

American Humane notes the most extreme act of child sexual abuse includes sexual intercourse and acts of perversion. All offences involving sexually touching a child and sexual exploitation are harmful and devastating to a child's well-being. (13)

CHILD SEXUAL ABUSE INCLUDES
TOUCHING AND NON-TOUCHING OFFENSES

Touching Offenses:

- Being touched and fondled in sexual areas, including kissing in a sexual way
- Forcing a child or youth to touch another person's sexual areas
- Oral sex—when the mouth touches sexual areas: the penis, vagina, anus, or breasts. Many children believe that oral sex means to "talk dirty"
- Commercial exploitation through prostitution or the production of pornographic materials
- Intercourse—penetration vaginally, anally, or orally; can be with body parts and/or objects (the most common body parts used are the fingers, tongue, and penis)
- Frotteurism—the act of obtaining sexual stimulation by rubbing against a person or object
- Touching and fondling of genital areas was the most common form of substantiated abuse, involving 65% of sexual abuse cases. (14)
- Intercourse, both attempted and actual, accounts for 35% of the substantiated sexual abuse cases. (14)

Non-Touching Sexual Offenses:

- Masturbating in front of a child
- Talking to a child about sex—intrusive questions or suggestive comments in verbal conversations, on the computer, texting, other forms of writing, and by obscene phone calls
- Deliberately exposing a child to the act of sexual intercourse
- Exposing children to sexually explicit or pornographic material on TV, videos, magazines, billboards, photographs, etc. These can be shown in person, on the computer, cell phone, email, and other ways through the media and internet
- Exhibitionism—a perversion in which sexual gratification is obtained from the indecent exposure of one's genitals

Sexual parts of the body include buttocks, anus, genital areas, vulva, vagina, penis, scrotum, breasts, and mouth. [14]

Adults exposing genitals to a child accounted for 12% of substantiated sexual abuse cases [14]

Characteristics And Behavioral Indicators Of A Pedophile:

- Pedophiles can be either male or female, and any age.
- Most often, they are adult males.
- Some are married, some are single.
- Pedophiles who marry have a purpose, they want to appear as a responsible adult and avoid suspicion.
- Pedophiles often use their own children to lure potential victims. In this way, they can easily target the children of other family members, friends, or neighbors.
- In cases of juvenile sex offenders, the targeted victims may be siblings. [12]
- Child sexual abusers work in all occupations, from unskilled laborers to celebrities, to corporate executives, community leaders, authorities, and political figures.
- They often seek employment or volunteer roles in programs for children, making it easy for them to select victims.
- Pedophiles usually relate better to children than to adults
- Child sexual abusers can have specific age or gender preferences.
- Some commit offenses exclusively as homosexuals or heterosexuals while others are attracted to either gender [15]
- They frequently take photographs and collect a wide variety of children, in full-dress, various degrees of nudity, and engaged in sexually explicit acts.
- They collect child erotica and child-adult pornography for several purposes. When they see others engaged in these acts, it helps them to legitimize their evil deeds. In addition, the pornographic material excites them when no victim is available. They show pornographic images to others to help lower his or her inhibitions and they use it to blackmail victims into secrecy.

- It is common for pedophiles to give alcohol and drugs to their victims to lower their resistance and inhibitions.
- Pedophiles are often intelligent enough to recognize that they have a problem and they understand the severity of it.
- They will go to great lengths to conceal their illegal, immoral activity.
- Often, they will try to justify their criminal acts by telling themselves this type of sexual activity has a positive impact on the victim, thus, repressing responsible feelings for the harm they are doing.
- A pedophile is a manipulator and a liar who will often depict the child as the aggressor. This usually occurs after the child realizes that when they perform sexual favors, they can get whatever things they desire such as toys, money, or trips.
- This deviant will refer to children in a similar manner as normal adults who speak of an adult lover or spouse.
- Often they themselves are child molestation victims and frequently seek children at the age or stage of physical development at which they were molested.
- Pedophiles often seek out publications and organizations that support their sexual beliefs and practices.
- They usually correspond with other pedophiles and exchange child pornography and erotica.
- Many are non-violent and have few problems with the law. In most cases, pedophiles are respected community members.
- Approximately 71% of child sex offenders are under age 35 and know the victim, at least casually.
- About 80% of these individuals fall within normal intelligence ranges and 59% gain sexual access to their victims through seduction or enticement. (16)

As we define the various <u>Types Of Child Sexual Offenders</u>, Note that different types of offenders have various identifying characteristics:

Those who have committed sexual crimes against children, but do not have the typical characteristics that define pedophilia, are referred to as situational, opportunistic, or regressed offenders. (17)

According to **The Occult and Violent Ritual Crimes Research Center**, there are some significant differences in the characteristics of the situational or regressed offender and the fixed or fixated pedophile. (18)

<u>The Regressed Offender:</u>

Psychologically, the regressed offender considers the child as a pseudo (imaginary) adult. Because the victim is young, immature, and vulnerable, the abuser is able to be in control. This causes the perpetrator to feel adequate and secure. The offender finds a comfort zone in the abusive relationship where he or she can avoid coping with any overwhelming trauma in their life. This type of abuse is generally impulsive rather than premeditated. Often this type of child molester is married and living with his family, but

5

the circumstances of his life propels him into a state of mind in which he feels more comfortable in the presence of children, leading to the child sexual abuse." [18]

The regressed sexual molester will not only molest children but will also abuse the elderly, the impaired or the sick.

The regressed offender has been traditionally involved with adults in normal relationships, and certainly, some interpersonal problems exist, but from an outward perspective, they have no great problems in relating with adults on a personal level as well as sexual relationships.

The regressed molester may collect child pornography but is not as likely as the fixated pedophile to do so.

The regressed offender will begin offending in adulthood rather than in their early years, often victimizing children within the family.

In the typical scenario of the regressed offender, feelings of inadequacy, helplessness, and vulnerability immerge, induced by emotional trauma resulting from conflict, separation, divorce, illness, or death. Reacting to his or her loss, the regressed pedophile may spontaneously introduce an inappropriate sexual dimension into an otherwise platonic relationship with a child.

According to Holmes and Holmes, the regressed offender is more apt to sexually abuse children he does not know and the children are typically victims of opportunity. In addition, this adult is more apt to sexually abuse females. He may also have some problems with alcohol abuse and probably has low self-esteem.

Regressed child offenders are more apt to be geographically stable. The fixated offender may move from one area of the country to another in his search for victims, taking some time in each area to cultivate and find children to victimize.

The Fixed Or Fixated Pedophile:

Offenders primarily attracted toward only children are called structured, preferential, or fixated pedophiles, as their orientation is fixed by the makeup of their personality. It is estimated that 2 to 10% of perpetrators of child sexual abuse meet the regular criteria for pedophilia. [17]

Unlike the regressed offender who begins offending in adulthood, the fixed pedophile characteristically begins offending at an early age, and commonly has a larger number of victims who are frequently, but not always, outside the family. Fixed pedophiles also have more of an appetite to offend having values or beliefs that strongly support an abusive lifestyle. [19]

Fixed pedophiles prefer children as the providers of personal and sexual gratification. [18]

The Situational Or Regressed Offender:

He or she typically has fewer victims than the preferential or fixed type.

The situational or regressed child abuser does not have an exclusive interest in children but, under stress, will typically revert to children.

The Following Comments Are Written By Sex Offenders In Treatment: [20]

- I can be a parent, stepparent, relative, friend of the family, teacher, clergyman, babysitter, or anyone who comes in contact with children.
- I am can be stable, employed, and a respected member of the community.
- My education and my intelligence don't prevent me from molesting your child.
- I convince your child they are responsible for my behavior.
- I make your child think no one will believe them if they tell.
- I tell your child you will be disappointed in them for what they have done "with" me.
- I warn your child that they will be punished if they tell.
- I may threaten your child with physical violence, towards them, a pet, or a person they love.
- I can make your child feel sorry for me.
- I may "accidentally" expose myself or walk in on children when they are changing clothes or in the bathroom.
- I may use situations like tucking kids in at night to touch them sexually.
- I have told my own children "this is normal; this is what all fathers do."
- I am so good at manipulating children. I can convince them to protect me, because they love me.
- I am probably well known and liked by you and your child.
- I can be a man or woman, married or single.
- I can be a child, adolescent, or adult.
- I can be of any race, hold any religious belief, and have any sexual preference.
- I can be anybody.

Abusive Sexual Behavior By Sex Offenders Involves An Imbalance And Misuse Of Power In The Relationship—Misused Power Can Include:

- Misuse of trust
- Physical strength
- Force
- Threats
- Weapons
- Blackmail
- Peer pressure
- The difference in age
- The difference in *cognitive abilities *cognitive abilities: of, relating to, being, or involving conscious intellectual activity such as thinking, reasoning, or remembering.

Sexual Preference:

Most perpetrators are males who consider themselves heterosexual. (21)

More than 20% of men who molest little girls also molest little boys. (22)

In the **Abel and Harlow Stop Child Molestation Study**, male molesters who sexually abused young boys were asked about their preferences for adult sex partners, and men vs. women. The majority said they were heterosexual, married, and preferred women. (23)

Of a group greater than 1000 admitted male child sexual abusers, who had molested boys, only 8% said they were exclusively homosexual. More than 70% said they were heterosexual and another 9% said they were equally heterosexual and homosexual in their adult sexual preferences. (23)

The Preference For Small Bodies:

Able and Osborn agree that in most cases, sexual interest in children runs on a different track than sexual interest in adults. One has nothing to do with the other. For most molesters, it is the sexual desire for a child that is significant. Note the emphasis on the word "child." Some molesters victimize girls and boys. The sex of the child is far less important than the simple fact that the victim is a child. These molesters are sexually attracted to small bodies." (24)

Why Do Molesters Often Choose Boys?

- Boys are more accessible since adults rarely protect them as much girls
- Parents rarely suspect their sons are being molested
- Boys try to be "tough"; they'll keep the secret longer
- Boys are afraid of being called "gay" because of having a sexual experience with a male, so they often never tell
- Boys take more responsibility for sex acts, sometimes it is easier to convince a boy that it is his fault
- Boys offer molesters a bigger advantage; they can molest hundreds of boys without being caught. (24)

Homosexuality And Child Sexual Abuse

Pederasty:

The term for the crime of molesting a child of the same sex, while the term *pedophilia* is commonly used to refer to child sexual abuse in general. The term *pedophile* is typically used as a general term to describe a person who molests any child. (25)

The homosexual who molests a child of the same sex, therefore, is technically guilty of pederasty rather than pedophilia; yet both are child sexual abuse. (25)

WARNING

THE FOLLOWING INFORMATION ABOUT
THE SADISTIC PEDOPHILE IS GRAPHIC AND DISTURBING

Victimization Tactics Of The Sadistic Pedophile:

Unlike Regressed and Fixated Offenders who are known to the children they victimize, gaining their trust by being "friendly", the Sadistic Pedophile will choose a child at random, stalk them, and use force to entrap them. They often use the internet in their search for victims and abduct a child from locations where children gather. Some child victims are snatched from their bedrooms. (26)

It is not unusual for the Sadistic Pedophile to travel great distances to stalk "just the right victim." They often have an elaborate offensive attack or abduction plan worked out in advance, designed to sidetrack the parents and authorities.

Hideous perversions such as mutilating the genitals, other parts of the victim's body, and even acts as drastic as decapitation, sexually excite this type of predator. There have been incidences where a victim's penis was severed and inserted into either the child's mouth or anus.

They prefer anal sex; with other sadistic behaviors, including whipping, bondage, and intercourse after the victim is unconscious or dead and the use of urine and feces for sexual stimulation. In some cases, the Sadistic Pedophile kills and cannibalizes their victim.

Sadistic Pedophiles typically do not stay in the same place for long and are unlikely to form long-lasting personal relationships. They often can get a decent-paying white-collar job, and have a dependable car. Characteristically, they move to a different location after a fatal victimization.

One of the most popular themes of hardcore pornography is the control and sexual torture of children. These "snuff films" mostly feature teenage girls, but can also feature small toddlers of either sex being forced into perverted and violent sexual activity. Frequently included in sexually explicit materials that depict child sexual abuse and torture are bestiality (sex between a human and an animal) and Satanism, which includes torture and human sacrifice. Some of these films go so far as to record the actual killing of children and others. (27)

Police investigations have uncovered countless pornographic pictures and videos of children being raped, tortured, murdered, and mutilated. Such pictures and videos are circulated among Sadistic Pedophiles and used for their sexual gratification.

Characteristics of Sadistic Offenders:

- Because they are inclined to be violent, they are very likely to have some kind of a criminal record
- They are sociopathic, having an aggressive and antisocial personality
- They are meticulous planners, spending unlimited amounts of time fantasizing about and preparing for their next assault
- Characteristically, they hate surprises or any kind of spontaneity
- They rehearse every step of the intended crime repeatedly, and have considered everything imaginable to reduce the chance of failure
- They experience sexual gratification by inflicting physical and mental pain on helpless children, and by performing perverted sex acts with them. (18)

This type of offender, who is more often a male, is intent on molesting children with the express desire to physically and mentally torture the victims, and have made the vital connection between sexual arousal and fatal violence. (27)

Over three million children have been abused, tortured, raped, and killed. (28)

Sexual offenders are never fully inactive. Even when he or she is not sexually abusing an innocent child, they are making plans for their next move, targeting new victims and collecting lures, always thinking of ways to entice more naïve, innocent children. They are never dormant. (18)

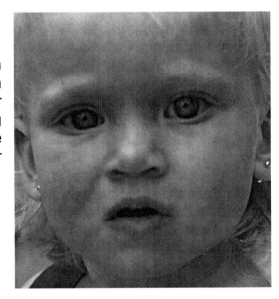

For more information on different offenders, see Chapter Three, Female Sex Offenders, and Chapter Four, Child and Adolescent Sex Offenders.

NOTES

Chapter Two

RECOGNIZING THE FRIENDLY ENEMY
AND HOW THEY GROOM CHILDREN FOR SEXUAL ASSAULT

Child Sexual Abuser—Monster Or Human?

In an article titled, "The Pedophile... Monster or Human?" a therapist who counsels sex offenders said, "When the average person hears the word pedophile, the word monster comes to mind. We must all, however, learn how to view a pedophile as a person, not just as a monster." (29)

When researchers asked groups of volunteers to pick out the child molester from pictures of different people, almost all of them chose an ugly, dirty old man in a trench coat. They didn't suspect a favorite aunt or uncle, the neighbor next door, the trusted church or community leader, family members, friends, or co-workers. Most don't think it can be a mom, a dad, or a single parent's significant other. The truth is—child molesters come from all lifestyles and from all socioeconomic groups. They can be male or female, rich or poor, employed or unemployed, religious or non-religious, and from any race or nationality."

Most parents feel they could detect a child molester, giving them a false sense of security. (30)

The "stranger molester" is a term used for an offender who, as the term implies, is a stranger to the child. This type of molestation is usually reported promptly to the police because the trauma to the child is readily apparent. (12)

However, only 4% of sexual assaults against children are by strangers, someone who is unknown to either the child or the child's family. (31)

About 30% of those who sexually abuse children are relatives of the child, such as fathers, uncles, or cousins. (29)

According to **Police Incident Data**, in 90% of child rape cases where victims were younger than 12, the child knew the molester. (32)

The American Psychological Association reports, in studies of who commits child sexual abuse, the majority of offenders are family members or otherwise known by the child. Sexual abuse by strangers is not nearly as common as sexual abuse by family members. Research also shows that men perpetrate children at higher percentages than women. (33)

Characteristically, a pedophile will seek employment and activities that give free access to a large number of potential victims. For instance, he or she may be a teacher, day care worker, camp counselor, doctor, clergy, coach, or several other positions where an adult can create opportunities to be alone with children. It is typical that much of his or her lifestyle involves children.

Strangers can be *good guys* or *bad guys*, just like seemingly normal people known to you and your children can be *good guys* or *bad guys*. It can be a male or a female. We do a great disservice to children when we teach "Stranger Danger" and leave out the important information we know about "The Friendly Enemy" in our midst.

Grooming The Victim:

In Chapter One, you learned about the Fixed or Fixated Pedophile. This person is attracted solely to children for sexual gratification. He or she takes the time to become the best friend or favorite relative, striving to be loved and trusted by the child, their parents, and concerned caretakers. About 95% of sexually abused children know their perpetrators. This makes it easy for them to become intimate with the young victim while adults are unsuspecting. In his article, "Grooming Children for Sexual Molestation," Gregory M. Weber tells us a predator will identify and connect with his victim to gain the child's trust, break down his defenses, and manipulate him into performing or permitting sex acts. If necessary, the predator will gain access to the child by using these same techniques with the child's parent or adult caretaker. This process is called grooming. (34)

Most sex offenders groom their victims prior to any sexual abuse. The following scenario came directly from an offender's treatment summary:

While playing the part of being the best friend, spending a lot of time with the trusting child, and telling her she could always come to him if she needed someone to talk to, the sexual predator gained his victim's favor by helping her do her homework and her household chores. He played games with her and took her to the park, to the mall, toy stores, clothing stores, and swimming pool. He gave her money and gifts such as toys, board games, a bike, and expensive clothing. At times when he was helping her mother by taking care of her, he told her she could do whatever she wanted to do. Once he gained her confidence, he told her that he would buy her more nice things if she would let him do anything that he wanted to do to her. To keep her quiet, he threatened her. If her mother found out what they were doing, she would be extremely enraged, and everything would be the child's fault. (34)

Showing special treatment and affection to the victim is the most common lure used by molesters. Grooming happens over a period of weeks, months, or even years. This is also a tactic used online to seduce unsuspecting youth who need love and attention. Ken Wooden, author of Sexual Assault of Young Children, puts it this way, "Pedophiles will smile at you, look you right in the eye, and make you believe they are trustworthy." (35)

Pedophiles prey on children with emotional difficulties, seeking out the lonely or unattended. Children from broken homes are prime targets. During treatment, a convicted child molester confessed that he sexually assaulted children, both male and female, since he was eight or nine years old. His victims ranged from age two to ten-years-old. As an adult, he groomed children by keeping candy, popsicles, and children's toys in his apartment. He raised birds to interest them, took them on trips to the park, the beach, the mall, and out to eat. By offering his services as a babysitter, he gained access to many children. He groomed the parents by sitting at no charge, providing them with transportation, and giving them money when they needed it. He gained access to his young victims by targeting single moms with several children who were sloppy housekeepers. In his words, "A mother who doesn't give a damn." (34)

Considering the nature of their sexual addiction, few pedophiles are able to resist their powerful urges. They will go to great lengths to initiate contact with children. Other common strategies include assuming a role where they can take advantage of children. Some activities are participating in community events that involve children, coaching children's sports, and volunteering in youth organizations, especially ones where they can chaperone overnight trips. They hang around places where children spend time such as playgrounds, malls, and game arcades. They also spend time on the internet learning about the online interests and lingo used by youngsters. (36)

Pedophiles are notoriously friendly, kind, and likeable. First, they select a victim, then gradually they cunningly infiltrate the life of the child through his or her family, school activities, house of worship, sports, and hobbies. They are professional con artists and experts at gaining the trust of children and adults. Through this deception, the offender becomes a very powerful influence in the life of the child. (30)

Once the child is groomed, meaning seduced by gifts and spending quality time together, the pedophile starts engaging in subtle foreplay such as cuddling and tickling. This gets the child accustomed to being touched and fondled. Typically, the next step is mutual masturbation. For some children, this experience is pleasurable, making it easy to continue the abuse. For others, the experience is frightening, confusing, humiliating, and even painful. Either way, the manipulative adult is now able to persuade or threaten the child into further sexual activity. (37)

Usually the pedophile will show the child homespun and hardcore pornography, including pictures of other children in degrees of nudity and in sexually explicit situations. He often uses drugs and alcohol to break down the child's resistance and to keep them from revealing the abuse and forces the child to pose for pictures and videos. (37)

At the high point of the seduction, penetration of the anus and vagina is made possible by using lubricating gels then stretching the muscles of the tiny openings with fingers, vibrators, or other objects, leaving little or no evidence of physical damage. However, the invisible mental and emotional injury inflicted upon these innocents is long lasting and life altering. Sexual victimization may profoundly alter the development of a healthy attitude toward self, sexuality, and building trusting relationships.(38)

By now, most children instinctively long to escape their abuser, but through fear, misdirected loyalty, and undeserved guilt, the child often remains under the control of the sexual perpetrator. The abuse can sometimes continue for years. When describing his feelings about his personal experience as a victim of sexual assault, one young boy remarked that he felt as if he was falling deeper and deeper into a dark pit and he could not climb out. (37)

Misplaced Guilt:

There are different types of guilt associated with sexual abuse. Some, carried like heavy weights by the victims, include: feeling different from peers, harboring anger toward parents or guardians for not preventing it (even though they did not know about the abuse), feeling responsible, feeling guilty for not reporting it , and feeling disloyal to the family for causing trouble. (38)

They may want to confide in someone about the abuse, but are too fearful of what might happen if they do. Stated in her report on child sexual abuse, Linda Lebelle, Director of Focus Adolescent Services says, "The child of five or older, who knows and cares for their abuser, becomes trapped between affection and loyalty for the person and the sense that the sexual activities are terribly wrong. If the child tries to break away from the sexual relationship, the abuser may threaten the child with violence or loss of love. When sexual abuse occurs within the family, the child may fear the anger, jealousy, and shame of other family members, or be afraid the family will break up if the secret is told." (37)

The pedophile is often a familiar person or a relative who is routinely entrusted with the care of children. Over 42% of adult females and 33% of adult males, who were sexually abused in childhood, report they never disclosed the secret to anyone. Of all confirmed cases of child sexual abuse, 84% occurred in the privacy of the child's own home. (39) As a result, these victims grow up suffering with mental and emotional scars as well as significant damage to his or her sexuality. An estimated 35% enter the Cycle of Abuse and become a sexual abuser themselves. (See Chapter Eleven, The Cycle of Abuse.). Most, if not all, have extreme difficulty with intimacy even when they feel love for their mate. If the child victim does not resolve the trauma, sexuality usually becomes an area of great difficulty and dysfunction. (38)

Gregory M. Weber, an Assistant Attorney General for the State of Wisconsin, specializes in the prosecution of crimes committed against children. Here he illustrates the boldness of men who are convicted child molesters and says of them, "They, too, are experts in the field of child maltreatment, and they spell it out."

The Following Statements Are Made By Child Predators:

- *Parents are so naïve. They're worried about strangers, but should be worried about their brother-in-law. They don't realize how devious we can be. I used to abuse children while in the same room with their parents. They couldn't see it or didn't seem to know it was happening.*
- *I was disabled and spent months grooming the parents, so they would tell their children to take me out and help me. No one thought that disabled people could be abusers.*
- *Parents are partly to blame if they don't tell their children about sexual matters. I used it to my advantage by teaching the child myself.*
- *Give me a kid who knows nothing about sex, and you've given me my next victim.*

Although no child is absolutely immune to abuse, many abusers admit that attentive parents and guardians tend to deter any would-be offenders. Weber quotes one pedophile as saying, "Parents shouldn't be embarrassed to talk about things like this. It's harder to abuse or trick a child who knows what you're up to."

In interviews conducted by law enforcement officers, the majority of molesters cited a preference for children just on the brink of puberty. This is the age of sexual awakening, making it easier for molesters to prey on the sexual curiosity and ignorance of youngsters. [30]

The single most effective means of protecting your child is harboring safe, open communication. If a child feels they cannot share their true feelings or that they will be "put down" or "criticized" when trying to discuss sensitive topics, then you cannot expect them to tell you if they are put in an uncomfortable situation by a child molester. [1]

For information on how to talk to your children about sexual matters and child sexual abuse, see Chapter Fourteen, Inter Personal Communication (IPC) And Reporting Child Sexual Abuse."

For more information, review Chapter One, Child Sexual Abuse-How Serious is it? and Chapter Eleven, The Cycle of Abuse—Do the Abused Become the Abusers? and Chapter Thirteen, The Secret—Why Don't Children Tell?

NOTES

Chapter Three

FEMALE SEX OFFENDERS

Statistics show that females commit approximately 25% of all reported sex offenses against children. [20]

However, self-reported studies provide a very different view of the occurrence of sexual abuse and the substantial increase in the number of female perpetrators.

- 60% of male victims remembered being abused by females [40]
- 51% of the female victims were sexually molested by males [41]
- 60% of male college students reported females sexually abused them [42]
- In other studies of college-age males, the rates of perpetrations by females were as high as 72 to 82% [43]

For many years the assumption was that women would not sexually abuse children. However, studies show that female perpetrators represent over 50% of all childhood sexual abuse. [44]

In one study, at least three women charged or sentenced with child sexual abuse were pregnant by teenage boys or had delivered babies whose fathers were under the age of 18. [45]

Approximately 60% to 80% of male rapists and sex offenders have a history of having been sexually abused by female perpetrators. [46]

About 60% of male survivors of sexual abuse report, at least one of their perpetrators were a female. [1]

One in six men reported they were sexually abused as children. Almost 40% of the perpetrators were female. [47]

The majority of female offenders are family members who abuse within their role as caretakers. Investigations of mothers, as the alleged perpetrator, were 7% of all cases.

- 5% biological mothers
- 2% stepmothers

Other caretakers, babysitters, teachers, and day care workers were responsible for over 25% of the reposted abuse [48]

- Low self-esteem
- History of severe emotional and verbal abuse
- History of being sexually abused as a child (especially incest)
- History of promiscuous or compulsive sexual activity

- Mental health problems including post-traumatic stress disorder and mood disorders
- Absence of parent during childhood
- Loss of a spouse
- Responsible for supporting the family
- Feelings of isolation and alienation
- Poor social and anger management skills
- Fear of rejection
- Overly submissive to others and to outside influences
- History of drug and or alcohol abuse [49]

Research suggests that overall; both genders will commit many of the same acts and follow many of the same patterns of abuse against their victims. There are no significant differences between male and female perpetrators in terms of the location of the abuse or their relationship to the victim, most of whom are relatives. [50]

Like male offenders, females seem to use verbal intimidation rather than physical force. The most commonly reported types of abuse by female perpetrators include:

- Vaginal intercourse
- Oral sex
- Fondling
- Group sex
- Mutual masturbation
- Oral, anal, and genital sex acts
- Showing children pornography and playing sex games (Faller, 1987); [51]

Should Women Sex Offenders Be Treated Differently Than Men?

- Sexual abuse by women is rarely reported. Victims often have no understanding that what happened to them was abuse, until years later when they are adults. The following information explains why abusive behavior by female perpetrators is frequently unacknowledged. [52]
- Children are reluctant to report the person from whom they get care
- Inappropriate sexual behavior often takes place while the perpetrator is bathing, dressing, or comforting the victim and usually goes unsuspected as abuse
- When females sexually abuse children, they send a false message to their victims about how women and children should appropriately interact
- People find it difficult to believe that women could sexually abuse children
- Children and adolescents who disclose sexual abuse by female offenders are often told they are fantasizing

When the victim is a male adolescent, the sexual abuses often go unreported because of the popular attitude that sex with an older female is acceptable, and even something to brag about. But victimization by female or male sex offenders can have the same devastating results:

- Self-blame
- Low self-esteem
- Substance abuse
- Problems with sexual functioning such as avoidance of sex or sexual compulsiveness (52)

Categories Of Female Sex Offenders Can Be Classified Into Four Groups:

- The most common type is a lone female perpetrator with a history of victimization of intergenerational incest with more than one person. She continues the generational sexual abuse by victimizing children in the same way she was victimized.
- The next most common category is a female perpetrator who is coaxed into sexually offending a child by a male partner who initiates the abuse. The young women in this study knew their victims and none of these perpetrators experienced legal consequences for their actions. (53)
- The lone teenage babysitter who targets young male children to sexually assault; this type is called an Experimental Exploiter.
- The teacher/lover is a lone perpetrator who claims to fall in love with an adolescent male. (54)

Statistics For Teacher Sexual Abuse:

When you think about the thousands of hours that children and adolescents spend in the classroom and how vulnerable they are under their teacher's authority and influence, one can only imagine the damaging impact this betrayal has on the victimized student. Unfortunately, greater numbers than were recognized in the past are now reported. (55)

Estimates show that a member of the school staff will sexually abuse 15% of all students during their school career.

The American Association of University Women Foundation surveyed more than 1,600 students in grades eight through eleven and found that 25% of the girls and 10% of the boys said they had been sexually harassed or abused by a school employee. Between 1 and 5% of all teachers sexually abuse or harass students. At least 1/4 of school districts in the United States have dealt with a case of staff sexual abuse in the past ten years.

According to a study in 1996, of the 51,331,000 kindergarten through twelfth grade public and private school students, an estimated seven million either were or very likely would be sexually abused by a member of the school staff. The 2006 U.S. Census reported that 55 million children attended school that year. Of these students, 1 in 6 has already been sexually abused. In nearly half of the cases, suspected sex offenders are accused of abusing more than one student. Only two cases were false accusations; of all cases studied, less than 1%. (55)

Despite the double standards in teacher/student sexual offences—girls are thought of as victims and boys are considered lucky—the boys who are sexually molested are just as damaged as girls are by these inappropriate relationships. The younger they are the more long-term damage they are likely to experience. (55)

Responses To Allegations Of Sexual Abuse Of Students By Staff:

* 38.7% of teachers resigned, left the district, or retired
* 17.5% were spoken to, informally
* 15% were terminated, or not re-hired
* 11.3% received a formal, verbal or written, reprimand
* 8.1% were suspended, but later resumed teaching
* 7.5% were cases where the superintendent determined that the teacher had not meant to sexually abuse

Of the 54% of abusers who resigned, were not eligible for re-hire, or were terminated, superintendents report that 16% are now teaching in other schools. Of the remaining 84%, his or her whereabouts are unknown. All but 1% of these accused schoolteachers retained their teaching license.

According to one U.S. survey of students, 57% of teachers who had engaged in sexual misconduct with pupils were female and 42% were male.

In a U.S. Department of Education report released in June 2004, at least 20% of students reported verbal or physical sexual misconduct by a female teacher or aide.

Most cases of teacher sexual abuse on students are never reported.

No type of school is immune to abuse public or private, religious or secular, rich or poor, urban or rural. (55)

Legalities:

* In 20 states, it is not a crime for school employees, including teachers, administrators, and coaches, to have sex with students aged 16 and over
* In 23 states, it is not a crime for school employees to have sex with students aged 17 and over
* In 45 states, it is not a crime for school employees to have sex with students aged 18 and over
* In 16 states, it is a crime for adults in a position of trust and authority including, teachers, administrators, and coaches, to have sex with students under the age of 18. (55)

Today, female teachers sexually assaulting children is more often reported and it is common to read headlines such as these:

- A teacher who admitted to having sex with a 13-year-old student was fired from her job and sentenced to two years house arrest.

- Schoolteacher plans to marry former student, whom she was convicted of sexually assaulting when he was only 12 years old.

- A 41-year-old teacher was sentenced to 30 years in prison for supplying teen boys with alcohol and drugs, then having sex with them.

- The tables were turned when a schoolteacher sued a 13-year-old student for child support and ended up in prison, charged with sexually molesting the teenage father of her child.

In courtrooms across our nation, teachers receive sentences for having sex with young boys, girls, and teenagers.

Research shows that there is no difference in the severity of abuse by female sex offenders as compared to male sex offenders [56]

For more information, see Chapter Seven, Male Victims of Child Sexual Abuse.

NOTES

Chapter Four

CHILD AND ADOLESCENT SEX OFFENDERS

Shocking Facts:

As shocking as it is, the fact remains; children as young as four years old are known to sexually abuse other children. In this chapter, you will find out why this happens and how to differentiate between sexual abuse and normal playful activity between children.

Sexual assaults committed by youth are a growing concern in this country. Adolescents, average age bracket 13 to 17, commit up to one-fifth of all rapes and one-half of all of child sexual molestations each year. (57)

In 1995, youth were involved in 15% of the arrests for forcible rape and 25% of exploiters of children are other children. In the same year, approximately 16,100 adolescents were arrested for sexual offenses, excluding rape and prostitution. Approximately 18 of every 100,000 adolescents are arrested for forcible rape. (58)

What Makes A Child Sexually Offend Another Child?

Children act out what they experience, repeat what they see and hear, and experiment with new acts or behaviors have been taught. (57)

Typically, children who molest other children are acting out their own sexual victimization; often, there is physical and emotional abuse as well. When a child has been sexually abused, or overly exposed to adult sexuality, the child's sexual development is negatively altered.

In homes where domestic violence is present, children witness violent arguments between adults that are followed up with a "honeymoon period" of kissing and sexual activity. This sends the message to children that violence and sex go hand in hand.

Adolescent sex offenders are typically lonely and socially isolated from peers, preferring the company of younger children. Often they are naive and lack suitable sex education. (59)

Juvenile sex offenders have a wide range of mental and emotional problems that do not fit into any other category of mental illnesses. Characteristics include behaviors ranging from naive experimenters to sadistic rapists, with everything in between. Intelligence can be extremely high in some, while others may function so low in life-skill abilities that they are considered retarded. They rarely feel remorse or empathy for their victims, and will deny offenses or, at the very least, minimize his or her responsibility for the effects of the sexual acts and the damage they are causing. (59)

Factors That May Cause These Abnormalities Include: (59)

- Fear of rejection and anger towards women, or a specific people group
- Abnormal erotic sexual fantasies
- Poor social skills
- Feelings of male inadequacy; females may suffer in this way, too Low self-esteem

An overall explanation for the characteristic behavior of an adolescent sex offender is, due to the exposure to sexual behavior that victimizes others and the neglectful lack of normal bonding, these children learn to trust no one. Often, the family moves from place to place. Mom, Dad, or both may have had several sex partners who come and go, creating a total lack of stability and consistency. This kind of dysfunctional lifestyle causes the child to have a real sense of powerlessness within the family unit and confusion in relation to their own sexual identity. Severe emotional problems result with the child never learning normal acceptable sexual and social behavior. (59)

A summary on the characteristic behavior of adolescent sex offenders also suggests a history of emotional family and social instabilities, isolation and sexual victimization, and an inability to master age-appropriate behavior in the home, school, and community. As a solution to boredom, they may commit other crimes such as vandalism, stealing, arson, and other illegal behaviors. It should be emphasized, however, that not all adolescent sex offenders have been sexually abused.

In a study of 286 male adolescent sex offenders, 53% are frequently unmotivated, disruptive in school, and may have learning disabilities including attention deficit disorder. Of this group, only 55% are considered on schedule in grade placement.

The peak time for juvenile assaults is around the end of the school day, 3 p.m. Other increases in the number of incidents were 8 a.m., noon and 6 p.m. Most of these assaults happen in the home of the victim, the home of the offender, or another familiar residence.

By far, the most significant behavioral abnormality of an adolescent sex offender is cognitive distortion, the twisting or distorting of that which is considered acceptable public behavior and consciously forming an opposite opinion, feeling, or tendency contrary to normal social behavior. This misinformation, strange beliefs, bad attitudes, faulty perceptions, and overall wrong thinking causes the youthful offender to act out his or her inappropriate, deviate sexual and social behaviors. (59)

Youthful Offender Statistics:

In an **American Justice Department Survey** of 60,991 victims, child sex offenders aged 7 to 11 years old were responsible for 3.6% of all sexual assaults committed (60)

- 40% of the offenders of victims, under age 6, were juveniles
- 39% of the offenders of victims, ages 7 to 11, were juveniles

25

- 27% of the offenders of victims, ages 12 to 17, were juveniles
- 23% of all sexual offenders are under the age of 18
- 13% are age 7 to 11
- Among adults convicted of sex crimes, 30% began offending before age nine (61)

While many adolescents who commit sexual offenses have histories of being abused, the majority of youth who are sexually abused do not become adult sex offenders. (62)

Research suggests there is the difference between sexually abused youths who will become sexual perpetrators themselves and sexually abused youths who will never become abusers. Factors depend on the age of the child when he or she was molested, the number of incidents of abuse, the time between the abuse and its first report, how the child felt about the way the family responded to the disclosure of abuse, and exposure to domestic violence. (63)

Abusers With Documented Histories Of Being Sexually Abused:

- 72% began molesting between the ages of 4 and 6
- 42% were between the ages of 7 to 10
- 35% were between the ages of 11 to 12 (64)
- 42% of adult pedophiles begin abusing children before they themselves were 12 years old (65)

Children who are sexually abused by child sex offenders suffer the same severity of negative consequences as children who are sexually abused by adults. (66)

Adolescent Sexual Abusers:

In the following study, "private parts" refers to the genitals, the area around the anus and buttocks, and the breasts of a female. (67)

These Behaviors Qualify As Sexual Abuse:

- Touching another person's private parts against that person's will, either with hands, objects, or one's own genitals, dressed, or naked. It does not matter if people are dressed or naked
- Touching the private parts of a person significantly younger. For example, a girl aged 13 touching the genitals of a boy aged 8. In some states, children close to the same age participating in voluntary sexual activity is not considered a sexual offense. The exception to this would be if a child is unable to give consent because of a severe disability, being asleep, or was forced
- Exposing private parts to a much younger child, or to anyone without consent
- Forcing another person to watch while he or she masturbates
- Showing pornography to a much younger child or forcing someone to view porn
- Taking pornographic pictures of a child
- Rape

These Behaviors Are Not Sexual Abuse, But Should Be Noted:

- Possession of large quantities of pornography, or use of pornography at an age before puberty
- Early consensual sexual activity
- Bragging about sexual matters
- Calling sex talk numbers
- Making threats and intimidating younger children
- Close, friendly relationships with much younger children and a lack of friendships with peers
- Frequent deceitfulness and lying
- Physical abuse of others or cruelty to animals
- Knowledge of sexuality unexpected for one's age (67)

Characteristics Of Adolescent Sex Offenders:

- 9 out of 10 juvenile sex offenders are male; however, girls do sexually offend (67)
- On average, juvenile sex offenders are between age 13 and 17
- 60% exhibit learning disabilities and academic dysfunction
- Up to 80% have a diagnosable psychiatric disorder
- Many have difficulties with impulse control and judgment
- A significantly high number of adult sex offenders began their criminal offenses during adolescence.
- Typically, adolescent sex offenders are lonely and socially isolated from their peers
- They prefer the company of younger children
- They are naive and lack suitable sex education
- They frequently experience disturbed family relations. (67)

In a wide range of histories of physical abuse, 20 to 50% of adolescent sex offenders were physically abused as young children. Likewise, 40 to 80% of adults who are adolescent sex offenders were sexually abused as children. (57)

Male adolescent sex offenders who were sexually abused exclusively by female perpetrators, almost always chose only female victims. (68)

Young Offenders Under The Age Of 12 Were Responsible For:

- 23% of forcible sodomies
- 19% of forcible fondling
- 17% of sexual assaults with an object
- 7% of forcible rapes

Adolescent Offenders Ages 12 To 18 Were Responsible For:

- 36% of forcible sodomies
- 27% of forcible fondling
- 23% of sexual assaults with an object
- 17% of forcible rapes

The age of a perpetrator should not cause us to ignore unusual or aggressive sexual behavior, nor should other behaviors be dismissed. Some of note are exposing private body parts, sexual touching over the clothes, frotteurism (rubbing against another person's body against their will), obscene and sexually mature language, obscene phone calls, possession of pornography, "boys will be boys" attitudes, bullying in a sexual way, and forms of harassment, all of which can be signs of an abuser or potential abuser. (69)

Normal Sexual Behavior Verses Abusive Sexual Behavior:

The normal behavior and gradual sexual development of infants, children, and adolescents mentioned in these studies should not be misinterpreted as "sex acts." An infant plays with its hands, feet, ears, hair, and any other parts of the body it can reach, including the genital area. That is not a sex act, but simply exploring through the sense of touch. As children become older, they begin to experiment further, learning from outside stimuli such as things they see, hear and experience, both good and bad. It is at this point when normal or abusive sexual behavior develops, depending on the environment, lifestyle, and treatment of the child. (70)

There is a balance between sexual interest and curiosity about life. Normal sexual activity in children involves mutual interest between children of similar ages, size, and development. It is playful and limited in type and frequency. (69)

It is expected that 40 to 75% of children will engage in some sort of sexual behavior before reaching age thirteen. In these situations, children are exploring each other's bodies while also exploring gender roles and behaviors; it does not mean these children are child sex offenders.

Normal Sexual Development:

Infancy:

- Children begin to explore their bodies, including their genitals
- Touch is the primary method infants use for learning about their bodies and the bodies of others
- Other people's response to that body exploration is one of the earliest forms of social learning (71)

Childhood:

- Half of all adults, who were questioned, reported they participated in sex play as children
- Children respond to feelings, arousal, and touching their genitalia with the same interest and curiosity that may have in the light of the moon, a blooming flower, or the vast wonders of life that surround them. Children express general interest in the bodies of others and may touch out of curiosity. Adults teach children about modesty and appropriate touching and that privacy is important for certain behaviors
- Masturbation occurs naturally in both boys and girls, and begins in infancy. By the age of 2 or 3, most children have learned that fondling themselves in front of others is likely to get them in trouble (71)

Pre-Adolescence:

- An interest begins to develop in viewing the bodies of others though the media, photographs, films, videos, etc.
- Very few children become sexually active in pre-adolescence. When they do, it is usually initiated by adults (71)

Group 1—Juveniles Who Sexually Offend Peers Or Adults:

- Predominantly assault females
- Assault mostly strangers or only casual acquaintances (71)

Offense Patterns: (71)

- Are more likely to commit sexual offenses in public areas
- Commit sexual offenses combined with other criminal activity

Social And Criminal History: (71)

- Are more likely to have histories of non-sexual criminal offenses
- Are criminally minded and have behavior disorders

Behavior Patterns: (71)

- Display higher levels of aggression and violence
- Are more likely to use weapons and cause injury to their victims

Group 2-Juveniles Who Sexually Offend Against Children: (71)

- Are slightly more inclined to victimize females
- Nearly half of offenders will assault at least one male
- Up to 40% of victims are either siblings or relatives

Offense Patterns: (71)

- They seek the opportunity to offend and devise clever ways to entrap their victim, particularly when the victim is a relative
- They trick the child by using bribes or threatening loss of their relationship

Social And Criminal History: (71)

- Low self-esteem is apparent
- They often lack social skills necessary for forming and maintaining healthy relationships and the ability to interact with others

Behavior Patterns: (71)

- Often display signs of depression
- Adolescents with severe personality and or psychosexual disturbance may display high levels of aggression or violence

Treatment: (69)

In 1983, there were only 20 treatment programs in North America for juvenile sex offenders. Recent studies show there are now over 1,000 worldwide (72)

The majority of juvenile sexual offender treatment programs pattern after traditional adult sex offender programs. Standard interventions that help offenders to deal with their unique issues are:

- Prevention of re-offending and preventing the sexual abuse cycle
- Training offenders to have sympathy for others
- Anger management
- Social and interpersonal skills training
- Cognitive restructuring, thinking through the therapy process.
- Assertiveness training to boost self-esteem
- Keeping a daily journal and recording actions, feelings, etc.
- Sex education

Treatment can be a difficult task for juvenile sex offenders. Of the total number of youthful offenders who entered a particular community-based treatment program, 50% were expelled during the first year of participation, mostly for failure to comply with attendance requirements or for not following through with therapeutic assignments. The offender's failure to complete treatment can increase his or her chances of re-offending.

Recidivism (Re-Offending): (69)

Many juvenile sex offenders will re-offend, even after completing a treatment program; Juveniles who participate in treatment programs have sexual recidivism rates that range between 7 and 13%, according to follow-up interviews in 2 to 5 years. However, research suggests there is no compelling evidence that shows us the majority will become adult sex offenders. Juveniles who engage in sexual aggression frequently cease such behavior by the time they reach adulthood.

Youths participating in treatment programs have lower recidivism rates than either adult sex offenders or untreated juvenile sex offenders. An analysis of eight separate studies found that:

- Re-offending rates for adults averaged 13%
- Juveniles who participated in treatment programs had a re-offending rate that averaged 7.1%

A 3 to 5 year, large scale, follow-up study across Canada, found that only 5% of youths who underwent treatment were charged with another sexual offense within six years, compared to 18% of the youths who did not participate in treatment.

NOTE: Although treatment is widely acknowledged as helpful to juvenile sex offenders, and is an important component in the prevention of future sexual offenses, additional studies of the effectiveness of different treatment programs is required.

Where Does Normal End And Abnormal Begin?

A normal adolescent boy or girl is often self-indulgent and self-centered, but an adolescent offender is obsessively, totally absorbed in concentrating on satisfying his own needs with absolutely no thought of others. As puberty approaches, the normal adolescent usually begins to show interest in the opposite sex. This is also true of an offender; however, he or she may be attracted to both sexes; and the interest is not casual or respectful, but rather opportunistic, manipulative, and weighed down with inappropriate sexual fantasies. (59)

Like the normal adolescent, an offender may sincerely desire pleasurable peer relationships, but he or she lacks the social skills needed to begin or maintain such associations. Thoughts of gradually building up to a sexual relationship are nonexistent because immediate sexual gratification is the goal. Normal adolescents may rebel, but the rebellion is usually manifested in legitimate ways such as, piercings or a messy room, while the sex offender thrills to doing the radically forbidden (59)

Sex Between Siblings: (59)

Molested children will often re-enact their abuse with other children. Therefore, when a child has committed sexual offenses against a sibling, it is important to investigate whether the offending child suffered sexually abuse by another.

In cases of sexual activity between siblings, it is important to determine whether the behavior was normal childhood sex play or whether the older or stronger child was coercing, overpowering, intimidating, tricking, or manipulating a younger or smaller child. Normal sex play occurs between young children of the same developmental level and power.

Much incestuous behavior between siblings is actually sexually abusive where the older child has more strength, more authority, and more experience.

Children's Sexual Behavior From Normal To Disturbed: (59)

Adolescence is a good experience or a bad experience depending upon the way people around the adolescent respond to their developing sexuality. The way other people react to a teen's physical maturing, appearance of body hair, formation of breasts, deepening of the voice, beginning of the menstrual cycle, etc. has a profound effect on the young person's sense of self-esteem and the development of his or her ability to interact in society.

The adolescent develops a growing awareness of sexuality and of the place and value of sex in their life including such options as celibacy (no sex). Some feel confused and conflicted about sexual orientation. Most practice some type of interactive sexual behaviors with others such as fondling, open-mouth kissing, and simulated intercourse.
(69)

The Normal Sexual Development Of Adolescence:

Clinical observation and experimental research indicates that juvenile sexual offenders fall into two groups:

- Those who sexually abuse children
- Those who victimize peers and adults

These two groups, as reflected in the following information, have clear differences. Not only in victim preferences, but also in offense patterns, social backgrounds, criminal histories, behaviors, and treatment required. (69)

Normal Sex Play: (69)

- Is exploratory in nature
- Characterized by lightheartedness and impulsiveness, rather than something planned
- The interest in sex is not an infatuation, but a curiosity
- Sex play may cause embarrassment, but not fear or anxiety

Disturbed Sexual Behavior: (69)

- Self-stimulating acts such as masturbation, done frequently or in view of adults
- Coercing other children, without making threats or hurting anyone, but the other children dislike or are bothered by the behavior of the offender

- The offence could represent a form of or re-enactment of sexual abuse, a way of dealing with the shame, guilt, anxiety, and fear related to the aftermath of an abusive sexual experience they suffered.

Children Who Molest: (69)

- Abnormal sexual behaviors occur often and essentially become the main thought and objective in the life of the youth
- Intense sexual confusion dominates their emotions
- Sexuality and aggression are closely linked
- They are manipulative, luring their victims with bribery, trickery, etc.
- Many of their behavioral patterns are impulsive, compulsive, and aggressive leading to problems in all areas of their lives

Behaviors That Cause Concern: (69)

- Sexual behaviors between children of different ages or developmental levels
- Unusual sexual behavior for the child's age, lifestyle, and normal interests
- Vast knowledge of sex and behaving in ways more consistent with an adult's sexual expression
- Sexual behavior that is significantly different from those of other children
- Sexual behavior that continues after consistent requests to stop
- Sexual behavior in public places or where the child has been told it is not acceptable
- Sexual behavior that is causing complaints from other children
- Sexual behavior that is directed at adults
- Sexual behavior that progresses in frequency, intensity, or intrusiveness
- When fear, anxiety, deep shame, or intense guilt is associated with normal sexuality
- Sexual acts or displays that cause physical or emotional pain and discomfort to others
- When anger precedes, follows, or accompanies the sexual behavior
- When verbal and/or physical aggression precedes, follows, or accompanies the sexual behavior
- When coercion, force, bribery, manipulation, or threats are associated with sexual
- Behavior

For more information, see Chapter Eleven, The Cycle of Abuse—Do the Abused Become The Abusers?, and Chapter Twelve, Indicators and Effects of Child Sexual Abuse

NOTES

Chapter Five

INCEST

This chapter is dedicated to my dear friend, Vicki.
Your story brought all of this to a realization that will forever affect my life's work—fighting the sexual victimization of innocent children worldwide.

Incest between an adult and a related child or adolescent is now recognized as the most prevalent form of child sexual abuse, and as one with enormous potential for damage to the child. [73]

- 43% of sexually abused children are abused by family members
- 33% are abused by someone they know
- 24% are abused by strangers
- Other research indicates that over 10 million Americans have been victims of incest [74]

The sexual abuse of a child by a relative, or other person in a position of trust and authority over the child, is a violation of the child where he or she lives, literally and in the sense of invading the very being of the child. A child molested by a stranger can run home for help and comfort. A victim of incest cannot. [74]

A nationwide study of prisoners serving time for violent crime in 1991 showed that, of those prisoners convicted of rape or sexual assault, two-thirds victimized children and almost one-third of the victims were the children or stepchildren of the assailant. [74]

Before age 14, 1 in 8 females are incestuously abused, and 1 in 6 before age 18. [75]

Clinical findings of adult victims of sexual abuse include problems in interpersonal relationships and mistrust. In general, adult victims of incest have a severely strained relationship with their parents that are marked by feelings of mistrust, fear, betrayal, and strong love/hate feelings for the abuser. These feelings may extend to all family members. [75]

Characteristics Of Incest:

- Sexual contact or interaction between family members who are not married
- Oral-genital contact
- Genital or anal penetration
- Genital touching of the victim by the perpetrator
- Any other touching of private body parts
- Sexual kissing and hugging
- Sexually staring at the victim by the perpetrator
- "Accidental" touching of the victim's body by the perpetrator

- Verbal invitations to engage in sexual activity
- Verbal ridiculing of body parts
- Pornographic photography, reading of sexually explicit material to children
- Exposure to inappropriate sexual activity (74)

Victims Are Extremely Reluctant To Reveal They Are Being Abused Because:

- All too often, pressure from family members, in addition to threats or pressure from the abuser, results in extreme reluctance to reveal abuse and to subsequently obtain help
- Their abuser is a person in a position of trust and authority for the victim
- Often the incest victim does not recognize sexual abuse
- They deny that anything is wrong with the behavior they are encountering because many young incest victims accept and believe the perpetrator's explanation that this is a "learning experience" that happens in every family
- Incest victims may fear they will be disbelieved, blamed, or punished if they report their abuse. (76)

In addition, some recent research suggests that some victims of incest may suffer from biochemically-induced amnesia. This condition can be triggered by a severe trauma, such as a sexual assault, which causes the body to incur a number of complex endocrine and neurological changes resulting in complete or partial amnesia regarding the event. Thus, any immediate and or latent memory of the incident(s) is repressed. (77)

Estimates of male incest may be low. While girls are extremely hesitant to disclose incest, boys are probably even more so. Boys may be especially reluctant to admit incest victimization because of the sexual details and fear it may indicate to others a weakness which can result in negative social stigmatization (78)

Less than 1% of victims of incest ever admit to the abuse. This is likely because the parent is the child's role model and often their hero (79)

A developing definition of incest takes into consideration the betrayal of trust and the power imbalance in these one-sided relationships. One such definition is the imposition of sexually inappropriate acts, or acts with sexual overtones, by one or more persons who derive authority through ongoing emotional bonding with that child. (73)

This Definition Expands The Traditional Definition Of Incest To Include Sexual Abuse By Anyone Who Has Authority Or Power Over The Child: (73)

- Babysitters
- School teachers
- Scout masters
- Priests, pastors and other religious figures
- Immediate and extended family members

Incest Occurs Between:

- Fathers and daughters
- Fathers and sons
- Mothers and daughters
- Mothers and sons

Perpetrators Of Incest Can Be:

- Aunts, uncles
- Cousins, nieces, nephews
- Stepparents, stepchildren
- Grandparents and grandchildren

As this abuse takes place within the confines of the family and the home environment, incest offenders can be persons without a direct blood or legal relationship to the victim such as a parent's lover or live-in nanny, housekeeper, etc. [74]

Incest does not discriminate. It happens in families that are financially privileged, as well as those of low socioeconomic status. It happens to those of all racial and ethnic descent, and to those of all religious traditions.

Incest Has No Age Limits:

Victims of incest are boys and girls, infants and adolescents [74]

Mothers Can Create Serious Risk Factors For Their Children Without Knowing It:

With the increase in divorce rates, more children are at greater risk than ever. Women may unknowingly put their children at risk for sexual abuse from the men they date. If the mother remarries, the stepdaughters are at high risk, over eight times greater, of sexual abuse by stepfathers than are daughters raised by their biological fathers. As some researchers have begun to suspect, a growing number of stepfathers are really "smart pedophiles," men who marry divorced or single women with families as a way of getting close to the children. [73]

Dysfunctional Family:

The term dysfunctional family is very typical in today's society. As stated by Krugman, "Adults take it out on children when they cannot manage tension and conflict, a pattern commonly associated with sexual abuse; the child is elevated to the role of the parent and the family system takes on a whole new function through role reversal. The child may also be assigned the role of substitute parent for the other children or, in the case of father-daughter incest, the role of substitute wife." [73]

Parents in these families usually have unhappy marriages, and sex between spouses is unpleasant or non-existent. Fathers are often controlling and physically abusive with the entire family, and incompetent as providers. [80]

Mothers, for their part, are either unwilling or unable to fulfill parental functions, feeling uncomfortable with the responsibilities of motherhood. In addition to the tension between themselves and their husbands, they are often on bad terms and have strained relationships with their daughters. In this situation, incest is a possible outcome and sometimes even viewed as a solution to the family's dysfunctional problems. Many mothers are unable to provide any protection for their daughters because they are depressed, incapable, and submissive to the extreme; and are considered unimportant or inactive family members. [81]

Such family systems that deny the normal functions of a family create certain unconscious rules, family messages, and learned behaviors in victims. These are virtually the same in study after study on incest. Without the benefit of counseling, adult survivors tend to function more or less according to these same rules in adulthood. [80]
The following are some of the major assumed "family rules" that form the basis of the dysfunction and abuse in the family where incest exists, and later may continue to operate in the behavior of the adult survivor. [81]

Never Ending Cycle Of Torment:

Certainly, the command to deny one's actual experience is the root of the problem.

Denial:

- Do not think, see, hear, feel, reflect on, or question your experience
- Do not believe the obvious—accept the lie
- Don't trust yourself or others

Be Loyal:

- You must protect the family
- Keep the secrets
- Obey
- You must not fight back, disagree, or get angry
- Don't have needs
- Love means being hurt or used
- Don't ask for help

Don't Show Pain:

- Minimize all situations
- Hide symbolic psychosomatic manifestations and complaints
- Hide self-injury and mutilation

Don't Be A Child:

- Don't play
- Don't make mistakes
- Be adult-like but without power or authority
- Be responsible for everyone else
- There is no capacity for innocent, curious, developmental exploration

It Is Your Fault:

There is an underlying general assumption that while others do the best they can and cannot seem to help themselves, you don't ever do the best you can and you do what you do on purpose

They Are Not Responsible For Their Own Behavior:

- It is not their fault
- You are bad, evil, immoral, to blame (guilty)
- You are responsible for other's behavior

They Make You Think That You Must Help Them:

- Stay in control of yourself and those around you
- Stay on guard
- Hyper-caution

Anything Bad That Happens Is Your Fault And Thus Your Responsibility To Prevent:

- You are incompetent
- Don't reflect, question, or process

"Think Outside Yourself" Mentality:

- No time, safe place, or safe harbor to reflect or process; especially traumatic experiences

Because the rules of logic in such families depends on unquestioning loyalty and the capacity of members to behave as if in hypnotic realities, there is a powerful restriction to keep all matters on the surface without analysis or critical judgment.

This Leads To:

- Extreme leaps of unquestioning interpersonal faith
- Frequent re-trauma, characteristic of adult survivors
- Denial and dissociation are the fundamental organizing principles of family life.

The family learns to live with the strict rules made up for them, maintaining a relatively stable state of balance, and taking on adaptive but dysfunctional roles. (82)

Vital Decisions:

There are women who feel they have no choice but to stay in a relationship with a perpetrator and try their best to prevent further victimization of their children.

These Are Some Reasons Many Women Do Not Leave The Perpetrator:

- They may end up on welfare if they have no job skills or limited job skills
- She may enter the dreaded "cycle of poverty" and doom her offspring

If she works, she probably will not find a job that pays enough to pay for childcare. Most communities do not provide childcare at reasonable costs to working mothers. (73)

Often women are manipulated and overpowered by the perpetrator.

CAUTION: Because of these findings, women, especially with daughters, are warned to be more cautious about re-marrying and be able to recognize the consequent risk to their children. (83)

Serious Long-Term Effects On Incest Victims:

Incest can have serious long-term effects on its victims. One study concluded that among the survivors of incest who were victimized by their mothers:

- 60% of the women had eating disorders, as did 25% of the men
- Of the 93 women and 9 men included in this study, 80% of the women and all of the men reported sexual problems in their adult life
- Almost two-thirds of the women stated they rarely went to the doctor or the dentist as the examination was too terrifying
- Posttraumatic stress disorder (PTSD), which includes amnesia, nightmares, and flashbacks, also remains prevalent among incest survivors (84)

There is additional research indicating that children who have been sexually abused by a relative suffer from even more intense guilt and shame, low self-esteem, depression, and self-destructive behavior such as substance abuse, sexual promiscuity, and prostitution, than children who have been sexually assaulted by a stranger. (85)

Whether an incest victim endured one incident of abuse or ongoing assaults over an extended period of time, the process of recovery can be exceptionally painful and difficult. The recovery process begins with admission of abuse and the recognition that help and rehabilitation services are needed. For both children and adult survivors of incest, there are services and resources available such as books, self-help groups, workshops, short and long-term therapy programs, and possible legal remedies. Many survivors of incest have formed self-help-support groups where they along with other incest survivors can discuss their victimization and find role models who have survived incest. (86)

In addition to believing, listening to, and helping victims of incest in their process of recovery, we need to simultaneously search for ways to prevent future generations from enduring such abuse and from continuing the cycles of abuse within their own family and relationships. (74)

Perpetrators of Incest:

Taken From Interviews With Incest Perpetrators.

Most incestuous sex offenders have similar belief systems: (75)

- Incest was defined as love and care
- The sexual experience was described as extremely pleasurable, using words such as "blissful", "thrilling" and "exciting"
- Some incestuous sex offenders actually saw themselves in love with the child
- About half claimed the love was mutual
- These incestuous sex offenders were unresponsive to the children's attempts to stop the incest
- Most perpetrators knew their behavior was wrong
- Many did not view their sexual acts as incest
- Some not only manipulated and took advantage of the child's trust, but felt a sense of power from the trust
- Almost all the fathers expressed a sense of excitement that they "had special rights" as the father to have sex with their children

Common Characteristics Of Incest Offenders Include:

- Passive personalities
- Dependent personalities
- Physical and emotional maltreatment during childhood
- Marital dissatisfaction
- Sexual dissatisfaction
- Disturbances in empathy and attachment (87)

Because their sexual offenses are limited to family members, it is commonly believed that incest offenders pose only a limited threat to society, and as a result of this perception, they are often given less intensive treatment. This characterization may be the result of comparisons between incestuous and non-incestuous child molesters that suggest arousal patterns of incest offenders are less sexually deviant. (87)

A Comparison of Incest Offenders Based on Victim Age:

Infant And Toddler Victims:

Sexual abuse of infants and toddlers is not uncommon, with cases involving victims as young as 2 to 3 months old. (87)

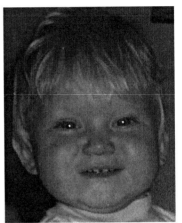

Of 270 Cases Of Sexual Abuse Of Children In Daycare:

- 6% occurred against children younger than 2 years
- 60% involved children less than 4 years of age (87)

Offenders who victimized younger children are significantly younger than those who victimized older children. Greenberg found that the offenders against younger children are observed to have characteristics similar to those who offend older children with the exception of the age. (87)

In addition, offenders against young victims were significantly more likely to deny their offenses and to have an anti-social lifestyle.

It is believed that a man who shows at least some aspect of sexual maturity and who sexually abuses an adolescent, while no less criminal in his actions, may be considered a less disturbed person than one who offends similarly against society's most vulnerable and least sexually stimulating individuals, infants, and toddlers.

Accurate estimates of the number of very young children who are sexually abused are difficult to obtain because of the limited verbal and associational skills of the victims, along with the damaging effects of the abuse itself presenting significant interference with full or even reasonable disclosure.

Characteristics Of Incest Offenders Of Younger Victims:

- Although there is difficulty with sexual function among all incest offenders, incest offenders of younger victims had poorer overall sexual functioning than offenders of older victims (89)
- Offenders of younger victims are significantly more likely than offenders of older victims to become drug and alcohol dependent
- Offenders against younger children exhibited significantly more psychiatric disturbance than those who offend against older victims
- A statistical trend suggested that the offenders of younger victims had lower full-scale IQ scores than the offenders of older victims
- In terms of family background, the group with younger victims was significantly more likely to have been raised in a family with a history of criminal activity
- Offenders of younger victims were more likely to have multiple victims
- 87.5% had 2 or fewer victims

- 12.5 % had between 3 and 7 victims (Having more victims may simply be the result of more opportunities for abuse in this particular study, but it may suggest that these offenders either possess less restraint or experience stronger inclinations to victimize)
- Men convicted of sexual offenses against younger children scored more poorly on nearly all measures studied, with the only exception being previous sexual offenses.
- The offenders of younger victims were more likely to have a male victim than the offenders of older victims. This observation does not eliminate the possibility that these same individuals also offended against girls. In fact, in the entire incest database from which the 2 groups in this study were sampled, only 19 of 342 offenders did not have a female victim
- Both groups showed clinically significant levels of deviant sexual preferences
- The largest proportions of incest offences are against females, specifically daughters and stepdaughters [90]
- Sons are extremely unlikely to be molested by fathers, even though other family members who molest often target boys [91]

Victim-Offender Relations In Younger Victims:

- Stepson/stepdaughter
- Biological son/daughter
- Sibling, and relative (grandson/granddaughter, niece/nephew)
- Offenders of younger victims were more likely than offenders of older victims to have been the grandfathers or uncles of their victims [92]

FOR ADDITIONAL INFORMATION
PLEASE CALL:

Family Violence & Sexual Assault Institute
1121 East Southeast Loop 323, Suite 130
Tyler, TX 75701
(903) 534 – 5100

Health Association
P.O. Box 13827
Research Triangle Park, NC 27709
(800) 342 - AIDS
(800) 344 - SIDA (Spanish)
(800) 243 - 7889 (TDD)

Incest Survivors Resource Network International
P.O. Box 7375
Las Cruces, NM 88006-7375
(505) 521 - 4260

National Children's Advocacy Center
200 Westside Square, Suite 700
Huntsville, AL 35801
(205) 533 - 0531

National Committee to Prevent Child Abuse
332 South Michigan Avenue Suite 1600
Chicago, IL 60604
(312) 663 - 3520

Survivors of Incest Anonymous
World Service Office
P.O. Box 21817
Baltimore, MD 21222-6817
(410) 282-3400

Voices in Action, Inc.
P.O. Box 148309
Chicago, IL 60614
(800) 7 - Voice - 8
(773) 327 - 1500

Washington, DC 20036
(800) 222 - 2000
(202) 429 – 6695

Additional Contacts:

STATE ATTORNEY GENERAL

COUNTY/CITY PROSECUTOR

COUNTY/CITY LAW ENFORCEMENT AGENCIES

See the BLUE PAGES of your local phone book under the appropriate section heading of Local Governments, County Governments, or State Government. (85)

Other important numbers:

_____

_____

_____

_____

Chapter Six

FEMALE VICTIMS OF CHILD SEXUAL ABUSE

Although both male and female children experience sexual abuse, there are similarities and differences in the way sexual abuse affects female and male children—both while they are young and as they grow into adulthood. This chapter addresses some of those issues.

A **U.S. Department of Justice** survey of twelve states by law enforcement agencies found that females were more than six times more likely than males to be the victims of sexual assaults. More specifically, 86% of all victims of sexual assault were female. (93)

- 69% of victims under the age of 6 were female
- 73% of victims under the age of 12 were female
- 90% of victims at age 13 were female
- A female is at her greatest risk for sexual abuse at age 14. Her risk drops to half the risk level by age 17

In one state, 126,000 children were victims of either substantiated or indicated sexual abuse. Of these:

- 75% were girls
- Nearly 30% of victims were between the ages of 4 and 7 (94)

Of women who reported they had been raped at some point in their life, 21.6% were under the age of 12 at the time of their first rape and 32.4% were between the ages of 12 and 17. Over half of all female rape victims surveyed in this study were under the age of 18 at the time of their first rape. (95)

A children's hospital reported that 58% of cases seen by the child abuse team involved sexual assault:

- 78% of the victims were female and 44% were under 5 years old (75)

Characteristics of Abuse	Male Victims	Female Victims
Threatened with physical harm	51%	37%
Physical force was used	48%	50%
Abused over a long period of time	43%	47%
Abused by multiple offenders	20%	13%
Victim resided with offender	21%	42%
Victim was abused by juveniles	56%	28%
Victim was abused by parent or guardian	8%	31%

Female victims are far more likely to be sexually abused in their own homes than are male victims. (75)

Eating Disorders And Psychiatric Disorders:

Young girls, who are sexually abused, have a greater dissatisfaction with their weight than girls who have not been abused. Many develop eating disorders as they approach adolescence.

- Characteristically, they diet excessively and continuously, purge by vomiting, use aids such as laxatives and diuretics, and avoid eating when they are bored or emotionally upset.
- Young girls who were forced to have sex are three times more likely to develop psychiatric disorders or abuse alcohol and drugs in adulthood. These disorders reflect efforts to cope with the trauma of sexual abuse. (96)
- In a study of 938 adolescents who were in residential, therapeutic facilities for the treatment of substance abuse and related disorders, 64% of the girls reported having been sexually abused. (75)

Other Serious Risk Factors:

- Women who had been raped as children were almost four times more likely than non-victims to make a serious attempt at committing suicide
- Women who report childhood rape are three times more likely to become pregnant before age 18
- An estimated 60% of teen first pregnancies are preceded by experiences of molestation, rape, or attempted rape. The average age of their offenders is 27 years
- Victims of child sexual abuse are more likely to be sexually promiscuous
- More than 75% of teenage prostitutes have been sexually abused (75)

Surprising Results From Pregnancy Risk Study:

In a pregnancy risk study among 200 women aged 18 to 20, female victims of sexual abuse reported that they wanted to become pregnant, had boyfriends who wanted them to become pregnant or feared that they might be infertile because of gynecologic and obstetric problems resulting from repeated sexual abuse. (97)

Why Girls Don't Tell:

Only 10% of child sexual abuse is reported. Here are some of the reasons why girls don't tell: (97)
- As with boys, if a girl's body responded sexually and there was pleasure or orgasm during the abuse, the victim feels she was somehow responsible for the offence.

There is a difference between the body responding naturally to sexual stimuli and being willing to participate in sexual encounters.

- If a female has a crush on the adult male who sexually assaults her, she may be accused of seducing him. However, the blame belongs to the adult offender. In one shocking case, a superior court judge accused a three-year-old of being seductive and dismissed the charges against the perpetrator.
- Female victims of sexual abuse often don't struggle. Some reasons: they have been manipulated into believing that the sexual activity is acceptable, they are too young to realize that they are being sexually abused, or there is fear that the abuser will become more violent if she does not submit.
- If a girl is promiscuous, she is usually blamed for the inappropriate sexual behavior, rather than seen as a legitimate victim of sexual abuse. If she dresses in a provocative way, some say she is "asking for trouble," or if she receives money for sex she is less likely to be perceived as a victim; although, promiscuity and prostitution are just a few of the many signs and effects of sexual molestation.
- If a girl looks or acts more sexually mature than her years, society may excuse the offender's behavior, rather than acknowledge the fact that the girl has been sexually abused. Pre-mature knowledge of sexual matters is yet another sign of having been sexually abused.

Statistically, 80% of female prisoners were victims of childhood physical or sexual abuse. Women, who suffered violent victimization as adolescents, are at greater risk for becoming victims and or perpetrators of felony assault, domestic violence, and property offenses as adults. (97)

What's Wrong With This Picture?

In a study where the beliefs and attitudes of school administrators about child sexual abuse was observed, participants viewed sketches of a 10-year-old female responding to her father's sexual advances:

- One sketch portrayed the child encouraging the sexual advances
- Another sketch implied that the child was passive about the advances
- In another sketch, the child was resisting the sexual advances of her father.

For the most part, participants did not attribute blame to the child. However, 16% of the teachers and 8% of the school psychologists attributed some blame to the child victim. (98)

The Truth Is:

Regardless of how a child or adolescent responds to sexual advances, sexual abuse is never the child's fault. The blame lies entirely with the offender. (99)
The Problem Is:

Young women who did not participate in a school sexual abuse prevention program in childhood were twice as likely to become female victims of sexual abuse as those who had participated in a prevention program." (100)

The Answer Is:

Along with **Adult Training Workbooks and Workshops, The Friendly Enemy Program** has workbooks and workshops for the awareness and prevention of child sexual abuse for children and adolescents. For more information, please visit *www.TheFriendlyEnemy.org*

Chapter Seven

MALE VICTIMS OF CHILD SEXUAL ABUSE

Male victims of sexual abuse constitute an extremely under-identified, under-served and frequently misunderstood population. Incidence rates for males range from 3 to 29%. (75)

Sexually abused boys are less likely to report sexual abuse to authorities than girls who are sexually abused. (101)

Facts About Sexual Abuse Of Boys And The Aftermath

As many as 1 in 6 men report unwanted direct sexual contact with an older person before age 16. If we include non-contact sexual behavior, such as someone exposing him or herself to a child, up to 1 in 4 men report boyhood sexual victimization. (102)

On average, boys first experience sexual abuse at age 10. The range of age at which boys are abused, is from infancy to late adolescence. (102)

At greatest risk for sexual abuse are boys living with neither or only one parent, those whose parents are separated, divorced, and/or remarried, boys whose parents abuse alcohol or are involved in criminal behavior and those who are disabled. (101)

Between 50 and 75% of the sexual perpetrators of boys are males. However, it is difficult to estimate the number of female perpetrators who abuse boys, since abuse by women often goes unreported. When a woman initiates sex with a boy, he is likely to consider it a "sexual initiation" and deny that it was abusive, even though he may suffer significant trauma from the experience. (103)

Treatment Response For Boys:

Girls are sexually abused three times more often than boys are. However, boys have a greater risk of emotional neglect and serious injury than girls do. (104)

When boys are victimized, they are blamed more often for the abuse and are viewed as less needy for care and support. As a result, boys have a greater risk of emotional neglect and serious injury than girls do. (105)

- Boy are perceived as needing protection less often than girls
- Sexually abused boys are thought to need less treatment than girls
- Boy victims are removed less often from the family than girls are (106)

Astounding Statistics:

When sexually abused boys are not treated, society must later deal with the resulting problems, such as high rates of crime, suicide, drug use, and sexual abuse. Statistically, 1/3 of juvenile delinquents, 40% of sexual offenders, and 76% of serial rapists report that they were sexually abused as children.

The suicide rate among sexually abused boys is 2 to 14 times higher than for those who were not sexually abused. Reports of multiple substance abuse among sixth-grade boys who were molested are 12 to 40 times greater than for those who were not victims of sexual abuse. Dr. Holmes states that studies lead him to believe that 10 to 20% of all boys are sexually abused in some way. [107]

Undeserved Guilt:

Boys often feel physical sexual arousal during abuse even if they are repulsed by what is happening. [108]

If boys are physically aroused, they feel that they are responsible for the sexual abuse. If he receives money or favors for sex during the grooming period, he is less likely to be perceived as a victim. [108]

Characteristics Of The Sexual Abuse:

- Boys are fondled less than girls
- Boys are more likely than girls to be subjected to anal penetration
- Boys are anally penetrated at any age
- Girls are typically abused anally when very young; later, around age ten, the abuse tends to be vaginal
- Anal penetration may be easier to identify than vaginal penetration
- Sexually abused boys usually suffer more physical abuse than girls
- Boys experience less masturbation during abuse
- Boys may experience more oral-genital abuse
- Boys may experience more repetitive abuse
- The severity of abuse in boys is usually greater than with girls
- Boys are less recognized as victims [109]

Characteristics Observed In Male Sexual Abuse Victims:

- They have difficulty recognizing that what happened to them was sexual abuse
- They have a high need for control in interactions with others
- They frequently engage in power struggles, or may seem passive, co-dependent, and conforming. Both are protection from feelings of vulnerability [110]
- They suffer from feelings of guilt
- Anxiety

- Depression
- Interpersonal isolation
- Shame
- Low self-esteem
- Self-destructive behavior
- Post-traumatic stress reactions
- Poor body imagery
- Sleep disturbance
- Nightmares
- Anorexia or bulimia
- Relational and/or sexual dysfunction
- Compulsive behavior like alcoholism, drug addiction, gambling, overeating, overspending, and sexual obsession or compulsion (108)

There is no compelling evidence that sexual abuse fundamentally changes a boy's sexual orientation, but it may lead to confusion about sexual identity and is likely to affect how he relates in intimate situations. (108)

Confusion Of Emotional Needs With Sexual Activity:

All children have a need to be nurtured and cared for. As a vulnerable young boy being groomed and nurtured by a manipulative pedophile, many of these needs may seem to have been met through sexual activity. As a result, the confused victim often identifies sex with his emotional needs being met; and therefore, sex continues to be viewed as the only way to be nurtured. Meaningful, non-sexual relationships with other men and women are often seen as threatening, so sexual behavior may actually be one of the few ways for the victim to relate on the surface, and still have some emotional needs met within him. Our normal societal values encourage men to determine how much of a man they are by their sexual activity and capability and discourage them from expressing their emotional needs. Some men give the impression they are "super studs" as a way of proving to themselves and the world that they are not abnormal or weak because of their history of being sexually abused in childhood. (110)

Confusion And Anxiety Regarding Masculine Identity—The Male Victim:

- Is extremely uncomfortable around other men
- Does not like to be touched by men
- Often avoids situations where he may be seen unclothed
- Because he does not feel part of the group, he is often isolated, having only a few male friends
- Shame is especially powerful regarding feelings about masculinity; "real men" don't get abused, they can protect themselves
- Internalized feelings about himself are either nonexistent or filled with shame
- May exhibit more feminine characteristics as an attempt to separate from negative masculine image of himself or to avoid identifying with the male abuser (110)

Multiple Compulsive Behaviors:

Sex, food, chemical substance abuse, and work are examples of common compulsive behaviors used to satisfy an internal drive to continually push oneself to avoid feeling pain and to meet dependency needs; but usually these compulsions are not productive or helpful. [110]

Physical and Emotional Symptoms:

- Hypertension and frequent chest pains
- Recurring dreams or nightmares of being chased or attacked, choked or stabbed
- Difficulty urinating in public restrooms
- Depression and anxiety [110]

Pattern Of Victimizing Self Or Others: [110]

Most victims do not become child sexual offenders, although many dysfunctional behaviors may be an attempt to punish oneself or to feel more powerful or do whatever it takes to numb the unwanted feelings connected with their abuse. This sometimes involves passive-aggressive behaviors such as exposing themselves, making obscene phone calls, or viewing pornography.

Anger toward self can involve suicide attempts or putting oneself in high-risk situations, which could lead to injury or death without actually attempting suicide. Some victims are known to react to a current situation that reminds them of their childhood abuse experience, leaving the victim feeling powerless and unable to assess the reality of the current event. They may use coping mechanisms typically used by victims to survive while being abused. They may actually become involved in abusive relationships as an adult that are in many ways similar to the childhood sexual abuse experience.

Victims often feel unsafe and unable to protect themselves resulting in difficulty establishing even the smallest amount of trust in others. They have an unrealistic fear that everyone can see their failures and vulnerability. Many victims also have a history of physical and emotional abuse leaving them filled with anxiety and rage, frequently causing them to suffer withdrawal.

Poorly Defined Sense Of Self:

For countless male survivors of child sexual abuse, self-protection becomes a matter of trying to hide from the world in an attempt to avoid feelings of confusion and vulnerability. The ability to look within one's self and find self-worth and self-dependability has been wiped away by the memory of the control that the sexual perpetrator gained over the victim. The victim longs to be independent, but at the same time is emotionally unable to achieve that independence. Behaviors are similar to co-dependency. For many survivors of sexual abuse the perpetrator remains in control of the victim's emotions for a lifetime.

Chaotic Relationships: (110)

- Victim has difficulties with intimacy
- An inability to be self-sufficient
- Has difficulty with commitments to relationships
- Experiences extreme and intense emotional confusion in having a need for closeness with others and at the same time fearing that closeness
- The need to be cared for and dependent upon others for their needs to be met is in conflict with their fear of being vulnerable and re-victimized
- This behavior repeats the victim-perpetrator experience when, in the mind of the victim, their spouse or partner becomes the perpetrator and at other times their protector

How Boys And Girls Respond To Sexual Abuse:

Girls may have a greater tendency to "act in," internalize, and become anxious or depressed (106)

Boys seem to have a greater tendency to "act out," and externalize their emotions with disruptive behaviors and attempts to prove their masculinity. This is perhaps the most common behavioral reaction of boy victims of sexual abuse. (106)

Typical Aggression—Acting Out Behaviors Of Boys Who Have Been Sexually Abused: (106)

- Picking fights
- Being destructive
- Anxiety disorders
- Suicidal tendencies
- Relationship problems
- Showing marked disobedience
- Having a hostile or confrontational attitude
- Increased tendency towards compulsive sexuality
- More likely to turn his rage outward in aggressive and anti-social behavior
- There may be a tendency for male victims of sexual abuse to repeat their own victimization, only this time in the role of perpetrator, victimizing a younger child.

Abuser Characteristics:

- Boys and girls are equally as likely to be abused by someone inside the family
- Boys and girls are equally in danger of abuse by strangers
- Adolescent abusers more often chose boys as victims
- Fathers, more often than stepfathers, sexually abuse boys
- Females are more likely to chose a boy than a girl to sexually abuse
- It appears that when the abuser is a professional person, they are more likely to chose a boy over a girl
- If the father is unemployed, he will typically molest the boy rather than the girl (109)

56

- Most perpetrators tend to be males who consider themselves heterosexual. (21)

Two Trends Are Evident In The Existing Statistics On Male Victims Of Sexual Abuse: (111)

- The more recent the research, the higher the incidence of abuse.
- With growing awareness, more men seem willing to disclose their abuse.

Over 80% of sexually abused boys never become adult perpetrators, while a majority of perpetrators (up to 80%) were themselves abused. (106)

For more information, see Chapter Eleven, The Cycle of Abuse—Do the Abused Become The Abusers?

NOTES

Chapter Eight

SEXUAL ABUSE VICTIMS WITH DISABILITIES

A TRUE STORY

Susan was born with cerebral palsy. The oldest of four children, she and her siblings grew up in a poor rural neighborhood. Susan's mother worked nights in a factory. As a young child, Susan could get around by walking and holding onto objects. By the time she was nine, crawling was her only means of movement. When Susan was ten, she got her first wheelchair.

It was around this time Susan's mother remarried. On many occasions, Susan's stepfather was the adult in charge. Susan did not like her stepfather; he was always trying to hug and kiss her when she did not want him to. Susan tried to stay away from him by going to her room. She frequently pretended to be asleep to keep her stepfather away.

One Saturday night when they were alone, Susan's stepfather came into her room and started touching her. She told him to stop, but he just kept doing it. He then turned her so she was lying on her back. In this position, her disability made it impossible for her to move. Susan's stepfather then forced her to engage in oral sex, followed by vaginal intercourse. After that, he also penetrated her anally.

Susan wished she would die. For the next two years, her stepfather continued to sexually abuse her, forcing her to engage in sexual acts. In addition, he took pay from his male friends and they had sexual relations with Susan. Not long after that, Susan's mother started to show Susan sex magazines. She also began to invite other male friends over to have sex with Susan.

Susan felt like a prisoner in her home. She felt there was no one she could tell about this terrible thing that was happening to her. After all, her mother had told her many times that their life was hard because of Susan's disability. Susan did not feel she had any right to complain.

It is estimated that children with disabilities are 4 to 10 times more vulnerable to sexual abuse than their non-disabled peers. (111)

Children And Youth With Disabilities Are At Risk Because Of:

Powerlessness:

Children and youth with disabilities often do not make choices for themselves; caregivers make decisions for them and they are taught to obey their caregivers. Their dependence on others puts them at risk for becoming sexual abuse victims. (97)

Need For Personal Care:

People with certain physical disabilities require someone to bath them and help them use the toilet. They have little control over who touches their bodies, and in what manner.

Isolation:

Often times, children with disability are isolated from the rest of the community, which increases the likelihood that sexual abuse will take place, and it increases the likelihood that the abuse will go undetected.

Physical Defenselessness:

Children who have physical, visual, and hearing disabilities, as well as other limitations, have difficulty defending themselves against offenders.

Language, Speech, Or Vocabulary Barriers:

Children with disabilities in communicating have difficulty asking for help or revealing abuse, which in turn puts them at greater risk for ongoing sexual abuse.

Impaired Or Limited Cognitive Abilities:

Young people with intellectual disabilities, having trouble reasoning or remembering, may not understand an abusive situation, and are more easily manipulated.

Lack Of Abuse Prevention Education:

Lack of knowledge about sexual abuse makes it difficult for children with disabilities to understand and recognize abusive situations.

Care Facilities Without Protection-Structures And Policies:

Care facilities that have inflexible routines and a high number of children per staff, lack clear "abuse guidelines and policies." They often do not have adequate background checks and proper screening of the staff and volunteers. These factors put people with disabilities at greater risk for abuse. (97)

Sexual Abuse And Disability—Myths, Realities, And Stereotypes:

- MYTH: Sexual abuse victims with disabilities are non-existent because people with disabilities are neither sexual nor attractive. (97)
  REALITY: Sexual abuse is primarily motivated by power and control. Individuals with disabilities may be easier to manipulate and less likely to report.
- MYTH: People with disabilities are either over-sexualized or unable to control their sexual impulses, or are asexual (void of sexuality).
  REALITY: Young people with disabilities go through similar stages of development as their peers without disabilities.
- MYTH: If young people with disabilities are protected and kept away from strangers, they will be safe from sexual abuse.
  REALITY: Most young people are sexually abused by those they know and trust.
- MYTH: Young victims with disabilities don't fully understand what is happening to them so they will not feel emotional pain when they are sexually abused.
  REALITY: A young person with a disability may not have the same words to describe their pain, but their emotional anguish is very real.
- MYTH: Young people with disabilities are incapable of understanding and relating information, and they are prone to fantasizing and lying.
  REALITY: They may process and communicate in different ways, but they are no less credible and truthful.
- MYTH: People with disabilities are child-like; they never really become adults, therefore cannot become sexual abuse victims.
  REALITY: While those with certain disabilities may not mature in the same manner or at the same rate as others, they do not remain children; therefore, they can indeed become sexual abuse victims. (97)

How To Help Prevent The Sexual Abuse Of Children With Disabilities:

- Train them in safety
- Teach them self-protection
- Teach them healthy sexuality
- Teach them to be forceful when they feel threatened and to tell
- Children need to know that they have a right to protect themselves and a right to tell an adult if they are not being protected
- Children need to know they have a right to tell someone if their needs are not being met

- Children need to understand clearly that they deserve to be treated with respect in every situation, at home, at school, in hospitals or treatment centers, in their social environments, etc. (112)

Parents And Caretakers Responsibility To Children With Disabilities:

- Parents, and other adults who contribute to a child's care, need education, support, and special training relevant to a child's particular physical, sensory, or intellectual needs.
- Parents and other caregivers also need education regarding the potential risks and signs of abuse. Their child may be at an increased risk of abuse from caregivers and others in the community.
- Learning to listen to a child is always important, especially if a child has a communication or intellectual disability.
- Children may communicate about abuse in indirect ways, such as regressive behaviors, resistance, "acting out," or excessive anger.

Parents Must Be Careful When Choosing Caregivers:

- Observe the child's response to these individuals
- Ask questions to help judge the openness and professionalism
- Be continually involved in the child's care and development (112)

NOTES

Chapter Nine

FOSTER CARE AND CHILD SEXUAL ABUSE

According to the American Academy of Child and Adolescent Psychiatry, in 2006 over 500,000 children in the U.S. currently reside in some form of foster care. Each year, an estimated 20,000 young people reach age 18, and typically "age out" of the foster care system. (113)

A study of reported abuse in Maryland found the rate of substantiated cases of sexual abuse in foster care more than four times higher than the rate in the general population. (113)

A study in Indiana discovered there are three times more physical and two times more sexual abuse cases in foster homes than in the general population. (113)

Even in an exemplary foster care program, where caseloads are kept low and case workers and foster parents get specialized training, sexual abuse still occurs. Results from one group of girls questioned about their experiences in the foster home of the longest period:

24% said they were victims of actual or attempted sexual perpetration
Officials at the program claim they have since lowered the rate of all forms of abuse to 12%. This is based on an in-house survey of the program's own caseworkers, not outside interviews with the children themselves. (115)

Types Of Abuse In Confirmed Cases:

- Neglect — 55.9%
- Physical Abuse — 25.6%
- Sexual Abuse —12.4%
- Psychological Abuse — 6.1% (115)

In another report from an urban foster care program, it was established that almost 50% of the substantiated maltreatment was sexual abuse, with the remainder being physical abuse and neglect. Problems in health, development, and functioning were reported in the social services record for a large number of all children. Children sexually abused while in foster care were significantly more likely to have a non-kinship placement, and to have mental health and development problems. (116)

Characteristics Of Foster Homes Where Maltreatment Of Children Is Reported:

- Homes that had younger foster mothers
- Homes in which children shared bedrooms with other family members
- Homes where case-workers felt uncertain or uneasy
- Homes that were restricted for placement of children with certain needs

Kinship-Care Homes Were Found To Present Decreased Risk:

Kinship Care is a program designed to help support a child who resides outside of his or her own home, either temporarily or for long term with a relative such as an adult brother or sister, a first cousin, a nephew or niece, an uncle or aunt or a grandparent, among others. (117)

Kinship Care supports the concept of children living with a relative to ease family stress or temporary family problems rather than placing the child in a foster home or other type of placement. For children who do come to the attention of the child welfare system, Kinship Care creates another placement option for a child who may not be able to continue living at home with his or her parents. It should not, however, be used when a foster care placement is in the best interest of the child. (117)

From a report of 290 incidents of abuse and neglect within family foster homes, group homes, residential treatment centers, and institutions in Colorado, it was revealed that 38% of the reported incidents took place in foster homes: (118)

Studies revealed that males were the predominant victims of both physical abuse and neglect while females were the predominant sexual abuse victims. (119)

Sexual abuse cases typically result in removing the child from the abusive facility, most of which are family foster homes. (120)

One Study Revealed That Foster Caregivers Were Identified In:

- 45 cases of physical abuse
- 34 cases of neglect
- 20 cases of sexual abuse (120)

Causes That Lead To Abuse:

Shortage of foster care homes because of low monetary support, creating pressure to issue foster care licenses to sub-standard sources

Emphasis on putting children in the least restrictive setting, placing difficult children with behavior disabilities in foster care.

A lack of adequate support systems for foster caregivers because of large caseloads Stressful situations in the foster family home can cause the foster child to react with aggressive behavior, leading to his or her being abused. The child is removed, placed in another home, and the cycle repeats. (119)

These affects and indicators of child sexual abuse were observed among youth incarcerated, living in group homes, and placed in foster care:

- Guilt
- Shame
- Feeling of helplessness
- Feelings of emptiness and grief
- Loneliness
- Feelings of separation
- Feelings of entrapment
- Confusion
- Feeling that the abuser has won and still dominates
- In adulthood, women with a history of child sexual abuse live with the fear that their own children may fall prey to a sexual predator. (121)

Children Sexually Abusing Children:

An important discovery is the number of foster children who are being sexually abused by foster brothers and sisters. (120)

A Broward County, Florida attorney reported in a sworn affidavit that over a period of only 18 months, he became aware of 50 instances of child-on-child sexual abuse involving more than 100 Broward County foster children. During a previous 18-month period, only 7 such reports were filed. When an epidemic of child-on-child sexual abuse was exposed, a study revealed the child abuse hotline had been neglecting to report child-on-child sexual abuse. (122)

In group homes, there was more than 10 times the rate of physical abuse and more than 28 times the rate of sexual abuse as in the general population, partly because so many children in the homes abused each other. (114)

Fostering Sexually Abused Children:

Research shows there are more difficulties and problems involved in fostering children who have been sexually abused.

Of particular importance is the evidence of sexualized behavior on the part of the children in 80% of the 80 cases reviewed.

Sexually abused children make sexual advances including touching the foster or adoptive parents' genital areas, demands for sexual intercourse, and in over 50% of the placements, some type of sexual activity was directed from one foster child towards another child in the family. (123)

The most dangerous problem for many foster families is that the sexually abused child will teach other children in the home sexual play. Very young children may be

particularly vulnerable to this type of abuse while at the same time; older children in the home may be coaxed into a sexual relationship, which they do not understand. (120)
How This Behavior Affects The Ongoing Sexual Abuse In Foster Care:
A U.S. study found that younger children who were sexually abused in foster homes were likely to have already been victims of sexual abuse; this finding did not seem to include older victims. (120)

Russell suggests that perpetrators of sexual abuse may be able to identify and exploit children who have already been sexually abused. MacFarlane reports that approximately 25% of the children in one study, who were in treatment for sexual abuse, were re-victimized during the treatment period there were in foster care. In linking inappropriate sexual behavior to the possibilities of further sexual abuse, caution must be taken not to bring up the argument that the child is "seductive." Responsibility for the abuse must remain firmly with the perpetrator and not with the innocent, naïve child. (124)

Stress Factors:

It was noted above that stress could trigger the sexual abuse of children, and Macaskill points out that fostering children who have been sexually abused is extremely stressful:

- Disrupting family life
- Unsettling established role models and relationships
- Sapping the energies of those caring for them.

Foster and adoptive parents are especially vulnerable as their tolerance level is often stretched to its ultimate limits. Several foster parents admitted that it was virtually impossible to realize in advance how heavy the personal toll would be when caring for an abused child. (123)

Consequently, experts place a great deal of importance on regular reviews that evaluate levels of stress in the foster home. This also raises important issues about the need for additional support and resources for foster caregivers who are caring for troubled, disturbed children and young people. Foster care advocates feel that foster care should be considered a professional, salaried government service. (125)

Allegations Of Abuse Against Foster Caregivers:

The National Family Caregivers Association stresses the importance of a Code of Practice when foster families are accused of abuse. (120)

There is a serious problem when foster caregivers have to cope with allegations of abuse being filed against them. A study of 36 foster caregivers, who were dealing with unsubstantiated allegations of abuse, showed that foster caregivers were often not told the exact nature of the allegation and therefore, did not know exactly what they were being accused of. Investigations were prolonged, and foster families frequently received little or no support. (120)

Foster Families Should Have The Following:
- The right to be told the details of the allegation
- The right to be heard by people not directly involved in the complaint
- The right to express and document their view point of the allegation
- The right to a second medical opinion where physical abuse is alleged and medical evidence is being presented
- The right to have competent, experienced, and unbiased people conduct a fair, proper investigation
- The right to counsel and support during and after the investigation
- The right to receive decisions in writing
- The right to appeal (120)

Suggested Characteristics Of An Effective Policy Format:

- Staff members and foster caregivers should be prepared and trained to expect and deal with allegations
- A statement should be provided insuring that the foster care agency will investigate all reports of allegations
- Information needs to be available about the procedure of the investigation and the decision-making process
- Foster caregivers should know what rights they have, and do not have

Throughout the investigation of allegations of abuse, foster caregivers should be informed about what resources are available for their support, what the foster care agency is willing to do, and know the approximately time frame

An effective policy format should avoid unnecessary or unplanned removals of children The foster family should be guaranteed that their input into a fair and thorough investigation and support for the family will be provided for interviews and hearings.

They should receive timely information on the progress of the investigation, a written notice of the final outcome, and what it means should be provided (126)

Following the outcome of the report, the foster family should be informed about agency procedures for this phase of the investigation, what is likely to take place, and what avenues there are for review and appeal of decisions (127)

Macaskill noted that in over 1/3 of foster families, the thought of being accused of sexual malpractice had not occurred to them, and they were therefore unprepared. A lack of basic information resulted in some families taking on the responsibility of fostering children without inquiring about their sexual abuse history; putting emphasis on the importance of professionals believing the child's story.

Macaskill states that it is grossly unfair to expect substitute families to take on a sexually abused child without first explaining how crucial the child's words will be in the event of an allegation. It is important to help them realize that these allegations do occur, and to know how to deal with this problem.

Macaskill recommends that foster families have all opportunities and considerations to create changes in their lifestyle, which may be essential to protect all family members against allegations. She further advises that caregivers should repeat this plan of action each time a new foster child is placed in their care, while taking into consideration the unique personalities and special needs of each child. [123]

Preparation And Training For Foster Parents:

Experts agree; it is essential that foster parents receive training on child sexual abuse to prepare them for the many challenges that go along with fostering children who are troubled and who may be victims of sexual abuse. [123]

The **Friendly Enemy Workbooks and Workshops** can provide adequate and professional education to help stop child sexual abuse in foster care.

<u>NOTES</u>

Chapter Ten

CHILD SEXUAL ABUSE AND THE CHURCH, WHEN A SACRED TRUST IS BROKEN

Child Sexual Abuse By Catholic And Protestant Clergy:

Allegations and confirmed cases of sex abuse by priests against children in the Catholic Church are now reported in the media since widespread reports of abuse first surfaced in the Boston area in the early 2000s. [128]

However, tracking allegations and confirmed cases of misconduct by protestant clergy is a difficult task because different church denominations are independent of each other, as compared to Catholicism's centralized chain of command.

The Association of Statisticians of American Religious Bodies estimates there are 224,000 protestant denominations across the country.

With so many different organizational structures, which may or may not include a centralized chain of command, it is sometimes impossible to accumulate all-inclusive data about sex abuse allegations with these protestant denominations.

Similarly, governed denominations include United Methodists, Lutherans, Episcopalians, and Presbyterians. Others carry a national name, such as Baptists, but may govern themselves at the local level. Countless others are independent, with no affiliation with any unit beyond their local church.

By contrast, Catholic bishops commissioned the Center for Applied Research in the Apostolate (CARA) at Georgetown University to track and publish an annual report on credible allegations of sexual misconduct among priests and deacons. In 2006, CARA showed 635 new and "credible allegations" were lodged against 394 priests or deacons from January 1 to December 31. That compares to 695 in 2005 and 898 in 2004. [128]

Protecting Children:

Since child sex abuse by Catholic clergy began making headlines, both Catholics and Protestants have taken steps to protect children from predators. [128]

In New York, the Syracuse and Rochester Dioceses have victim assistance coordinators who handle complaints of suspected sexual abuse of a minor, involving clergy, church employee, or volunteer. Syracuse has a Safe Environment Program that requires all priests, paid employees, childcare providers, coaches, and other volunteers to complete a training session, background screening, and agreement to adhere to a strict code of conduct.

The Wyoming Conference established a Safe Sanctuary program that required clergy and an estimated 3,000 local church volunteers who work with children to complete training.

In reply to one reporter's inquiry, United Methodist Bishop Susan W. Hassinger of the Wyoming Conference issued a statement saying allegations are taken very seriously and credible complaints would result in temporarily or permanently removing a pastor from a church assignment and possibly asking the clergy to surrender ministerial credentials. At that point, the accused would be identified through an announcement to the church, and the complaint would be inserted into the pastor's personnel file, possibly available for review by potential church or private sector employers.

In the Wesleyan Church, allegations are investigated by the local church and reported to the district. The Wesleyan Church has zero tolerance for clergy abusing children. If a pastor is found guilty, that person is dismissed immediately and forbidden from accepting a pastor's position again.

Episcopalians in Central New York, who serve in roles where they work with children, must participate in safe church training and undergo background checks.

"We ask ourselves why this happened in our church and in our community," said Adams, about a recent case of child sex abuse by clergy. "I have faith we will see the effect of God's reconciling grace in and through one another."

Priest Or Clergy Sexual Abuse, Trauma And Healing:

Family Safety And How Social Workers Help:

As of 2007, over 900 Catholic priests and other members of the clergy were found guilty of sexually molesting a child. Most of these offenders had multiple victims. (129)
Several priests publicly admitted their offense, and many more were found guilty in criminal or civil trials. The Catholic Church has paid over $2 billion as compensation to victims of abuse.

In past years, priests caught in child sexual abuse went into treatment programs, and then returned to their duties where, sadly, in most cases, criminal sex acts were repeated. Rarely were the offenders prosecuted or defrocked. Since the scandals of the early 2000s, laws in most states now require clergy to report any childhood sexual abuse of which they are aware.

Extent Of The Abuse:

- A random survey of over 7,000 active Catholics in the U.S. and Canada found:
- 1.7% of females and 3.3% of males admitted they were sexually abused by a priest as a child
- 1 in 5 alleged victims of priest sexual abuse are female
- 4 % are teens

- 2 % are preteens
- The majority of the victims were between the ages of 13 and 17

Traditionally, priests were expected to be "role models" to young males. Statistics are much higher regarding the number of boys vs. girls sexually abused by priests. Bear in mind that until recent years, only males could be altar boys (servers) who work closely with priests. (129)

Power Dynamics In Clergy Sexual Abuse:

In the Roman Catholic Church, the ordained priest holds a position of sacred trust. Not only is the priest considered the church's representative, but also the representative of God. This religious position and the rituals they lead in mass increase the clergy's power of influence over members. Their robes and adornments call attention to their authority. Both young and old Catholics address the priest as "Father," who carries out his duties largely without supervision. Frequently, congregations idolize their spiritual leaders and view them as God's representative on earth. (129)

The Psychological Impact:

What about the individual victim's response? To find answers to this question, Van Wormer examined unpublished transcripts from ethnographic interviews with nine female survivors of clergy sexual misconduct. Dealing with the scientific description of individual cultures, all the women in the study were white and Roman Catholic from birth. Each had been sexually exploited and/or abused by a Catholic priest and lived in a cloak of secrecy.

Faith In God Shattered:

These survivors reported that their faith in God was shattered. They not only endured personal violation, but also found themselves without a spiritual home that they could turn to for comfort and safety. Each woman either lost their fathers early in life or are estranged from them. Significantly, several of those surveyed had experienced some kind of sexual violation earlier in life, even before the priest encounter. This increased their vulnerability. (129)

All who were interviewed reported that they were forced into secrecy, often after a few failed attempts to get help. Some were accused of being seductive with an innocent priest. Most responded to the trauma either by repressing the memory or by blaming themselves. Several of the women were successfully healed— after suffering through many years of pain—with therapeutic and social support. Some turned to a Heavenly Mother, Mary, for solace.

A review of the literature on priest/clergy abuse reveals that for either gender the typical survivor became disillusioned with the church and suffered a loss of religious faith because of the abuse. Those that revealed their abuse suffered yet more traumas by

73

the non-supportive response of the church body to their allegations. There is an inadequate amount of research to determine the full extent of suicide attempts or completed suicides of victims from this form of abuse. One estimate in the literature is that 20% of children who were abused by religious authorities considered suicide at some point. (129)

Prevention:

The institutional church has only reluctantly acknowledged the magnitude of the damage that has been done through the years of denial and deception. Today, the trend is a strict crackdown on the crime of sexual abuse committed against children and adolescents. The understanding of Catholic Church members and the reporting of criminal cases to the authorities would further guarantee the integrity of the Catholic Church. (129)

A recent survey, in conjunction with U.S. Bishops and released to the public, provides some hope that the situation is improving. However, of the 70% of incidents against minors reported in 2006, the actual abuses occurring between 1960 and 1984, the findings are that the majority of victims are now deceased.

The Report Also Showed The Following:

Money spent on child protection efforts by the Catholic Church increased 35% from the previous year

Allegations of sexual abuse against minors by clergy fell by 9% from the previous year Allowing women to become priests, coupled with a re-evaluation of the enforced celibacy rule for clergy, are changes that might prevent further abuse, although this will likely take time—time some children at risk don't have. Both steps might help provide a larger pool of qualified candidates. The Vatican's response, which is to remove known homosexuals from the priesthood, is not helpful since there is not a significant link between homosexuality and pedophilia, other than the fact that some pedophiles are also homosexual. (129)

Once an allegation of priest sexual abuse is reported, all parties involved need to seek professional treatment. The victim needs immediate support and reassurance. The priest also therapeutic attention and support with an opportunity to make amends, so that, even if he is dismissed from the priesthood and/or imprisoned, he may find a way to discontinue his criminally, deviant behavior.

How Social Workers Help:

Grass roots organizations are helping church authorities address the issue of priest sexual abuse. Activist Barbara Blaine is a social worker and attorney who is the founder and president of Survivors Network of Those Abused by Priests (SNAP). Ms. Blaine reported her abuse in 1985 to church leaders, but to no avail. She decided to find other survivors, hoping they would help each other cope with the effects of the abuse and work together toward an institutional change. (129)

Since its foundation in 1988, SNAP has grown to over 8,000 members in 50 states and is now in other countries besides America. Today, over 65 support groups are affiliated with this organization. At the policy level, SNAP is sponsoring a nationwide push for all states to end the statutes of limitation on the crime of sexual abuse against children and to extend the amount of time victims of childhood sexual abuse have to seek justice in both civil and criminal courts.

As we know from studies of rape survivors, a crucial factor in the recovery process is the immediate response from significant others and authorities. If this crime and resulting trauma is to be prevented, early intervention is essential. A teenage female survivor, in contrast to the male survivor of any age, is often at least partially blamed for the sexual involvement; therefore, support by church and community is vital for her successful healing

Counseling sessions with an expert on trauma and healing can be tremendously helpful. Such an individual can help all violated children, men, and women regain their faith in human nature, in their religious beliefs, and in themselves. Referral to a self-help activist group such as Crusaders Against Clergy Abuse can be extremely helpful. (130)

Justice can begin when offenders take full responsibility for what they have done to the victim/survivor and the community as a whole. Social workers are becoming increasingly familiar with restorative justice techniques in bringing about justice and reconciliation when a wrongdoing has occurred. From this approach, society has accountability to the victim to help him or her restore what was lost. Offering apologies and compensations are vital to the restorative justice viewpoint. (131)

Social workers can play an active role in helping youths express their feelings of disillusionment; loss of trust and innocence and in some cases religious faith. Social workers have two obvious advantages over others who are helping through their professional training. The first is their systems orientation and willingness to involve family members in the counseling process, which is crucial to help survivors rebuild their self-esteem. A second advantage, unique to social work, is the profession's holistic approach that addresses human behavior from a psychological, social, and spiritual perspective. The social worker addresses the spiritual side of pain and healing as well as the psychosocial aspects of the trauma. (132)

The Survivors Network Of Those Abused By Priests (SNAP):

SNAP is a self-help organization of adult survivors of clergy sexual abuse and their supporters. Along with the founder, Barbara A. Blaine, this organization works to end the cycle of abuse in two ways:

- By supporting one another in personal healing

- By pursuing justice and institutional change through holding individual perpetrators and the church accountable

SNAP has local chapters and support groups in over 50 cities across the country and provides resources such as peer counseling, contact information for local support groups, online discussion boards, a library of educational materials, and news stories and ways to support their mission, both in the local community and on a national level.

Stop Baptist Predators.Org:

"THIS LITTLE LIGHT OF MINE... I'M GONNA LET IT SHINE"
This little light shines for the many other clergy abuse victims whose voices have been silenced; silenced by shame; silenced by the false instruction of religious leaders; silenced by church shunning or bullying; silenced by church contracts for secrecy; silenced by suicide.

The mission of StopBaptistPredators.org is to break the silence of Baptist clergy sex abuse. (133)

The Cost Of Sexual Assault Upon The Church Around The World:

Across the nation of Australia, Catholic dioceses have paid out an estimated $800 million in settlements of clergy sexual misconduct lawsuits in the past 15 years. Estimates of the number of priests involved range from 400 to 1,000 out of a total priest population of about 50,000. (134)

The Anglican diocese of Caribou, Canada is near bankruptcy due to sexual abuse compensation payouts. In December 2002, the Catholic Archdiocese of Boston considered filing for bankruptcy for the same reason. The Catholic diocese of Santa Rosa, California took heavy loans to pay off compensation suits. (135)

The Anglican diocese of Brisbane considered bankruptcy, resulting from paying sexual abuse claims. This is consistent with the Archbishop's statement that the proposed inquiry into the diocese's handling of abuse claims between 1990 and 2001 would be approximately 40 to 50 cases. (136)

One researcher claims that the problem is greater among Protestant churches than among Catholic churches, stating that 1.7% of Catholic priests are abusers, but 10% of Protestant ministers are abusers. (137)

NOTE: In all of these cases named, legal action was a last resort for the victims. Most, if not all, approached the church for help and counsel and it was the unsympathetic stalling of the church that drove the victims to lawsuits. The fact that they won their suits is testament to the legal validity of their claims. (135)

Jewish survivors of sexual violence speak out with information for and about sexual assault, rabbinical sexual misconduct and those who care about them. (138)

IN THE BASEMENT, BEHIND A CLOSED DOOR

by Aviva Lori Haaretz

A community psychologist Avrohom Mondrowitz, age 60, was probably born in Poland and settled in Israel with his family after World War II. He grew up in Tel Aviv, but in the 1950s, the family immigrated to Chicago. He attended the Telshe Yeshiva, in Wickliffe, Ohio, run by the Lithuanian branch of Orthodox Jewry. In the 1970s, he came to Brooklyn, saying he held a master's degree in the sciences, a Ph.D. in clinical psychology from Columbia, and another Ph.D. in educational administration from the University of Florida, in addition to being an ordained rabbi. The Jews of Brooklyn were impressed, and Mondrowitz began to acquire social status. He wrote articles on education for the Haredi press, had a radio program on which he gave listeners advice on how to treat children, established a yeshiva for children in distress and was active in Ohel, a large New York organization for orphans and children from broken homes. Finally, he hung a "psychologist" sign on his door and started to receive patients. (138)

"He made a name for himself and was much respected in the community," says a Brooklyn Hasid." Children were referred to him, hard cases from Ohel, and he treated them. Rabbis also referred children to him for treatment. His expertise was treating children who had been sexually molested."

Children who visited his office, which was located in the basement of his home, remember him boasting about the "bragging wall," on which hung his diplomas and certificates, all finely framed. But his diplomas turned out to be fakes, including his rabbinical ordination."

The police suspect that in that office, behind a closed door and drawn curtains, he sexually abused children, including acts of sodomy. In many cases, the parents were waiting in the next room for the treatment to end so they could take the children home. Those are the facts as collected by the Brooklyn police and told by the children.
At the time of this report, Rabbi Avrohom Mondrowitz was sitting in a jail in Jerusalem, Israel awaiting an extradition trial scheduled for November 27, 2007.

Prevention Efforts:

Narrow Bridge is a controversial, acclaimed film, which has been making waves in the Orthodox Jewish community. It is the first film of its kind to break the silence on the issue of sexual abuse in the Orthodox Jewish community. (138)

The Awareness Center is the Jewish Coalition Against Sexual Abuse/Assault (JCASA), the only international Jewish organization dedicated to addressing sexual violence in Jewish communities around the world. JCASA acts as a clearinghouse of information and resources on the topics of childhood sexual abuse, sexual assault, clergy abuse (in the Jewish community), and sex offenders. JCASA offers a speaker's bureau to discuss these topics, an international conference on sexual violence in Jewish communities, and a certification program for rabbis and other professionals interested in working with survivors of sexual violence. Lastly, JCASA seeks to develop a treatment center and ongoing educational programming in Israel, the United States, and throughout the world.

The Awareness Center
P.O. Box 65273
Baltimore, MD 21209
Voice Mail (443) 857-5560

Vicki Polin, Executive Director
vickipolin@aol.com
Email: info@theawarenesscenter.org
www.theawarenesscenter.org

Vicki Polin, MA, LCPC, NCC, ATR-BC, is the founder and executive director of The Awareness Center. Vicki is a Nationally Certified Counselor (NCC), Licensed Clinical Professional Counselor (LCPC) in the state of Illinois, and is a Board Certified Art Therapist.

In the past, Vicki has qualified as an expert witness and provided testimony in juvenile court on cases related to childhood sexual abuse and neglect. She has presented educational and experiential (based on experiences) seminars to community groups, universities, and at professional conferences on both a local and national level. Vicki served as a board member of several non-profit organizations, which included VOICES in Action, Inc., and Alternative Behavior Treatment Centers for Juvenile Sex Offenders and Sexually Reactive Youth. Vicki also served on the planning committee of Jewish Women International's (JWI) 2nd International Conference on Domestic Abuse. [138]

What The Church Is Doing To Secure The "Sacred Trust":

Creating Safer Havens, Donalda Shepardson, President/Founder:

Our mission is to combat child abuse and specifically child sexual abuse, by challenging churches, schools, and youth organizations to "take a stand" to better protect children and youth. Through the implementation of Creating Safer Havens child protection program, there will be "Safer Havens in an Unsafe World." [139]

Why Is The Church Vulnerable To Liability?

- By its very nature, churches are trusting institutions.
- The Church provides a trusting atmosphere for child molesters.
- Willing volunteers are always needed. Often complete strangers are permitted to work with children.
- Background and screening checks are rarely implemented.
- The church may not have established policies and procedures to prevent child sexual abuse.
- Often, there is a lack of proper supervision.
- Church staff and volunteers lack education and training in child abuse, more specifically, child sexual abuse. They need to know the Church's child abuse policies and procedures.
- Most churches do not have insurance coverage that will protect the church from the liability created by child sexual abuse.

What Can The Church Do To Decrease Their Liability?

- Take a positive stand to protect children and the church.
- Implement a Child Protection Program that provides risk management.
- Screen all workers working with children and youth.
- Maintain watchful supervision over children and youth.
- Provide education in child abuse and more specifically, child sexual abuse.
- Provide training in policies and procedures adopted by the pastor and church board.
- Report to authorities all sexual abuse allegations or suspicions.
- Appoint a media spokesperson, preferably a senior pastor, to represent the church should there be allegations of child sexual abuse.
- Carry an insurance policy providing liability coverage for child sexual abuse allegations.

Son of man, I have made you a watchman for the house of Israel. (NIV)

Read Ezekiel 3:17, 33:7

The challenge of our churches is to take a stand for children and youth by protecting them from abuse by aggressively pursuing a risk management approach to end child sexual abuse.

Creating Safer Havens is a child abuse prevention, protection, and risk management-training program that provides consulting services and guided implementations.

Start with the overview-training workshop for clergy, staff, all volunteers, and anyone from your congregation or organization who may come in contact with children or youth. This workshop provides people with a broad brushstroke on the history of abuse, various types, and gives a solid foundation for policies, procedures, etc. It can help your church or organization be united in your stand on this issue. Implementing an overview training will show you are aggressively pursuing a risk management approach to combat child sexual abuse.

Additional training is done in phases, working with a team of 2 to 5 people from your church or organization. Each phase is a separate workshop to guide you through the following:

- Policies
- Procedures
- Screening/fingerprinting
- Supervision, i.e. watchman supervision
- Reporting (not a separate workshop). Reporting laws are briefly mentioned in the overview and covered again in each procedures workshop.

We advise that your team members be at the overview training to understand the justification for the entire program. Keep in mind this team will be implementing the program. It is critical to have competent people who will stay the course and follow through. Your team will become your future trainers.

In order for a child abuse prevention and risk management program to succeed you need overall church cooperation and a process to establish ongoing training. The Overview Training and Creating Safer Havens for our Children and Youth booklets accomplish that goal through education and awareness.

Booklets Provide Validation For The Need To Better Protect Children, Youth, Clergy, Staff, And Volunteers. They Are Used:

- During the Overview Training and in additional workshops
- During a brief presentation to the congregation
- Booklets may be provided for each individual family or household of your church
- To establish ongoing training
- Booklets are given to new members at orientation and are used during training of all new volunteers.
- If you have a child sexual abuse risk management program already in place to protect the children, youth, clergy, staff and volunteers, God bless you. If you do not, Donalda Shepardson, challenges the church and other organizations to take a stand and implement this program to help children.
- "God's blessings as we continue to move forward Creating Safer Havens for our children, youth, clergy, staff, and volunteers." (139)

NOTES

Chapter Eleven

THE CYCLE OF ABUSE,
DO THE ABUSED BECOME THE ABUSERS?

Several studies have been done on the cycle of sexual abuse, that is, the likelihood that child victims of sexual abuse will become adult abusers. (140)

These studies show that the majority of victims of sexual abuse during childhood did not become sex offenders as adults. Therefore, childhood sexual victimization does not necessarily lead to adult sexual offending. In addition, the majority of the studies concluded that most adult child sex offenders did not report that they were sexually victimized as children.

Sexual victimization in childhood may significantly increase the risk that victims will themselves become sexual offenders as adults. However, many other conditions and experiences may contribute to this increased risk. For example, one study found that children who are neglected are more likely to commit sex offenses as adults than those sexually abused as children.

Research is ongoing and greatly needed. There is work yet to do in determining what kind of experiences increase the chances that sexually victimized children will become adult abusers. The goal is to help prevent victimized children from becoming adult abusers. (140)

One theory developed in a study with 747 males and 96 females who attended a forensic psychotherapy service; shows the direct correlation between being a sexual abuse victim and becoming a sexual abuser. (141)

- 35% of male perpetrators were a victim of childhood sexual abuse
- Males who were sexually abused in childhood by a female relative often became perpetrators
- 51% of incest victims were perpetrators
- 61% of pedophile victims were perpetrators
- 1 in 10 victims of incest later perpetrated incest
- 3 in 10 victims of pedophilia later perpetrated pedophilia

- 75% of victims of both incest and pedophilia became perpetrators
- 1 in 10 victims of both incest and pedophilia perpetrated both incest and pedophilia
- Of the 96 females in the study, 43% were victims of childhood sexual abuse, but only 1 was a perpetrator [141]

QUESTION: Why are incest victims less likely to become perpetrators themselves than victims of sexual abuse outside the family?

The answer to this question is complex; there are many pieces to the puzzle. Incest often involves the cooperation of other members of the family to keep the abuse secret. Psychological preparation for the incest occurs within the family unit as a kind of mental foreplay. For instance, it is common for generational boundaries to be distorted by the father, who may relate to his daughter more as a husband than a parent in an emotionally close relationship, which later leads to sexual relations. Thus, incest victims are accustomed to this way of family interaction, in other words, groomed to receive these incestuous acts. Incest is a component of sadomasochism, which is the receiving of pleasure from inflicting physical or mental pain upon the victim. This is a familiar part of home life for many abused children. Consequently, the sense of betrayal (at the time of the abuse) may not seem as traumatic as when the abuse comes from someone outside the family. The treatment from the abuser inside the family often leaves the victim feeling isolated from everyone except their abuser.

Although the victim of pedophilia may be groomed and nurtured by the perpetrator, victims who are abused by offenders outside the family unit often feel helpless, unprotected, rejected, or abandoned by family members. This adds to the victim's sense of isolation, and ironically increases the dependency upon the pedophile. This, in turn, intensifies the feeling of shock and betrayal during sexual abuse.

In other words, since the victim of pedophilia feels more unprotected and betrayed than someone who has been abused within the family, it is possible for the victim of pedophilia to unconsciously protect themselves against the traumatic effects of sexual abuse by identifying with the perpetrator of the abuse. The victim of pedophilia may be more dependent upon the perpetrator than the victim of incest is because he or she is less isolated and has other family members, such as the cooperative or passive participants, with whom to identify. [141]

According to Garland and Dougher, emotionally deprived youth seduced by an adult will bond with them and later attempt to gain a position of power and control in contrast to his or her former position of weakness, becoming the aggressor instead of the passive or submissive partner in the relationship.

The abnormal sexual arousal begins with habitual sexual fantasies, coupled with masturbation that results in orgasm. The sexual experiences at an early age with an adult or another child, supply the mental sexual images for these sexual fantasies contributing to the inappropriate sexual behavior.

Reaching an orgasm becomes almost like a reward, which only encourages the youth to indulge more and more often, making the abnormal sexual activity develop into an obsessive behavioral pattern. Garland and Dougher also believe that the above experience prevents the youth from entering the normal developmental phase of typical peer sexual relationships. The masturbatory fantasy becomes the sexual outlet preference for the youth and in adulthood; he becomes fixed on what he has convinced himself was not an abusive act perpetrated against him in childhood, but more of an ideal sexual experience. (141)

There Is A Cycle Of Non-Sexual Violence Linked To Victims Of Sexual Abuse:

By studying official arrest and juvenile detention records of a specific group, we can establish that victims of molestation and other types of abuse and neglect in childhood are more likely to become involved in criminal behavior than those who were not victims of abuse or neglect. Childhood abuse increases the odds of future delinquency and adult criminal activity overall by 40%. (142)

Victims of child sexual abuse are 27.7 times more likely to be arrested for prostitution when they become adults than non-victims.

Some victims become sexual abusers or prostitutes because they have a difficult time relating to others except on sexual terms.

Official Criminal Records For 908 Children Were Traced And Placed Into Three Groups:

- Those with a confirmed history of sexual abuse
- Those with a confirmed history of physical abuse
- Those with a confirmed history of neglect

Researchers found that children who had been sexually abused were more likely to have an adult arrest for prostitution, while they were not more likely than the victims of physical abuse or neglect to have adult arrests for other sex crimes. Therefore, the link between childhood sexual abuse and becoming a child sexual abuser in adulthood may be difficult to establish because other childhood environmental and family situations are also a contributing factor. (142)

Seghorn (1987) carried out a study similar to that of Glasser, but with access to more detailed objective information about childhood circumstances. (143)

- Child sex abusers who were sexually abused in childhood were more likely than those who were not sexually abused to have had fathers with a criminal and or substance abuse history
- They had parents with psychiatric problems
- There was evidence of abnormal sexual activity within the family
- There was a high incidence of childhood neglect

In conclusion, it is difficult to distinguish the effects of sexual abuse alone without considering overall family abnormalities. (144)

Other possible explanations look at family dysfunction as a cause of emotional deficiency and isolation, putting children at risk for developing low self-esteem and weakened social skills. Family dysfunction can also lead to separation from family members who would otherwise be good role models, for instance being able to identify with the normal role of a father. (144)

The control the abuser uses over the victim appears to have more bearing on the likelihood of the child victim becoming an abuser in adolescence or adulthood than does the type of abuse itself. (144)

Obviously, there is not only one simple cause for a single outcome. An indicator of how children will be affected later in life by dysfunction or illness in childhood depends upon many factors and how they work together to affect each child. (144)

We question why two individuals with the same risk factors have different outcomes. A comparison of the affect that the same type of trauma has on different children was explained during an experiment using three dolls. One was made of glass, another constructed of plastic, and the third doll was made of steel. Each figurine was hit equally as hard as the other one with a hammer. The glass doll shattered, the plastic doll showed a dent, and the steel doll remained undamaged. (144)

Sexually Abused Males Who Do Not Enter The Victim-To-Abuser Cycle:

Prendergast focuses on sexually abused males who do not go through the victim-to-abuser cycle. He lists a series of factors which appear to protect some male victims of childhood sexual abuse from becoming sexual perpetrators and which should be addressed as having great importance to victim treatment: (145)

Protective Factors:

- Good self-esteem
- The availability of other important adults in the child's life, besides the abuser, including an adult with whom he or she could discuss the abuse, and also real friends with whom he or she could discuss anything
- Religious education stressing positive development and forgiveness rather than sin and damnation
- Success in schoolwork, sports, or other activities
- Parents showing pride in the activities of their child
- Personality strengths and social situation of the child that enabled him or her to have long-term goals as well as day-to-day short-term goals
- Supervision by the child's parents which reduces the possibility of repeated abuse
- Enough sexual knowledge at the outset of the seduction, so that any sexual pleasure is less likely to entrap the child in a downward spiral of guilt (145)

Stopping The Cycle Of Violence:

The National Center for Victims of Crime notes that early detection and appropriate treatment may prevent some victimized children from becoming adult perpetrators. In order to intervene early, parents should educate their children about appropriate sexual behavior and how to say no. (146)

An estimated 40% of sexual abusers were sexually abused as children and approximately 40% of untreated, non-incest offenders will re-offend. However, studies have also found that treatment can successfully decrease the rate of re-offending. (146)

For more information, see Chapter Twenty, Sex Offender Treatment...Is There A Cure?

Chapter Twelve

INDICATORS AND EFFECTS OF CHILD SEXUAL ABUSE

Sexuality is a part of self and not limited to genitals, discrete behaviors, or the biological aspect of reproduction. It is more properly considered as a component of the total personality that affects one's concept of personal identity and self-esteem. (147)

Keeping the secret of child sexual abuse causes devastating, long lasting, and life-altering affects. Therefore, it is very important to be able to recognize the indicators. (148)

Physical Indicators:

Visible Injury To The Rectum:

This is rare in sexual abuse. Most pedophiles go to great lengths not to inflict trauma so the physical abuse will remain undetected. The anus can expand to accommodate bowel movements larger than the adult penis. Still, some signs may be observed, especially followingf a violent rape. The area around the rectum should be examined for scars, warts, bleeding, bruising, and small skin tags. (149)

Any Injury To The Genitalia:

This should raise the question of abuse, although this area of the body is certainly susceptible to unintentional injury. The majority of children who have been sexually abused have no detectable genital injury. A negative physical examination never rules out sexual abuse. Only a minority of sexually abused children test positive for a sexually transmitted disease at the time of their initial physical examination. No single finding of physical evidence is conclusive of the occurrence of sexual abuse. Likewise, the absence of physical evidence is not conclusive of the absence of sexual abuse. (149)

Physical Injuries To Breasts, Buttocks, Lower Abdomen, Or Thighs:

Any of these indicators may be noted, particularly when extreme force was used. These injuries may include lacerations, bruises, contusions, hematoma, irritation, or bleeding. In severe forms, there may be partial or permanent disabilities resulting from physical abuse that caused serious physical injuries, such as fractures. (149)

Additional Evidence Of Physical Trauma

- Bruises, hematoma, or pain in the genital or anal region
- Genital or rectal bleeding
- Blood stains on the child's underwear
- Presence of semen or pubic hair on clothing, linens, body, or in the urine (149)

More Complicated Evidence Worthy Of Suspicion:

- Painful injuries or illness such as recurrent urinary tract infections, or urinary tract complaints, which may prompt medical attention. Symptoms like urinary frequency, urgency, incontinence (inability to control urine) and painful urination. The persistence of symptoms where there is no physical indication of urinary dysfunction calls for psychological or emotional issues to be considered as the involuntary discharge of urine, (Enuresis), is often a manifestation of psychological distress.
- Difficulty sitting or walking and painful urination may be related to the actual presence of a foreign body in the genital area or urethra, or it can indicate a secondary infection from the abuse.
- Disturbances in bowel movements such as constipation, pain during bowel movement, or involuntary bowel movements. These may be related to trauma in the rectal area. Like urinary tract infections, bowel movement disturbances may be a manifestation of psychological distress. Children, who continue to have these symptoms in spite of appropriate treatment, may need to be assessed for psychosocial and stress-related issues.
- Hemorrhoids are not common in children, and their presence or the presence of skin tags should be considered suspicious. However, it is important to remember that some tags in the anus may have existed since birth. (149)

Non-Specific, Multiple Psychosomatic Complaints:

These could consist of stomachaches , headaches or patchy hair loss, which may be secondary to self-destructive head banging or hair pulling. Patchy hair loss is a symptom.

Masturbation:

This may explain excessive redness of the external genitals as children do indeed masturbate. It can begin in infancy as soon as they discover their genitalia; it is a normal part of sexual development. This is true for both girls and boys. Boys who are circumcised can irritate their genitals and develop some difficulty in urinating by engaging in self-stimulatory behavior. The insertion of toilet paper and small foreign bodies into the female genitalia is also considered to be part of normal exploratory behavior. Girls would rarely insert objects that mimic a penis. This would be a strong reason to suspect abuse rather than self-stimulation. (149)

When Pregnancy Occurs In An Underage Child:

Particular attention should be given to those who refuse to talk about the father of the baby. There are considerable health and medical complications for the pregnant child or adolescent as well as for the infant. In addition, there are psychosocial dangers when children give birth to babies. The emotional damage accompanying the physical pain and scars of child sexual abuse goes beyond the pain and scars that are usually associated with childbirth. (149)

Sexually Transmitted Diseases (STDs):

In some countries, sexual exploitation of children and juvenile prostitution is relatively common. The occurrence of sexually transmitted disease is a major public health issue. The most commonly found sexually transmitted disease in children is gonorrhea. Symptoms, when they occur, are usually present within two to five days of contact with the genitals. The presence of symptoms however, seems to depend on the part of the body that has become infected and perhaps on the age of the patient. (149)

STDs and other body fluids or tissues may be transferred from the abuser to the victim during intimate sexual contact. Although this kind of evidence will be found only in a minority of cases, it must be looked for whenever sexual abuse is suspected. When found, it is compelling evidence that abuse has taken place, and may at times help to identify a specific individual as the abuser. STDs such as gonorrhea, genital herpes, venereal warts, trichomonas vaginalis, hepatitis B, and HIV may be a consequence of sexual abuse, especially among children exposed to prolonged sexual exploitation. When left untreated. Certain STDs, when left untreated, may lead to severe gynecological conditions that may affect childbearing at a later age. Adolescents with a history of sexual abuse are significantly more likely than their peers to engage in sexual behavior that puts them at risk for HIV infection.

- Genital or anal warts in children are strong grounds to conduct an investigation for sexual contact. Boys may suffer from the consequences of untreated genital warts.
- Herpes simplex virus infections are frequently found in children. Some herpes simplex viruses are commonly associated with wounds in the mouth, others with the genital area. Both types, however, may be spread sexually.
- Genital infections in children are strong presumptive evidence of sexual contact. These infections are often accompanied by tender swelling of the lymph nodes in the area.
- HIV is transmitted by sexual contact and has been reported to be involved in a number of cases of sexual abuse. Routine testing of sexual abuse victims may also be appropriate in areas where HIV exposure is prevalent among persons with other sexually transmitted diseases.
- Molluscum contagiosum is a contagious viral condition that can be sexually transmitted. It is also reportedly spread by other forms of close contact and from contaminated surfaces. If the disease is sexually transmitted, lesions usually appear in the genital area, abdomen, and thighs. Non-sexual spread can reportedly cause the disease to appear on almost every other part of the body.
- Genital itchiness, vaginal discharge, swelling, burning sensation, or redness in the genital areas are signs and symptoms of vulvar or vaginal infection.
- Bruising, redness or discharge from the penis may suggest abuse.
- Swellings or ulcers may be signs of sexually transmitted diseases. A swelling of the foreskin, called phimosis, may be caused by trauma or infection. In severe cases, such infection may be accompanied or preceded by unexplained difficulty walking or sitting, and/or bruising or irritation of the perineum (the area between the anus and

the back part of the external genitals). Poor hygiene, skin irritations, foreign bodies, or skin disorders can also cause the condition. If this is recurrent, persistent, or severe and accompanied by other behavioral symptoms, sexual abuse should be considered.

- Throat and rectal infections in children may be without symptoms, while urinary tract or vaginal infections usually do present symptoms.
- Syphilis is not common in sexual abuse but is regularly found whenever a large enough group of abused children can be studied. Occasionally, non-sexual transmission has been demonstrated through skin contact with contaminated materials. Wounds on the genitalia however, are highly suggestive of sexual transmission.
- One or more types of viruses that cause common skin warts also cause venereal warts. Genital warts in adults are highly contagious and are easily spread to sexual partners. Recently, genital warts in children have been found to be sexually transmitted. The presence of common warts on other parts of the body, such as the fingers or soles of the feet does not seem to be related to the development of genital warts. Although there is still some controversy at this time, it seems reasonable to presume that genital warts are mostly caused by genitally related types of virus. All available evidence suggests that genital warts in older children are sexually transmitted. Infection appears to require skin or mucosal damage. (149)

Victims of child sexual abuse are more susceptible to eating disorders, diabetes, heart disease, stroke, high blood pressure, and other chronic illnesses. Not only is this a threat to the lives of sex abuse victims, it also results in millions of dollars of health care costs to society. (154)

Research concludes that strong family relationships may decrease the risk for eating disorders among youth who experience sexual abuse. (150)

In a number of cases, sexual abuse is not the initial reason for seeking medical intervention; and only after doing the examination is it discovered that sexual abuse has taken place. Of all the types of child maltreatment, sexual abuse requires the most meticulous collection of evidence. A complete medical assessment should be conducted for every child suspected of being sexually abused. It is also important to reassure the child victim that he or she will receive the necessary medical attention and that the abuse will not occur again. (149)

Health practitioners, in particular, must be sensitive to the child's feelings, thoughts, and perception of the physical evidence of sexual victimization. In many cases, even in the absence of physical evidence, the psychological scars affecting one's mental and emotional health may be evident and long lasting. (149)

NOTE: Physical abuse resulting in bruises, broken bones and other physical signs is more easily identifiable than sexual abuse. Therefore, the crime of child sexual abuse usually must be proven without substantiation or physical evidence.

Behavioral, Mental, And Emotional Effects:

Although no single behavioral symptom is conclusive proof that sexual abuse has taken place, behavioral disturbances or changes may be the only clues that sexual abuse has occurred or is ongoing. (151)

Behavioral Indicators:

- Age-inappropriate sexual conduct is perhaps the most specific behavioral sign of sexual abuse. Although children have many opportunities to learn the motions of adult romantic behavior, the desire for others as sexual objects does not normally start until adolescence
- Acting out seductively
- Use of sexually explicit language
- Persistent and inappropriate sexual play with peers, toys, animals, self
- Preoccupation in young children with sexual organs of self, parents, or other children
- Sexual themes and fears in child's artwork, stories, and play
- Aggressive behavior such as hurting self and others, setting fires, and cruelty to animals
- Hysteria—lack of emotional control
- Fear of being alone or fear of particular places and people, even of going home, if that is where the abuse is taking place
- Lack of trust, particularly with significant others
- Withdrawal and chronic depression
- Sleep disturbances and nightmares
- Overly submissive behavior
- Role reversal—overly concerned for siblings
- Unexplained accumulation of money or gifts
- Unwilling to change clothes in front of anyone
- Decline in school performance
- Running away from home
- Adolescent prostitution or sexual promiscuity
- Substance abuse

Young Girls Who Are Forced To Have Sex:

- Are three times more likely to develop psychiatric disorders
- Are sexually active at an earlier age
- Seek out older boyfriends
- Are four times more at risk of substance abuse if their sexual abuse included intercourse. (152)

Common Coping Mechanisms By Adult Survivors Of Childhood Sexual Abuse:

- Minimizing the abuse history and the actions of the offender

- Rationalization of one's victimization "Oh, he or she just didn't know any better. They, too, were abused as a child."
- Denial—it is more comfortable for both the child and adult survivor to pretend the abuse never occurred than to face the emotional and psychological pain of the violation
- Regression (forgetting) is the mind's way of denying the victimization
- Seeing the facts of this life only in of black and white terms, with no shades of gray. This is common in survivors when the behavior of the offender was either abusive or loving, with no middle ground.
- Lack of integration—on the inside, a feeling you are bad or evil. On the outside, you are a super achiever. Thereby developing a "false self"
- Out of body experience—during the abuse, the victim feels they are watching the abuse occurring to their own body but are detached from their body
- Control Issues—the more disorganized family life is in childhood, the higher the risk that control issues will become a problem.
- Dissociation, spacing out—everyone does this at times. The difference is the degree and frequency that it happens to certain individuals. For example, driving a car and realizing that you are farther along than you thought you were.
- Hyper awareness- a super alert awareness of everyone and everything around you
- Workaholic lifestyle, being hyper-busy. Staying busy is one way to avoid "feeling"
- Escaping or running away—in passive ways this can include reading books, sleeping too much, and watching television. It is important to remember that fantasies can be the source of a rich creative life and can be vital to healing.
- Self-mutilation, self-harm, and self-injury—internalization of the offender. Instead of being hurt by the victimizer, the survivor hurts himself or herself. Mutilation often releases intense feelings and or numbness
- Suicide attempts—this often occurs when survivors feel trapped with no way out. Our message of hope is "Don't kill yourself, instead call a friend, your therapist, or a crisis hot-line!"
- Psychiatric hospitalizations can be used as a relief from intense feelings, flashbacks, or during compulsions to hurt or kill one's self.
- Isolation—the victim feels safer when they are alone..."No one can hurt me if I'm alone."
- Addictions are a common way of coping with the pain of sexual abuse. The victim is usually self-defeating and self-destructive by using drugs, alcohol, food, gambling, sex, etc.
- Lying—when children are told not to tell anyone about the offense, the offenders are teaching the children to lie. Many survivors are compulsive liars with the sexual offense being the biggest and most damaging lie of the all
- Religion—safety can be found in attaching one's self to a belief system that has clear boundaries and rules. Traditional religion can provide an anchor. The belief of divine forgiveness can be a powerful pull for the survivor who still feels the abuse was his or her fault. Unfortunately, destructive cults can also be alluring to an adult survivor for some of the very same reasons.
- Avoiding Intimacy can mean appearing open and friendly on the surface, but hiding their real feelings inside. The survivor of child sexual abuse keeps themselves safe

by avoiding intimacy and sometimes this leads to positive traits such as independence and autonomy, which is self-directing freedom and especially moral independence. However, it also means missing the rewards of healthy relationships. (153)

The Effects Of Sexual Abuse And Sexual Exploitation Greatly Depend Upon:

- The interaction between the victim and the perpetrator
- The nature of the abuse
- The environment where the abuse occurred
- Age of the child when the first abuse occurred
- Symptoms that the victim developed after the abuse
- Relationship between the victim and the perpetrator
- Number of perpetrators
- Number of sexual abuse incidents
- Type of sexual behavior involved
- Degree of intimidation used
- Whether the perpetrator admitted to the abuse
- Whether there were other forms of family violence
- Overall health status of the child
- Disabilities including intellectual impairment, communication impairment, blindness, deafness, mobility impairment or multiple disabilities
- Time it took the victim to tell others of the abuse (149)

Manipulation:

Adult survivors diagnosed with Borderline Personality Disorders often hear that they are manipulative. Once they are able to identify, process, and express feelings attached to manipulative behavior, and are taught other ways to get their needs met, the manipulation will usually cease.

Children need continuous support and reassurance that they were right to have told about the sexual abuse. Healing requires understanding and supportive care. (149)

Rate Of Recovery:

For Individual Children And Adolescents, This May Depend Upon:

- How well they learn to cope with their acquired sense of sexuality
- Their psychological vulnerabilities
- The degree to which they are able to recover from the abuse
- Their intellectual ability and perception of the abuse as a violation of a trusting relationship
- Their belief in the possibility of being able to develop future trusting relationships
- The strength of character that they have learned through proper guidance during childhood
- The support of their family

Tragic Results Of Child Sexual Abuse:

Invariably, a child victim of sexual assault feels damaged by the sexual experience; regardless of the presence or absence of, and extent of, any physical trauma. This "damaged goods" syndrome is not confined to the child's feeling for himself or herself, but also extends to how different societies respond to the abuse. Many cultures, after learning about the child's premature exposure to sexual activity, also consider the child as "being damaged." (149)

For more information see Chapter Thirteen, The Secret—Why Don't Children Tell?

<u>NOTES</u>

Chapter Thirteen

THE SECRET

Millions of victims of child sexual abuse, both male and female, live a life of loneliness, fear, insecurity, and pain, isolated in a world of secrecy. The dark truth of their victimization and the debilitating secrecy of that truth hurls them violently into adulthood, baring the unmerited yoke of guilt and shame that erodes self-esteem and builds brick walls where there should be loving and trusting relationships—as the secret continues to kindle the flame of the bitter memories of the sexual assault.

There are an estimated 60 million survivors of childhood sexual abuse in America today. (1)

The typical child sex offender molests an average of 117 children, most of whom do not report the offense. (79)

Only about 10% of child sexual abuse is reported. (154)

Reasons Why Children Keep Sexual Abuse A Secret:

- They fear that reporting it will bring consequences even worse than being victimized again. (155)
- Among victims of sexual abuse, the inability to trust is characteristic, which contributes to secrecy and non-reporting. (156)
- Victims may feel embarrassed or reluctant to answer questions about the sexual activity. (157)
- Sexual abusers tell the child that no one will believe them; and even if someone does believe them, the child will be blamed for the abuse. (121)
- Perpetrators tell the child that they (the abuser) will get into trouble if they tell on them. This is particularly fearful for the child when the perpetrator is a family member, because the child fears abandonment. (158)
- Sexual abusers promise gifts and rewards and offer bribes for the child to keep the secret. With young children, this can be candy, toys, and trips to their favorite fast food restaurant. For older youth, it can be videos, DVDs, car or motorcycle rides, sports tickets, sports equipment, clothes, makeup, jewelry, money, anything that is valued by the youth. (158)
- Another less obvious reason some children don't report abuse is they are too young and naive to recognize their victimization as sexual abuse. (159)
- Unavailability of intervention options. There needs to be appropriate, available channels for reporting the abuse and more help services provided by trustworthy adults
- Long-term sexual abuse of children involving relatives as perpetrators is most likely to occur in dysfunctional families. In many cases, the mental health of the victims is impaired by exposure to psychological or physical abuse or neglect. These children
- will find it difficult to report any abuse, particularly as they are likely to feel terrified that harm will come to them or to their family if they do tell. (149)
- The victims may also be dependent upon the perpetrators for their shelter and survival. This is particularly so in the case of children with disabilities. (149)

The longer the secret goes unrevealed, the more trapped in the abuse the child or adolescent becomes. (75)

Those children with a positive sense of self-esteem and a trusting and confident relationship with an adult are more likely to immediately report any attempted or achieved sexual abuse. (149)

Survival Means Learning To Adapt To The Abuse In A Variety Of Ways:

- Minimize the abuse by pretending that whatever is happening is not *really* that bad. This can emerge in the form of a tough sense of humor. (149)
- Rationalize the abuse by explaining it away and blame the assault on the offender's alcohol addiction, drug use, or other behavioral problems; thus convincing themselves that the offender is showing them love. In doing so, developing a twisted sense of what love really means. (149)
- Child victims tend to deny some facets or downplay their sexual experience when they do report the abuse. This is proven by comparing the interview notes to the police apprehended evidence of photos or videos made by the perpetrators recording the sexual molestation acts. (160)
- Sexual abuse victims are often in denial that the abuse ever took place, which is one of the most common and effective ways children deal with abuse. (149)
- Victims commonly blame themselves feeling that, "something is wrong with me," and believe they deserve the abuse or that somehow it is their fault. Nothing can be further from the truth! (161)
- Feeling out-of-control of their own circumstances, sexual abuse victims sometimes become manipulative. In an effort to re-gain control of themselves and others, they become super-alert and eager to please. (149)

Though these coping skills are largely self-destructing, they are also highly effective at helping to numb the pain and get the child through each day. (75)
Sexually abused children who keep the abuse a secret, or who "tell" and are not believed, are at far greater risk for psychological, emotional, social, and physical problems, which often last into adulthood. (162)

Children who feel compelled to keep sexual abuse a secret suffer greater psychological distress than victims who reveal the secret and receive assistance and support. (75)

A child's interpretation of the abuse, and how quickly they tell, is important to the short-and long-term effects. Children, who are able to confide in a trusted adult, and be believed, experience fewer traumas than children who do not disclose the abuse. Furthermore, children who disclose the abuse soon after its occurrence may be less traumatized than those children who live with the secret for years. (163)

Children need to be told, "I believe you, and it's not your fault." (75)

NOTES

Chapter Fourteen

INTERPERSONAL COMMUNICATION SKILLS (IPC)
AND REPORTING SUSPICION OF CHILD SEXUAL ABUSE

IPC SKILLS ARE USED TO "LISTEN AND REACT"

When a child is trying to open up about something as personal and as serious as sexual abuse, how you listen and react to what they are saying can make a difference in how well the child will be able to express what actually happened, and how well they will begin their journey to recovery (164)

Anyone who has been sexually abused will face enormous difficulties in attempting to cope, let alone being healed. With IPC skills, you will be able to more effectively guide children through the stages of grief and other emotions and reactions such as denial, anger, depression, acceptance, forgiveness, and healing. Ways in which we can respond to the problem of sexual abuse are as follows:

Trust, Prepare, And Listen:

Children need someone they can trust to feel safe enough to confide in. You, a caring parent, or other caretaker can serve as the confidant for the child.

- Remove all obstacles when talking with the child
- Keep interruptions and distractions to a minimum
- Pay close attention to what is being said
- Observe body language
- Maintain eye contact
- Reflect on what is being said and let the child know that you honestly care
- Don't rush things. Wait patiently through the silence, the anger and the tears
- Be slow to speak and quick to listen.
- When the child is finished talking, don't feel as if you need to make them say more
- Wait until they are ready to talk
- Be a patient listener (164)

Drawings:

A good way to bring out the inner feelings of a child is to ask them to draw pictures of the experience. If the drawings include people with genitals, this is a strong indication of a sexual encounter. Under normal circumstances, young children give little or no thought to the genital area.

Self-Control:

Children don't like to upset the people they love. A panicky reaction to what they are telling you can cause more harm than good. If your child, or a child you know, tells you that he or she has been approached or actually molested, be careful to act calm and keep your emotions under control... even though you may be shocked or feeling panic inside. Your reaction is important. It can encourage the child to continue talking about the sexual abuse or cause them to withdraw from the conversation. (164)

Reassure:

When a child reports they have been sexually molested, reassure them that they were right to tell, and that what happened to them was not their fault!

Believe:

Abused children are confused and filled with emotional pain. Always let the child know that you believe them. Young Children do not lie about sexual abuse because they do not have knowledge of sexual matters. Occasionally, an older youth may give false statements about having been molested, but very seldom do children lie about sexual abuse.

Empathize:

Be alert to the effects of sexual abuse such as the undeserved guilt and shame the victim carries. Be especially sensitive to ways you can communicate your *empathy and understanding. *empathy: the action of understanding, being aware of, being sensitive to, and vicariously experiencing the feelings, thoughts, and experiences of another.

Reassure:

The victim of sexual abuse needs frequent and sincere reassurance. Continue to use your IPC skills to reflect on their strengths and concentrate on their good qualities; for instance... "I think your feelings are natural," or "I'm glad you said that" are affirming. Reassurance reinforces self-esteem. Constantly reassure the child that they are somebody special and should never let anyone try to convince them otherwise. Let them know you are aware they have undergone a traumatic experience. Remind them they survived the actual abuse and explain that with proper counseling, they will move past these feelings and be able to go on with life. (164)

Protect:

Protect the child by encouraging their participation in programs that offer help and support. Reiterate that they never have to allow any kind of abuse.

Intervention:

Professional intervention is very urgent in the event of sexual abuse. Be aware that severe personality disorders can result from child sexual abuse. Healing from any type of abuse is possible, but sexual abuse in particular requires expert attention. Therefore, seek professional psychiatric care immediately, taking into consideration that some counselors have little knowledge in this area. Inquire as to the number of molestation victims they have counseled with, what type of treatment they use, what kinds of medication they prescribe and any other concerns you may have. If a child has been sexually molested and the therapist says he or she is all right after only a few sessions, find another counselor. Seek medical attention and be present in the room during examinations to calm the child's fears. It is important that you explain to the child the difference between sexual abuse and being examined by a medical doctor.

Support:

It is very important that the people who are closest to the abused child know how to cope with the emotional turmoil caused by the invasive sexual abuse. Healing is best accomplished with professional help from a therapist who can provide intense individual and group therapy with the victim and their entire family. Let the youth know that healing is a long and deliberate process and not instantaneous, so never give up hope.

According to the **American Psychological Association**, children, and adults sexually abused as children, have indicated that family support, good self-esteem, and spirituality were helpful in their recovery from the abuse.

Using Inter Personal Communication Skills, you will be equipped to guide the child into acknowledging the abuse did happen and help them to identify the responsible person and others who may be involved. Very young children will probably not be able to identify their experience as sexual abuse. (164)

Use These Skills:

- To ease a child into conversation ask them questions such as, "Do you want to tell me about something that has happened to you that makes you feel frightened, uncomfortable, and unhappy?" and/or "Has someone done something to you that you do not like"?

- Ask a few questions at a time. Under no circumstances should you add to the child's story. Instead, give the youngster the opportunity to explain the details about his or her own experience as it actually happened. Always write the details down so that they are available when filing a report with the authorities, so the child won't have to endure more questioning than is necessary.

- How you react is very important. Don't add to the pain the child is going through by saying things such as, "Mr. Friendly is so nice; you must be mistaken."

- Never question why the child did not tell you what was happening sooner. The important thing is that they are telling you now. You have learned about the controlling, manipulative nature of pedophiles. Understand that innocent, naive children are helpless to protect and defend themselves against these clever deviants. Do not make the child feel that you are blaming them by saying things like, "Why did you let him do that?" or, "What were you doing there anyway?"

- Don't cause the child to lose hope by saying things such as, "Oh, my poor baby; you're ruined for life. You'll never be the same." Instead, reassure the child that you will work everything out together and with a lot of love and the right kind of help everything will be all right.

Be careful not to betray a confidence between yourself and a child; respect their privacy. They do not want everyone to find out what happened. Let them know that the proper authorities must be involved in order to give them protection; but if too many others are told it will only add to the child's feelings of confusion, humiliation, and shame. If the word gets out that the child has told, the perpetrator will have the opportunity to flee or prepare a defense or in some extreme cases, cause additional harm to the child. (164)

Do And Don't Do—Guidelines:

DO use the child's language or vocabulary.

DO acknowledge that it is difficult to talk about such things.

DO tell the child that this has happened to other children and that they are not the only one.

DO tell them that they are not responsible for what happened and did not deserve it.

DO tell them that sometimes adults do things that are not okay.

DO make certain that the child feels safe following the disclosure. You might need to stay physically close to give an extra sense of security. Remember, the offender has likely used threats.

DO be careful about touching, such as hugging or cuddling the child if they have not initiated the contact. Some children may be upset for a while by physical contact.

DON'T make promises you cannot keep, especially if the child asks you to keep it a secret.

DON'T ask invasive questions. Listen, but don't pry. Respect the child's need for privacy. The details of the abuse need to be worked though with the help of a professional. Be aware that it takes time to reveal the full extent of their experiences. (164)

DON'T be overly protective. (165)

Reasons Children Are Often Fearful Of Telling:

- They blame themselves for the abuse and feel guilty for telling
- They are ashamed and embarrassed about the abuse
- They feel confused about their feelings for the perpetrator
- They may be afraid of the perpetrator and afraid that the abuse may reoccur (165)

CAUTION! In anger and desperation, you may want to seek revenge on the person who hurt a child you love. Exercise self-control, do not make threats, or attempt to approach the alleged perpetrator. If you take the law into your own hands, it will only complicate the matter for everyone, including the traumatized victim. Let the child know you are sorry about what happened to them and that you will do everything in your power to keep it from ever happening again. Show love and concern. Again, please do not try taking the law into your own hands, or it may be you who ends up in jail. The child will feel responsible for your fate as well as having to cope with the trauma of the sexual assault. Keep the child's best interests in mind and make cool-headed, wise decisions. (164)

Facts About Sexual Abuse Disclosures:

Most disclosures are delayed. Of those children and youth who do disclose, between 8 and 22% withhold some of the facts of the sexual abuse. (166)

Within a year of the first sexual molestation, 75% of child sexual abuse victims do not tell, and 18% waited more than five years to reveal the sexual abuse. (166)

Almost 3/4 of children in all studies did not reveal abuse had occurred when first questioned. (167)

First time sexual abuse disclosures may sound unconvincing and be full of inconsistencies. Often they are compounded by feelings of anxiety. The coping skills that helped the child survive may be the very thing that now alters an accurate memory and perception of the abuse. In addition, other destructive and delinquent behaviors that child sexual abuse victims often display, leads some adults to invalidate the disclosure, which intensifies the anxiety, guilt, fear, and confusion of the abused child. (168)

Even if adults do believe the disclosure, often the threats that were made upon the child by the offender, in order to keep the abuse a "secret," actually come true. The family becomes divided, and when the perpetrator is a family member, he or she should be removed from the home, splitting the family unit further. The youth's world begins to fall apart and if there are no supports and effective intervention for the sexual abuse, the youth will retract the sexual abuse disclosure. (162)

Fabricated sexual abuse reports make up only 1 to 4% of all reported cases. Of these reports, 75% are reported by adults and 25% by children. Children only fabricate 0.5% of the time. (168)

If you suspect that someone is a sexual predator, but you are not acting upon a disclosure, before you make an official report, you should ask yourself this question; "On what evidence am I basing my suspicions?" For instance, if a person loves children and works well with them, this is not necessarily an indication that they are a pedophile. Count the cost to the person you suspect if he or she is innocent—without delaying your decision to report the suspicion in the event that there is a possibility that other children are being sexually molested by an alleged perpetrator. (164)

Even if the abuser is a relative or a close family friend, always report your knowledge or suspicion of child sexual abuse, as no one benefits from keeping these horrible secrets. If the perpetrator keeps getting away with this crime, it is usually the case that he or she has assaulted more than one child and will continue this pattern of sexual abuse. (164)

It is vital that you are discrete about your suspicions. Keep them confidential, except to report to the proper authorities. Do not take a chance of either ruining the reputation of a person who may be innocent or giving a guilty person an opportunity to flee or prepare a defense. (164)

When the evidence of child sexual abuse is obvious, so is the responsibility to report it immediately. (164)

In all 50 states, it is mandatory that medical staff, schoolteachers, and childcare workers report any knowledge or suspicion of child sexual abuse. If anyone refuses or neglects to report any kind of child abuse, they become an accessory to the crime and can be fined and imprisoned.

Who To Call To File A Report Of Child Sexual Abuse:

- The local police department
- The local sheriff's department
- The local child protection agency

The designated agency for reporting child sexual abuse varies in most counties. The best place to call first is your local police department.

NOTE: According to law, your call will remain confidential and anonymous and no one needs to know who reported the incident. (168)

For more information, see Chapter Twenty-Two--The Law.

NOTES

Chapter Fifteen

VICTIM TREATMENT—FORGIVENESS AND HEALING

Medical Treatment Of Child Sexual Abuse Victims—What You Should Know:

It should never be taken for granted that medical personnel can always recognize and treat the symptoms of child sexual abuse. This information will help you to choose the right pediatrician or other medical practitioner. You may want to have the doctor read over this information to determine if they are qualified to treat the victim of child sexual abuse correctly and affectively. (169)

Pediatricians and health care providers involved in the medical care of children and adolescent victims of sexual assault should be trained in the *forensic procedures required for documentation and collection of evidence. Details of the required examination and documentation are presented in a handbook titled, Evaluation and Management of the Sexually Assaulted or Sexually Abused Patient, by the **American College of Emergency Physicians**. Another help for diagnoses—professional medical personnel should refer patients to an emergency department or rape crisis center where there is staff experienced with adolescent rape victims. New **colposcopic procedures allow examiners to better document genital trauma, including micro trauma, seen in rape cases. There is ongoing research demonstrating the patterns of genital injury in sexual assault victims. *forensic: belonging to, used in, or suitable to a court of justice or to public discussion and debate. **colposcopic: using a magnifying instrument designed to facilitate visual inspection of the vagina and cervix.

Pediatricians who treat sexually abused/assaulted patients need to be aware of the legal requirements, including proper forms and reporting procedures specific to their state and county. With the advances in DNA magnification technology, we can more accurately identify assailants; however, forensic examinations need to be conducted as close as possible to the 72–hour period after the sexual contact, which was previously considered the cutoff for such examinations.

The diagnosis and management of sexually transmitted diseases (STDs) is an important part of treatment of the assault victim. Blood and tissue specimens should be obtained to detect Neisseria Gonorrhea and Chlamydia Trachomatis. Vaginal secretions should be microscopically examined for Trichomonas species. Specimens should be tested for herpes virus if there is a clinical indication, e.g., vesicles. Serum samples should be obtained to test for syphilis, hepatitis B virus (HBV), and human immunodeficiency virus (HIV). These tests serve as a baseline, indicating the presence of any STDs in the victim that may have been present before the assault, but are considered controversial by some authorities who prefer performing the initial STD tests 2 weeks after the assault. All authorities agree that the syphilis and HBV tests should be repeated in 6 weeks and that the HIV test should be repeated in 3 to 6 months.

Pregnancy prevention and post-coital (after-intercourse) contraception should be discussed with every adolescent female rape and sexual assault victim and should include risks of failure of the contraception. The victim should also have the opportunity to choose the options for pregnancy management. It is important that a baseline urine pregnancy test be performed because the adolescent could be pregnant from sexual activity that occurred before the assault.

Current recommendations are to provide preventative treatment for chlamydia and gonorrhea infections in adolescent sexual assault victims and to supply them with educational materials on pregnancy prevention. HIV preventative treatment is not generally recommended but should be considered when there is mucous membrane exposure in the oral, vaginal, or anal areas. Factors to consider include: [169]

- The risks and benefits of the medical treatment
- Whether there was repeated abuse or multiple perpetrators
- If the perpetrator is known to be HIV-positive
- If there is a high prevalence of HIV in the geographic area where the sexual assault occurred.

HBV vaccination is recommended for those who have not received a complete HBV series or who have a negative surface antibody despite previous vaccination. [169]

The Centers For Disease Control And Prevention

Provides The Following Guideline:

The identification of a sexually transmissible agent from a child beyond the neonatal period suggests sexual abuse. In other words, sexual abuse should be strongly considered when a gonorrheal infection is diagnosed in the genital, rectal, oral, or eye areas in a child from the age of newborn to before the onset of puberty. A sexually transmitted disease may be the only physical evidence of sexual abuse in some cases. Sexually abused children may deny that abuse has occurred.

This statement does not address gonorrheal infection in adolescents, which may result from sexual abuse or consensual sexual activity. **The Committee on Adolescence Statement on Sexually Transmitted Diseases** provides additional guidance for the pediatrician evaluating adolescents as follows: [170]

The American Academy Of Pediatrics Guidelines:

- Pediatricians should be knowledgeable about the *epidemiology of sexual assault in adolescence. *epidemiology: a branch of medical science that deals with the incidence, distribution, and control of disease in a population.
- Pediatricians should be knowledgeable about the current reporting requirements for sexual assault in their communities.

- Pediatricians should be knowledgeable about sexual assault and rape evaluation services available in their communities and when to refer adolescents for a forensic examination.
- Pediatricians should screen adolescents for a history of sexual assault and look for potential aftereffects of child sexual abuse.
- Pediatricians should be prepared to offer psychological support or referral for counseling and should be aware of the services in the community that provide management, examination, and counseling for the adolescent patient who has been sexually assaulted.
- Pediatricians should provide preventive counseling to their adolescent patients regarding avoidance of high-risk situations that could lead to sexual assault. (170)

Dentistry And The Victim Of Child Sexual Abuse:

A study posted in **The Journal of the American Dental Association,** conducted by a team of Canadian researchers, suggests that in consideration of the prevalence of child sexual abuse, dentists, knowingly or unknowingly, probably see patients several times a week who are victims of sexual abuse. Therefore, it is important for dentists and dental office staff members to gain some insights into the unique challenges of working with these patients more effectively. (171)

During a personal interview with an adult female victim of child sexual abuse, she reported that she was frightened of the control that she felt the dentist had over her while she was laying back in the chair with all of the dental instruments hanging out of her mouth and the dentist bent over her. She was unable to keep her appointments unless her husband was in the same room to give her the feeling of being protected. (172)

There seems to be one other obvious parallel between the characteristics of a certain aspect of dental care and the characteristics of abuse that could result in boosting the anxiety level of the victim, often leading to canceled appointments. Dentists ask their patients to trust them to do what is best for them, assuring them, much as the abuser did, that while the experience may be painful or unpleasant, in the end it will be good for them. (171)

The JADA study offers tips dentists can use to help abuse victims become more comfortable with dental treatment all tips supplied by the patients themselves:

- Avoid asking patients about the history of their abuse. Ask instead whether any aspects of dental treatment are particularly difficult for them
- Offer "same-day" appointments to cut back on cancellations and rescheduling
- Allow the patient to observe part of the treatment using a mirror to reduce the feeling of vulnerability
- Explain each treatment step in advance, "inform before you perform"
- Allow for frequent breaks

- Avoid reprimanding patients for neglecting their oral health. Instead, dentists should ask how they can help patients take better care of their teeth
- Substitute vinyl gloves for latex gloves with patients who may associate latex with condoms and condoms with abuse. (173)

Psychological Treatment:

Researchers have begun to take a serious look at the issue of healing from child sexual abuse. What they have discovered from interviews with victims is that a strong factor of the child's recovery from the abuse is a high level of maternal, family, and extra-familial support and interaction; this is assuming that the abuser is not a member of the immediate family and is not living in the household. (174)

Other factors of healing are to help the child give up any feeling of guilt about the abuse, promoting high self-esteem and encouraging Spiritual soundness. In addition, attending workshops and conferences on child sexual abuse, learning all you can about it and undergoing psychotherapy are all helpful strategies. Research has shown that often, along with all of the other therapy, the passage of time is a key element to healing. Family counseling is always the best way to overcome the systems of family dysfunction. (174)

When Seeking A Good Counselor Always Ask:

- How many other sexual abuse victims have you counseled? Make sure that the counselor is experienced in this area.
- Do you counsel the entire family? Family counseling is always recommended.
- How long will you counsel the victim? The correct answer to this is until symptoms of distress have been resolved, which can take years. (121)

Undeserved Guilt:

The definition of guilt is the state of one who has committed an offense meriting condemnation or blame.

Almost all victims of child sexual abuse commonly experience guilt. (175)

In group therapy with women who were sexually molested as children, Tsai and Wagner listed one of two primary therapeutic goals for helping victims of sexual abuse; eliminating sexual guilt and shame. (176)

Courtois and Wafts described the "sexual guilt" as "guilt derived from experiencing sexual pleasure" Courtois, C. A. & Watts, D. L. (1982). Counseling adult women who experienced incest in childhood or adolescence. (177)

An adult victim of childhood sexual abuse reported that she was left feeling guilty because she experienced orgasm during the sex act. (178)

Adolescents do not understand that orgasm is a normal physical reaction to sexual stimuli and not necessarily an indication of "sexual pleasure" during sexual abuse. Reassuring all victims of sexual assault that they are not at fault for what happened to them and encouraging them to forgive themselves is essential to the success of the healing process. (121)

The parents and other loved ones of sexually abused children also suffer agonizing feelings of helplessness and undeserved guilt. "Why didn't I recognize the signs that something was terribly wrong? I should have suspected that something dreadful was happening! My children depend on me to protect them and now I've let them down, how can I ever forgive myself"? (121)

The truth is that in most cases, everyone is taken by surprise when sexual assault occurs. It is difficult to recognize an enemy when you are unaware that there is one laying in wait for the right time and place to strike. Even when you are very protective of your children, it is impossible to be with them every moment of every day. Babies stay in day care, eventually start school, begin to spread their wings playing outside, and visit a neighbor's house or trusted relative or friend. (121)

An average of 5.5 children per 10,000 enrolled in day care are sexually abused, an average of 8.9 children out of every 10,000 are abused at home. (179)

No one wants to believe that someone they know and trust could be capable of such a vile crime against a child they are supposed to love. There is no way to describe the pain inflicted upon the entire family or explain "why" this type of immorality takes place. (171)

Abused children commonly feel they are partly responsible for the abuse and the pain that it causes their parents and other family members. These afflicted children need love, acceptance, renewed self-esteem, trust, and reassurance that the sexual assault will not continue. (121)

Types Of Guilt Associated With Sexual Abuse Include:

• Feeling different from peers
• Harboring vengeful and angry feelings toward both parents
• Feeling responsible for the abuse
• Feeling guilty about reporting the abuse
• Bringing disloyalty and disruption to the family (180)

As important as it is for the victim of child sexual abuse and their loved ones to forgive themselves, it is equally important in the healing process to let go of hatred and to encourage forgiveness of the abuser. Naturally, you may think this is impossible and too much to ask. But consider this, forgiveness is not so much for the abuser as it is for the victimized child and everyone else concerned. Often, the offender does not ask for, nor do they seem to care about, forgiveness. The victim can make a decision to exchange hatred for forgiveness and personal pain for peace and healing. (121)

Giving up hatred and choosing to forgive does not mean that anyone is condoning the sexual offense or canceling out the guilt of the offender; nor does it mean that you have to get back into a relationship with that person. Sexual assault is very demeaning and due punishment by the judicial system and by a higher power is justified. However, hate is as destructive as cancer, festering and devouring the one who persists in hatred. (121)

FORGIVENESS AND HEALING

Vicki Lynn

A True Story

Vicki, an adult victim of childhood incest, puts it this way: "It's the nature of man to try to find a logical explanation for everything that happens. We cannot seem to just say that this act of sexual abuse that leaves the abused feeling guilty is from an evil source, and just leave it there. Instead, we do our best to analyze it and try to make sense out of it. There is no logical explanation for the way abused children take on the guilt and try to protect the abuser.

Forgiveness," says Vicki, "allows you to put your spirit in a better place to equip you to face tomorrow, because unless your spirit can get to a place of peace within yourself, you cannot move forward. You cannot stop being a victim. You continue on, in the same condition. You run, hide, and put on a happy face, but underneath you have this frightened and tormented child that controls your life and you're stuck there trying to make adult decisions based upon a child's mentality. There are so many out there drinking and hopping from one man to another because a frightened child is running their mind, saying that this time it will work. Forgiveness has to come for complete healing to take place and it has to come from within. It also has to be a logical choice made by an adult decision. You have to ask yourself, do I continue on with what is not working, or do I summon the courage to do something that might change my life, instead of always thinking it's never going to change."

Vicki is a dear friend of mine with whom I shared this book in 1983. After she read it, she broke down, and for the first time in her life told her incredible story. Though she was grown and had a family of her own, and though her abuser lived miles away, her stepfather still had control of her through her fear and hatred for the man who betrayed her and stole her childhood in the worst possible way.

Vicki called me one afternoon and choking back tears, whispered into the phone, "I'm not afraid of him anymore." After a long silence I asked, "What happened?" Without hesitation she bravely replied, "I forgave him."

112

Vicki describes forgiveness as a choice to move in a positive direction. "Like unconditional love," says Vicki, "forgiveness requires action in spite of how you feel. The bile still comes up in the back of my throat when I think about my step father and I don't feel like I have forgiven him, but you don't invite that thought to live inside of yourself... because that's how you get robbed of your soul.

For many years, I didn't dwell on what happened to me; I just left it there, buried deep down inside of me. I may not have reveled in it, but I let it live there. By the time I was fifty-four years old, my children were grown. My beloved mother, whom I cherished, died and left me to my own thoughts and fears. My only saving grace was my wonderful, compassionate husband. But even he was not enough to keep me from reaching the end of my rope. I knew that if I didn't do something, the hatred would destroy me. I had to make a conscious decision to forgive in order to save myself."

In the summer of 2008, Vicki, a retired Registered Nurse, took her stepfather into her home to care for him during the last six months of his life. He had Alzheimer's disease. She will tell you that it was the most horrible yet most blessed time of her life as she poured herself out with compassion and unconditional love, proving to be so much a part of her healing process.

Forgiveness is an indication of willingness to give up hate in exchange for something far better. Love and trust are the two things that were so cruelly stolen by the destructive nature of sexual abuse. Letting go of hatred makes room for new life, new love, and new trust, making whole that which was torn apart.

Is Healing From Sexual Abuse Possible?

Yes, healing from child sexual abuse is possible. The lives of children who have been sexually abused will forever be changed, but we have many wonderful examples of children healing from the abuse and living out caring and productive lives. Some children may be ready to talk about the abuse and deal with it soon after it happens; others may need to move more slowly, gradually testing the safety of addressing the issues that arise. Children do best with a combination of love from caregivers and support from a counselor with special training to work with children who have experienced sexual trauma. (181)

NOTES

Chapter Sixteen

SEX TRAFFICKING INVOLVING CHILDREN

Trafficking Sex Rings:

Buying sex with a 12-year-old girl in Cambodia takes less time and effort than changing money in a bank or paying a telephone bill.

Svay Pak is a brothel village where immigrant child prostitutes from Viet Nam offer "boom-boom" (intercourse) and "yum-yum" (oral sex) for $5 in cramped, clammy rooms and makeshift plywood cubicles.

Sex with a girl aged 10 to 13 costs about $30. Younger girls cost more. A virgin costs a few hundred dollars. (182)

Child Prostitutes Have As Many As 40 Customers Per Day:

Child Prostitutes are subjected to as many as 40 customers per day in red-light districts often leaving them with untreated injuries and illnesses. (181)

Additional Forms of Sex Trafficking:

- Child Pornography (child engaged in sexually explicit conduct)
- Child Sex Tourism (organized networks effect a commercial sexual relationship by the tourist with residents at the destination.
- Sexually Explicit performance (live or public acts or shows)
- Forced Marriage (by payment and/or the husband transfers her to another person)
- Mail-Order Bride (exploited by illicit agencies to traffic women into sexual exploitation) (114)

***The Initiative Against Sexual Trafficking**, accessed October 31, 2007* states that, each year sexual traffickers lure, coerce, trick, drug, kidnap, and sell millions of vulnerable women and children into the multi-billion dollar sex trade. In their daily lives victims of sexual trafficking endure unspeakable acts of physical brutality, violence and degradation including rape by "customers and pimps", undergo forced abortions, acquire drug and alcohol dependencies, live in fear of their lives and in fear for the lives of their family and friends. They suffer acute psychological reactions as a result of their extreme physical and emotional trauma, and contract sexually transmitted diseases which all too often bring life-long illness or hasten death. If they survive, the physical, psychological and spiritual impacts of these experiences on victims are devastating and enduring.

Big Money Generated At The Expense Of Children:

Billions of dollars are generated annually on the street from human trafficking. (183)

The United Nations estimates the total market value of illicit human trafficking to be in excess of $32 billion.

<u>*Trafficking Statistics Worldwide:*</u>

- According to ***UNICEF***, more than 1.2 million children are trafficked every year.
- Approximately 30 million children have lost their childhood through sexual exploitation over the past 30 years
- ***The Department of Justice*** reports, the average age of a trafficked victim is 12-14 years old.

<u>*In the U.S.*</u>

- ***The U.S. Dept of State*** reports that, almost 300,000 American children are at risk for trafficking into the sex industry
- There are girls as young as 5 and 6 years old in the U.S. that are forced to do sexual acts for economic gain by their pimp
- Statistics from ***The Department of Justice, Child Exploitation and Obscenity Section, accessed October 31, 2007***, state that younger children, many below the age of 10, have been increasingly drawn into serving tourists

<u>*In The U.S. A Child Is Reported Missing Every 40 Seconds*</u>:

- That is over 2,000 per day
- Over 800,000 per year
- 500,000 missing children are never reported
- **The National Incidence Studies of Missing, Abducted, Runaway, and Thrown-away Children** report that 450,000 children run away from home each year. (184)

One out of three teens of the street will be lured into survival sex within 48 hours of leaving home. <u>Catholic Charities USA</u> has been a leader in developing services and advocacy for U.S. citizen children and youth who have been caught up in the sex trafficking trade. (184)

<u>*Trafficking In Persons—Legal Definition:*</u>

The federal **Trafficking Victims Protection Act** of 2000 defines severe forms of trafficking in persons as sex trafficking in which a commercial sex act is induced by force, fraud, or coercion, or in which the person induced to perform such act has not attained 18 years of age; or the recruitment, harboring, transportation, provision, or obtaining of a person for labor or services, through the use of force, fraud, or coercion for the purpose of subjection to involuntary servitude, convict labor, debt bondage, or slavery. (184)

<u>*There Are Three Phases In The Trafficking Process*</u>:

- The recruitment phase—luring or kidnapping the victim

- The transit phase—transporting the victim
- The destination phase—assigning the victim to their fate

Reasons Children Are So Easy To Victimize:

- They are tempted by the chance to earn money and believe the stories they are told
- Many young people who fall victim to traffickers believe that they are going to get a real job in a hotel, a bar, or a private home
- Some believe that they will be getting married
- Some are unhappy in their home situation and are trying to find a better life
- Many have suffered abuse from their parents and want to escape
- Many have not succeeded at school and see no future for themselves in their own environment
- Sometimes they are members of a minority that suffers discrimination in their own country
- Some want to escape their poverty
- Sometimes they are kidnapped by the traffickers and sold Child Prostitution, Child Pornography and Trafficking in Children for Sexual Purposes. (190)

Common Ways Traffickers Keep Young People Submissive:

- Taking away their identification documents
- Threats of reporting them to the authorities
- Claiming that the young person owes a debt of money
- Not allowing the young person to have money
- Violence or threats of violence
- Threats of violence towards members of the young person's family
- Keeping the young person locked up or limiting their freedom in other ways (185)

The Underlying Causes Of Trafficking And The Commercial Sexual Exploitation Of Children Are Diverse And Include:

- War
- Natural disasters
- Economic injustice
- Fundamental differences between the rich and the poor and lack of harmony between them
- Large-scale migration and urbanization
- Societal and family disintegration
- Lack of protection available to children at risk
- Underfunded or failed social services

The common factor that identifies a child victim of trafficking is that they are being exploited or used unfairly. The child is forced to either earn money for another person or is being used to work for no pay. Either way, someone is taking advantage of him or her. Since the wishes of the child do not matter and the child is used for the profit of another person, the child is the victim of trafficking. (185)

117

Legal systems commonly fail to prevent injustice toward children or to protect them from criminal acts, and systems of governance more often than not display indifference toward the exploitation of children. Further, discrimination, gender gaps in education, and a double standard of morality for men and women contribute to a climate of inequality and exploitation. (186)

Children Trafficked Within The United States:

Children who are U.S. citizens are trafficked within the United States. An estimated 300,000 American children are sexually exploited each year. Exploiters include criminal networks, family members, acquaintances, strangers, local pimps, other youth, pedophiles, and transient males. Commercially, sexually exploited children cut across socio-economic, race, ethnic, and gender lines. Over 75% of the children are from middle class backgrounds. (187)

Traffickers might be part of a well-organized criminal network or individuals who play a part in one or more of the various stages of the operation, such as providing false documents, transporting victims, or offering his or her home as a place to keep victims until they are transported. These criminals are very dangerous and willing to commit serious crimes of violence to avoid detection and protect their financial interests. (185)

A 2011 *TIP (Trafficking In Persons)* report reveals that, "With estimates of 1.5 million people enslaved in the United States alone, it is imperative that this nation is seen as a leader in the fight against human trafficking and in the care for the survivors." (185)

Vanishing, Forgotten Children:

Both girls and boys are trafficked for a variety of purposes, not just sexual exploitation, but very little is known about them: whom they are, where they are, or under what conditions they suffer because very few of them have been found. (185)

In much of the world, there is virtually no data about child trafficking victims. The U.S. government has begun paying attention to the problem of international trafficking in children, but does not pay as much attention to the problem of sex trafficking of children here in the United States. Many people are unaware of human trafficking, including people who should know about it, such as law enforcement and service providers. In October 2002, ECPAT-USA, in partnership with the **International Organization for Adolescents** (IOFA), launched an unprecedented, citywide outreach and educational project to address this problem. (185)

Supply And Demand:

Human traffickers operate in circumstances where there are large numbers of people who are desperate for relief from poverty, lack of real opportunities for improvement because of personal difficulties, and when there is a demand for their labor or services in other places. (185)

As with adult victims, traffickers abduct children and young people in many different ways. It is a complex crime, which is committed by clever, devious people quite good at deception. Though much of the demand is for sexual services, the victims do not always know that they will be sexually exploited; often they believe that they are going to a respectable job, only to find the true nature of the work after they arrive.

For example, a young person might answer an advertisement for what appears to be legitimate work as a food and drink server or perhaps as a cleaning and maintenance worker, but instead they become prisoners, forced into prostitution. Some are promised work as a model, but are used to make pornographic movies instead. A young girl may fall in love with a young man who promises to take her to a foreign country and marry her, but his real intention is to sell her to his friends for sex. A small boy might be offered a chance to go abroad and get an education, but find that he is put on the streets to beg and to steal for his "master."

Demand For Increasingly Younger Children:

Children can become the victims of a trafficking operation at any age, depending on the type of exploitation they will suffer. Teenagers are often trafficked for sexual exploitation. Older children sometimes know they will provide sexual services to adults; however, they are completely unaware of the level of abuse to which they will be subjected or of the physical and psychological damage. Younger children can begin as beggars and thieves and exploited in the labor market in several ways. (185)

The sex sector involves pornography, prostitution, and trafficking in children for sexual purposes and for profit. Child exploiters deliberately seek occupations that bring them into frequent contact with children and can often be found among the most highly esteemed members of a society. Pedophiles constitute a significant group of the offenders. The child victims of commercial sexual exploitation are both boys and girls, although they are primarily girls between 10 and 18 years of age. Research suggests that the age of the children involved is decreasing, and sexual exploitation of children as young as age 6 is documented. (188)

In Fayetteville NC, a woman sold her 5 year old daughter into sex slavery for drug debts. The little girl was raped, and then killed.

Since there is a demand for, and taste in young children of all ages, the exploiters will supply these children to their customers; especially on the internet.

Those Who Are Supposed To Protect Children Are Often The "Worst Enemy":

The unlawful recruitment and sale of children across international borders, is an organized industry ranging from small businesses to large enterprises. The business involves deception, kidnapping and enslavement, smuggling, false passports, bribery, and corruption. (188)

For instance, Nepal, located between India and China, has powerful interests that control and maintain the structures within the sex sector (area of sexual operation). National case studies indicate sexual exploitation of children continues to flourish there, partly because it is protected and supported by corrupt politicians, police, armed forces, and civil servants who receive bribes, demand sexual favors, and are themselves customers or owners of brothels. (189)

The commercial sexual exploitation of children is an atrocity. It has rightly been called "the ultimate evil." It denies children their fundamental rights. It has devastating psychological and physical consequences for them. It is a perversion of the natural order—adults should be there to protect and nurture children, not take advantage of their emotionally and physically vulnerable state. (190)

By the very nature of the practice of human trafficking, all victims are in horrible, life threatening conditions, but children are arguably the most vulnerable. Children lack the strength and maturity to escape from traffickers or to cope with the harmful effects of trafficking. (184)

<u>NOTES</u>

Chapter Seventeen

CHILD PROSTITUTION

There are 10 million child prostitutes worldwide. The Global Coalition to End Human Trafficking Now

Approximately 95% of teenage prostitutes were sexually abused as children. (191)

Globally, prostitution is one of the most hostile forms of child labor. Force is used to confine the children so that they can rarely seek help or be reached. They have no ability to negotiate the terms of their employment; they are commonly sold, trafficked, tricked, or lured. The child victims of the industry are most often from the poorest sections of society. Family or community members may knowingly sell children to brothel agents or pimps or unwittingly sell them into prostitution in the mistaken belief that the go-between will find them work in a factory or as domestic help. Some children are kidnapped or lured by traffickers with promises of employment only to end up in brothels. (192)

Child Prostitution—A Growing Global Problem:

Child prostitution is a growing problem worldwide. In Asia, alone, more than one million young boys and girls are engaged in commercial sexual activity. In every part of the world, the number of children harmed in this way is growing. Child prostitutes are found in virtually every country, including the United States, France, United Kingdom, Germany, and Japan. There is an increasing demand for child prostitutes, globally. This may be partly out of the fear of AIDS and the inaccurate belief that younger sex partners are free of disease. (185)

Child Prostitution And Trafficking Encouraged As "Economic Activity":

The growth of the sex sectors (areas of operation) is closely tied to economic progress and modernization. It may be an intentional policy of some countries to promote prostitution as an economic activity. Government policies for the promotion of tourism, migration for employment, and the export of female labor provide significant sources of foreign exchange earnings and may have indirectly encouraged the growth of prostitution and sale and trafficking in children. Other policies may also have led to the growth of the sex sectors through their impact on poor families and the strategies adopted by them for survival, especially in the absence of social welfare. (186)

Due to the criminal nature of the sex sectors, precise figures on the number of children involved are difficult to obtain. In Asia, because groups working against the commercial sexual exploitation of children have been active for a relatively long time, data is more complete. The 1996 **United Nations Special Report on the Sale of Children, Child Prostitution, and Child Pornography** estimates that about one million children in Asia are victims of the sex trade. According to the International Labor Organization, the problem is especially alarming in Korea, Thailand, the Philippines, Sri Lanka, Vietnam, Cambodia, and Nepal. (193)

A 2011 report from the **Protection Project** states that, in South Asia alone, 74 million women are reported missing; nearly 20 million are reported to be "whoring" in brothels, and 20-25% of the women trafficked for sexual exploitation are under 18 years old.

*There Are Approximately **2.5 million** Victims of Human Trafficking:*

- 1.4 million - 56% in Asia and the Pacific
- 250,000 - 10% in Latin America and the Caribbean
- 230,000 - 9.2% in the Middle East and Northern Africa
- 130,000 - 5.2% in sub-Saharan countries
- 270,000 - 10.8% in industrialized countries
- 200,000 - 8% - are in countries in transition

People are reported to be trafficked from 127 countries to be exploited in 137 countries, affecting every continent and every type of economy.

The Victims:

- An estimated 1.2 million children are trafficked each year
- 95% of victims experienced physical or sexual violence during trafficking
- 43% of victims are used for forced commercial sexual exploitation, of whom 98% are women and girls
- 32% of victims are used for forced economic exploitation, of whom 56% are women and girls

Child Prostitution In The U.S.:

A recent US survey on the business of child prostitution turned up very little information. Although news accounts describing children forced into prostitution rings, trafficked internationally, arrested on the streets, or abused by respected members of society seeking to buy the sexual services of children are regularly reported, gathering the facts about prostituted children is still very difficult. (185)

ECPAT-USA Working To Collect Data:

Until these facts are collected and presented in a way that holds more evidence and conclusive proof it will be difficult to ensure that the rights of children exploited in the prostitution and pornography business in the United States can be properly protected. End Child Prostitution, Child Pornography, and Trafficking in Children for Sexual Purposes, (ECPAT-USA), works to see that this is done. (185)

Tourist's Demands For Child Prostitutes Bringing In Millions Of Dollars Annually:

Globally, child prostitution originated partly as a response to a demand from tourists and is now an organized industry with clients, traders, distribution routes, and outlets that bring in multi-millions of dollars each year. International tourism has become a leading division in world exports and is the biggest employer in the world with 1 out of every 6 jobs somehow being dependant on, or related to, travel and tourism. Tourism is not the cause of sexual exploitation of children but it does provide easy access to vulnerable child victims. (185)

U.S. And Europe Travel Agencies Set Up Sex Tours:

U.S. and European travel agencies set up sex tours for thousands of travelers every year. The flow of sex tourists is mainly from economically developed countries. To date, clients are mainly men from the United States, Germany, Sweden, Australia, and Japan. In addition, the impact of local tourism is increasing and many customers are from neighboring countries. (194)

Sex Tourism Seen As "Economic Development":

International tourism organizations have been unanimous in condemning the use of tourism for the purpose of sexual exploitation of children, and discussions are ongoing on how the tourism industry can help bring the end to this practice. However, many countries struggling with weak economies rely on tourism as their primary industry, and while some countries view sex tourism as an unwanted but unavoidable part of tourism development, in many cases the governments directly tolerate sex tourism in pursuit of economic development. (194)

The Law And Protective Measures For Children Are Lax:

Commercial sexual exploitation of children is old and new; old in that it includes traditional practices and new in that, globalization and advances in technology are posing a different set of challenges to the problem. Sexual abuse of children entails economic, social, and political aspects. It takes place in most countries. The global sex sector is growing, as is the demand for increasingly younger children, facilitated by inadequate government interventions and lax law enforcement particularly in terms of protective measures for children. (194)

Child Prostitution—A Growing Industry Worldwide:

According to the U.S. Department of Justice, prostitution in the U.S. is growing dramatically among young people with the problem of teenage prostitution being particularly severe. In Europe, trafficking is increasing rapidly, and the ages of the women and girls involved are getting younger and younger. The problem is particularly severe in the East European countries where the **Defense for Children International** has reported an alarming growth of prostitution among Russian, Polish, Romanian,

Hungarian, and Czech children. Trafficking routes are extending and there is evidence to suggest that children are trafficked across continents and into the sex industries of industrialized countries such as Japan, Australia, and throughout Scandinavia. (195)

In Africa, many countries face a rising child prostitution problem and the linkage with tourism is evident. Algeria is a place of transit for traffickers, and Senegal, Kenya, Sudan, and Libya are on the list of countries where child prostitution is increasing. Visible increases of children in prostitution are noted in Ghana, Cote d'Ivoire, and Burkina Faso. (195)

Younger Children Being Prostituted:

In Central and South America, there are large numbers of street children; and the link between that and prostitution is strong. Child victims of sexual exploitation are present in large numbers in Nicaragua, Venezuela, Bolivia, Chile, Ecuador, and Peru. In Brazil, UNICEF estimates that the number of prostituted children exceeds 500,000. The average age is 13 through 17, but there are cases of children as young as age 6 documented in Brazil. Concerns have been raised regarding the visible increase in child sex workers in Honduras, El Salvador, Mexico, Costa Rica, Panama, Guatemala, and Argentina. (196)

How It Affects The Child Victims:

The commercial sexual exploitation of children is an issue of health and it is a concern for public health. The consequences for abused and exploited children include profound physical, developmental, emotional, and social problems. (197)

The Symptoms Experienced By Child Prostitutes Are Similar To Those Reported By Other Sexually Abused Children:

- Depression
- Self-destructive tendencies
- Inability to enter the mainstream of society
- Isolation

Child Victims Of Prostitution May Have A Lifetime Of Recurrent Illnesses:

- Venereal diseases
- Fertility problems
- Pregnancy complications
- Malnutrition
- Tuberculosis (197)

Many Suffer From A Range Of Illnesses:

- Respiratory problems

- Headaches
- Exhaustion
- Recurring infections and wounds
- Substance abuse
- Sexually transmitted diseases
- Injuries—inflicted by those involved in controlling and organizing the sexual transactions or through self-harm
- Malnourishment or debilitation due to inevitable hazards of a poor living environment, poverty, or neglect
- Many attempt suicide [198]

Myths That Children Are Less Susceptible To Sexually Transmitted Diseases:

The demand for children for sex has increased dramatically in recent years. This may be partly due to the belief that children are less susceptible to sexually transmitted diseases and that sex with children is safer. To meet the demand for virgins, agents have intensified the recruitment of very young girls from remote villages and across borders, particularly in Asia. In reality, children are especially vulnerable and are biologically more susceptible to sexually transmitted diseases, infections, and injuries. [199]

UNAIDS reports that, "at the end of 2001, an estimated 40 million people globally were living with HIV. In many parts of the developing world, the majority of new infections occurred in young adults, with young women being especially vulnerable. About one third of those currently living with HIV/AIDS are aged 15 to 24, most of whom are unaware that they carry the virus."

The link between prostitution and the increased risk of contracting HIV/AIDS is now well established and well recognized; even in those countries for which any discussion of sexual activity has traditionally been taboo. **UNAIDS** also reports that, "significantly higher rates of HIV infection have been documented among sex workers and their clients as compared to most other population groups within a country."

However, when children are involved, many myths persist; both as to the child's susceptibility to the virus, and to that of his or her abuser. It should be noted that the reporter of this information does not use the term "sex workers" in the context of children involved in prostitution.

In the years since the discovery of the HIV/AIDS virus, the demand for increasingly younger children for purposes of prostitution has continued to grow. Their abusers are no longer only Pedophiles but also individuals who believe that sex with younger partners is a safer option. They believe that younger people are less likely to have the virus as they have had fewer sexual partners, and some reports allege the persistence of myths in certain cultures that sex with a virgin or with a child will actually cure HIV/AIDS infection in the older partner.

However, children in prostitution are at greater risk of contracting the virus than adults. The forced penetration of a child by a larger individual is more likely to cause injuries and bleeding by which HIV is transmitted. Children are physically weaker, less experienced and therefore less empowered to negotiate the terms of the abuse, such as an insistence on the use of a condom or refusal to be subjected to particularly violent and physically damaging

126

sexual activity. Children working in brothels generally live in very poor conditions, often deprived of adequate food, water and medical treatment, factors which increase a child's vulnerability to contracting infection. This is particularly the case in the countries of Africa, Asia and South and Central America.

Even in countries where children and their abusers are more likely to have access to and actually use condoms, the risk of infection with HIV/AIDS is still high. This results from the almost systematic links between prostitution and dependency on hard, injectable drugs, often administered with unsterile or shared needles. For example, *UNAIDS* also reports that three quarters of infections in Ukraine are caused by injecting drug abuse. In many countries, children enter prostitution in order to feed their drug addiction, and the role of their drug dealer merges with that of pimp.

Children And Aids—A Public Health Concern:

Child prostitutes may pose a greater public health danger than adult prostitutes, because children are weak, vulnerable, and uninformed. In addition, they may not be in a position to seek out medical care if they contract a sexually transmitted disease. There is a significant link in the chain of transmitting diseases from an infected child prostitute to our population at large. This is because their clients have unprotected sex with their spouses or significant others. (197)

Children involved in the sex trade face new and potentially fatal dangers in light of the spread of HIV/AIDS. It is estimated that 7,000 young people aged 10 to 24 are infected with HIV every day. In 2000, ten million children were orphaned because of AIDS, placing a severe burden on health services. (199)

Most Recent Statistics Are Devastating:

- In 2007, approximately 2.5 million people were infected with HIV
- Every day, over 6800 people become infected with HIV; that's almost five people per minute
- 5700 people die from AIDS every day
- One child dies every minute
- Every fifteen seconds, another person age 15 to 24 becomes infected with HIV/AIDS (200)

In 2008:

Worldwide, it is estimated that more than 15 million children under age 18 have been orphaned as a result of AIDS. Around 11.6 million of these children live in Sub-Saharan Africa. In countries badly affected by the epidemic such as Zambia and Botswana, it is estimated that 20 percent of children under 17 are orphans, most of whom have lost one or both parents to AIDS. (197)

<u>NOTES</u>

Chapter Eighteen

EFFORTS TO STOP TRAFFICKING
IN CHILDREN AND CHILD PROSTITUTION

To Combat The Problem, Customers And Exploiters Need To Be Targeted:

In the past, emphasis was placed on addressing the supply side of the problem through poverty measures, social development, and income generation schemes for families. However, it is increasingly recognized that the demand side is also a crucial area of concern; the sex exploiters, customers, sex sector, and its participants need to be targeted as we develop measures to combat the problem. (199)

Lack Of Research And Monitoring Is Both A Cause And A Symptom:

Determining the extent of commercial sexual exploitation of children, and how to document it, continues to be a challenge as there is no clear definition of what child sexual exploitation involves. There are very few examples of thorough, accurate research. Moreover, data that does exist is characterized by a poor understanding as well as the use of information with which to annualize its severity and additionally hindered by a lack of information on how child sexual exploitation fits into different cultural societies and the changing worldwide characteristics of sexual exploitation of children. Most countries collect information about children, but few are able to produce wide-ranging and up-to-date statistics on the health of children. The data is commonly concerned with two age groups; children under 5 years of age, concentrating on health aspects, and adolescents over the age of 15, focusing on employment, sexuality, and drug use. Researchers recommend that data be collected for the age group 5 to 15 years, especially with regard to information on violation of rights, exploitation, abuse, accidents, injuries, child homicides, and illnesses related to the work environment. According to UNICEF, "this failure to monitor the effects of economic and social changes on those most vulnerable is both a cause and a symptom of the lack of political priority afforded to children at task." (197)

The Best Interests Of Children:

Where children are victims, the international legal standards recognize that because children are still developing both physically and emotionally, special protection measures are needed. Under international human rights law, especially recognized by and outlined in the **Convention on the Rights of the Child**, children are recognized as persons having certain indisputable rights of their own. (185)

The possibility of contradiction between safeguards required to protect children from harm, and choices the individual child is entitled to make in his or her own right, is resolved in modern jurisprudence by having regard to "the best interests" of the child. This means that in any decision regarding a child, the "best interests" should be the primary consideration. Thus, any situation should be looked at from the child's own perspective, seeking to take the child's views into consideration, and with the objective of ensuring that his or her rights are respected. Any decision concerning a child should therefore be guided by what is objectively best for that child, given his or her age and maturity.

Within the past decade, human trafficking (use of force, fraud, or coercion to transport persons across boundaries or within countries to exploit them for their labor), has re-emerged as an issue of major concern for governments and non-governmental organizations alike. The United States is itself a destination country for trafficking victims.

Official estimates indicate that 50,000 women and children are trafficked into the U.S. every year from many parts of the world, and the average age of the victims is 20 years old.

The passage of **The U.S. Victims of Trafficking and Violence Protection Act** (VTVPA) in 2000 signals the U.S. government's commitment to treat trafficked persons as victims with eligibility for services, to prosecute traffickers and their associates, and to work to prevent human trafficking in source countries. (185)

The Work Of ECPAT-USA

Since 1997, **End Child Prostitution, Child Pornography, and Trafficking** (ECPAT) has worked to try to understand the problem of the commercial sexual exploitation of children in the United States. This problem is virtually undocumented and barely acknowledged. (185)

ECPAT-USA, along with **Girls Educational & Mentoring Services** (GEMS) and **International Organization for Adolescents** (IOFA), has initiated the **New York City Task Force Against Sexual Exploitation of Young People**. It brings together diverse groups and individuals in New York City to focus on working on NYC policies and programs for ending commercial sexual exploitation.

ECPAT-USA works to stop the involvement of Americans in the child sex trade through research, education, and advocacy on the following issues:

- Child sex tourism
- Child prostitution in the United States
- Child trafficking
- U.S. military involvement with child prostitution

ECPAT-USA supports the **UN Convention on the Rights of the Child** and its optional protocols as tools for protecting children from sexual exploitation.

The International Organization For Adolescents (IOFA):

IOFA is an independent, nonprofit organization with 501(c) (3) status in the United States. IOFA was founded in 1999, in response to a gap in services for adolescents around the world. With offices in Chicago and New York, IOFA is currently working in partnership with local organizations in over 20 countries to develop and implement sustainable programs and services for youth. Their mission is committed to advancing the health and well-being of adolescents throughout the world. IOFA's activities seek to foster the physical, mental, emotional, and psychological development of adolescents. (201)

IOFA is dedicated to improving the lives of young people by addressing critical and emerging issues affecting vulnerable adolescents around the world.

Youth, Their Rights, And Our Responsibility:

IOFA envisions a world where youth are no longer subject to exploitation, violence, and neglect; a world where every young person is able to exercise their human rights and realize their full potential as positive and productive members of society. (201)

- IOFA is an established leader in identifying critical and emerging issues that threaten the well-being of the world's most vulnerable youth. From child trafficking in the former Soviet Republics and in the US, to girls being forced to drop out of school in Africa, IOFA has worked in more than 20 countries to improve the lives of young people.
- Conducting peer-led research, IOFA documents the negative impact of these critical and emerging issues on the well-being of vulnerable adolescents. By involving youth in IOFA's research, the results provide great insights into developing innovative and practical approaches to solving complex and difficult problems confronting the world's adolescent population.
- Developing youth-participatory and rights based solutions, IOFA works at the community, national, and international levels to conduct advocacy and develop sustainable programs and initiatives that empower and involve young people to play an active role in solving their problems.
- IOFA mobilizes support for implementing sustainable solutions by establishing collaborative partnerships and building the capacity of affected communities. IOFA has established hundreds of effective partnerships across the United States and the world. (201)

Why Focus On Adolescents?

Startling Report:

According to the **United Nations World Youth Report** 2005, today's generation of young people is the largest in human history. Nearly half the world's population (more than 3 billion people) are under the age of 25. Nearly 45% of all youth (or 515 million children) survive on less than $2 a day, and some 238 million on less than $1 a day. Even with these harrowing statistics, adolescents are not mentioned in the **UN**

Millennium Declaration and are barely discussed in the Millennium Development Goals. While adolescence should be a time for growth and learning, it is a time of heightened risk. During this critical phase of their lives, adolescents are faced with questions about health, safety, goals, and aspirations. Decisions made and actions taken during this period can often have lifelong consequences. Yet, it is obvious that adolescents continue to be overlooked and underserved in many of the countries around the world. (201)

IOFA's Unique Approach To Serving Adolescents:

IOFA seeks to tackle emerging problems facing young people through partnerships, coalition building, and the innovative approach of social connectivity. Social connectivity is the magnet that brings networks of people and information together with the goal of advancing the health and well-being of adolescents. Social connectivity extends beyond what has traditionally constituted a social network of family, neighbors, and peers to include the global community. (201)

Prevention Of Youth Trafficking Initiative:

Each year 1.2 million adolescents are trafficked. The trafficking of young people for prostitution and forced labor is a serious and growing global problem. These youth are subject to sexual exploitation, forced marriage, domestic slaves, bonded labor, and other atrocities that are dangerous to their short and long-term mental health and physical well-being. IOFA is an international leader, working both in the United States and abroad, to develop and implement innovative strategies to combat this heinous crime. (201)

The UN protocol to prevent, suppress, and punish trafficking in persons, especially women and children, defines trafficking: Trafficking in persons shall mean the recruitment, transportation, transfer, and harboring or receipt of persons by means of threat or use of force or other forms of coercion: abduction, fraud, deception, abuse of power, position of vulnerability, or the giving or receiving of payments or benefits to achieve the consent of a person having control over another person for the purpose of exploitation. (201)

More specifically as it relates to children: The recruitment, transportation, transfer, harboring or receipt of a child for the purpose of exploitation shall be considered "trafficking in persons" even if this does not involve any of the means set forth in subparagraph (a) of this article. "Child" shall mean any person less than eighteen years of age. (201)

IOFA's Youth Trafficking Prevention Projects In The United States:

- Assessing the Extent of Human Trafficking, A Community Outreach Approach: In conjunction with the **Vera Institute of Justice**, IOFA will conduct a test of a new data collection instrument that will identify and gather data on victims of trafficking in

New York City (NYC); and provide critical information to law enforcement and service providers on how to effectively respond to the problem in NYC, and elsewhere.

- **Freedom Network to Empower Trafficked or Enslaved Persons** (USA): IOFA is a founding member of the Freedom Network (USA), a coalition of 25 US-based organizations working to advocate for the rights of trafficked and enslaved persons in the United States.
- Freedom Network Trafficking in Persons Training Institute: Freedom Network members are providing national training, specialized hands-on capacity building, and mentoring for organizations providing services or advocacy for victims of trafficking in the United States. IOFA serves as Northeast Regional Coordinator for the Training Institute.
- NYC Community Response to Trafficking Project: In collaboration with ECPAT-USA and partners from the New York City (NYC) **Task Force Against Sexual Exploitation of Young People** seeks to raise awareness about human trafficking in NYC and to increase the capacity of community-based organizations, public and private service providers, members of at-risk communities, other NGOs, and local law enforcement to identify and provide services to victims of human trafficking in the NYC area. The project has been featured on **National Public Radio** and has been lauded by NYC Mayor Michael Bloomberg as an exemplary anti-trafficking effort.

Trafficking in Persons Information and Referral Hotline: IOFA, in coordination with various partners, provides training and technical assistance to the management staff and hotline operators of the Trafficking in Persons Information and Referral Hotline, the first national 24-hour hotline for victims of human trafficking, which is operated by **Covenant House**. IOFA has also developed a Trafficking Quick Reference Guide to assist hotline operators with answering calls and referring potential victims. (201)

Joint Media Release ECPAT International, UNESCAP, UNICEF:

Delegates Agree To Strengthen Efforts To Reduce Demand For
Commercial Sexual Exploitation Of Children:

Representatives from more than 20 countries met in Bangkok to report on their governments' progress toward commitments made at the 2001 East Asia and Pacific Regional Consultation against Commercial Sexual Exploitation of Children. (202)

The meeting was organized by an Inter-agency group comprising End Child Prostitution, Child Pornography and Trafficking of Children for Sexual Purposes (ECPAT) International, the United Nations Economic and Social Commission for Asia and the Pacific (UNESCAP) and the United Nations Children's Fund (UNICEF), in cooperation with the governments of Italy, Japan and Thailand and the NGO Group on the Convention for the Rights of the Child, represented by the Save the Children Alliance.

From November 8–10, delegates from government and civil society, as well as young people, reported on a draft of new measures and improvements to existing interventions designed to protect children from commercial sexual exploitation, assist victims, and punish exploiters. They noted that while progress had been made, the region also confronted challenges such as new technology, new victims, and new exploiters, as well as the spread of HIV/AIDS and greater global integration.

At the meeting, participants committed themselves to addressing the behaviors, beliefs, and attitudes that cause males to demand commercial sexual exploitation of children; this includes seeking virgins and mail order child brides. They also recognized that until demand is reduced, the supply of children will continue and they called for more men to join the fight to end this inhumane violation of young lives.

Participants also considered strategies to stop the extremely rapid increase in the supply and demand of child pornography over the internet. New technologies including the internet, digital cameras, and mobile phones have increased the spread of child pornography, the demand for it, and the risk for children of sexual exploitation.

National laws have not kept pace with these trends. Most countries in the East Asia and Pacific region do not have laws that refer specifically to child pornography and few criminalize its mere possession. This means that the end user of child pornography is not considered a criminal and is subject only to minimal penalties, even though consumers of child pornography further the abuse and exploitation of more children because their demand fuels the incentive to make it.

Other efforts discussed included the world's first multi-country **Memorandum of Understanding** (MoU) against trafficking, which was signed by ministers from Cambodia, China, Lao PDR, Myanmar, Thailand, and Viet Nam in Yangon, Myanmar. The MoU covers the prevention of trafficking, the victim's return to the country of origin, rehabilitation and sensitive treatment of victims, and the extradition and prosecution of exploiters.

Action has also been taken to address the prostitution of children within their home countries. Community-based projects in the Philippines and Thailand, for example, have empowered local people, including children, to resist exploitation through greater awareness of child rights and methods of exploiters. Local monitoring systems mean that members of the community can report abuse, while local officials have been trained to respond with greater sensitivity and effectiveness.

Despite this progress, a lack of reliable data remains a major hindrance to the implementation of well-targeted and effective measures to stop the commercial sexual exploitation of children. New research designed to address this shortcoming and better support the need for monitoring was presented for discussion.

Young people remained active throughout the meeting. The youth delegation presented statements assessing the situation of commercial sexual exploitation of their peers and multi-level efforts to address the problem. They expressed support for various actions, but they also identified many problems and gaps, and then urged action to address them. In particular, they stressed that high-level policy decisions such as cross-border agreements require raising greater awareness and having tangible action at the grassroots level in order to ensure positive change.

Delegates included representatives from Australia, Cambodia, China, Fiji, Indonesia, Japan, Kiribati, the Republic of Korea, Lao PDR, Malaysia, Mongolia, Myanmar, New Zealand, Papua New Guinea, the Philippines, Samoa, the Solomon Islands, Thailand, Timor Leste, Vanuatu, and Viet Nam. (202)

International Collaboration:

Human trafficking is a very profitable crime that extends beyond national borders and has acquired vast resources. In our modern world of sophisticated communications, no government can address the problem of human trafficking alone. The task is difficult because countries have different legal systems, different types of police forces, different levels of resources available, and speak different languages. However, following international agreements, governments are making efforts to work together to uncover these criminal networks by using their laws and their law enforcement methods, and to increase their partnership so that human traffickers will be arrested and victims can be rescued. (185)

Names Of Foreign Pedophiles Published:

End Child Prostitution in Asian Tourism is an international organization, founded in 1991 with headquarters in Thailand. The core members of ECPAT's plan are working hard to persuade other governments to pass laws protecting children and then follow-up to make sure the laws are enforced. In addition, ECPAT works with rural leaders to convince parents not to sell their children into prostitution. The organization also campaigns to discourage tourists from the sexual exploitation of children and publishes the names of foreign pedophiles found in Asian countries. (185)

Child Victims And International Law:

In the year 2000, an international treaty was adopted by the states that are members of the United Nations at the **UN Convention against Transnational Organized Crime**. *A* supplementary part of that treaty is the Protocol to Prevent, Suppress, and Punish Trafficking in Persons, Especially Women and Children. (185)

In the protocol, states have agreed to combat human trafficking related to organized crime, to protect and assist victims, and to cooperate with each other within the context of combating organized crime.

European states have gone even further. Among the states members of the **Council of Europe**, a Convention on Action against Trafficking in Human Beings is being implemented. This agreement is corresponding to the United Nations treaty but has a wider application. It does not apply only to organized criminal trafficking operations, but considers that any form of trafficking in human beings is a violation of human rights and an offence to the dignity and integrity of human beings. (185)

European States Have Agreed:

- To combat all forms of trafficking, whether national or transnational, and whether or not it is related to organized crime
- To extend protection to all victims: men, women and children
- To apply the protection of the convention to all forms of exploitation: sexual, forced labor, services, etc.
- Where the age of a victim is uncertain and there are reasons to believe that the victim is a child, it is presumed that the victim is a child (185)

In addition to the international treaties that specifically address the crime of human trafficking, children have special protections under other international provisions. The most important one is the **Convention on the Rights of the Child** (CRC). Under this treaty, every country in the world (except for the United States of America and Somalia) has agreed to protect children against all forms of sexual exploitation and sexual abuse and to prevent children from being abducted, sold, or trafficked for any purpose. Additionally, the CRC sets up minimum requirements for a national law that will protect children from sale, prostitution, and pornography. Countries that have already approved the CRC are now trying to ensure that their national laws are in line with the requirements of the CRC rules so that the children within their jurisdictions can be properly protected against trafficking and exploitation. (185)

Prostitution is illegal in Thailand. Nevertheless, like all crime, it still exists. Sexual contact with minors is a criminal offense; sexual intercourse with a minor is statutory rape and is punishable by imprisonment.

In 1996, Thai laws were strengthened by new legislation, which significantly increased the penalties for those caught engaging in sex with a minor. The law targets customers, those who provide the children, pimps, owners, and operators of brothels as well as parents who sell their children to exploiters. The Thai law also calls for prison terms of up to ten years and heavy fines for anyone convicted of being involved in international commercial sex trade. The new legislation also eased restrictions on the police, making it easier for them to enter and search suspected brothels and make arrests.

The Royal Thai Government also works closely with government and law enforcement agencies in other countries and with international organizations to attack the problem from the outside. Part of this effort is aimed at preventing known sex offenders and publishers of pornography from entering Thailand. The government also monitors the activities of tour agents abroad who promote sex tours in an attempt to prevent their customers from entering the country.

Foreign nationals are not exempt from Thai law. Those who engage in sexual activity with minors are subject to arrest and imprisonment. The Thai police have stepped up surveillance of suspected child molesters and have made numerous arrests resulting in convictions and long-term prison sentences. This information is available to all tourists visiting Thailand, and advises them of the law and the penalties for violating it. (185)

The Root Causes Of Child Prostitution:

Poverty is probably the most important factor contributing to the growth of child prostitution. Children offer themselves, desperate for money, or they are sold for sex in return for money. In developing countries, the lack of workable economic opportunities, mostly in rural areas, are combined with the rising expectations of the people and the desire to acquire modern goods. All this contributes to the potential for exploitation. (185)

Counteraction To The Problem:

To counteract this, the Royal Thai Government has taken initiatives, which are designed to provide training and economic opportunities to youngsters who may be tempted or lured into prostitution. To reach these vulnerable children, the **Department of Public Welfare** has opened vocational training centers in every region of the country. These centers, aimed particularly at young women, provide job skills, training, and other services to more than 5,000 youth annually. (185)

The department also distributes information to households throughout the country, alerting parents to the dangers of prostitution and the scams used by those who look for children and recruiters (those who lure and transport children for exploitation).

Additional government efforts are aimed at locating women and children who have been forced into prostitution and assisting former prostitutes; rehabilitation shelters run by the Department of Public Welfare offer counseling and vocational training for some 1,200 former prostitutes each year.

The Center for the Protection of Children's Rights is an international human rights group that distributes information to parents in poor, rural areas about the horrors suffered by children sold into prostitution. This group uses printed material, radio, television, and staff visits to rural villages to deliver its messages

The **Thai Business Initiative in Rural Development** (TBIRD) is an organization that encourages businesses to create job opportunities in remote areas. (185)

Multi-National Projects:
Preliminary Global Assessment of Shelters Serving Victims of Human Trafficking:

For this project, IOFA surveyed existing shelters that serve victims of human trafficking and created a "best practices manual" for governments and NGOs that are interested in establishing new shelters that serve this population. (201)

Girls Leadership Development Initiative

Throughout the world, growing up as a girl comes with unique challenges. Across cultures, the experiences and needs of girls are constantly undervalued. In response to these challenges, IOFA developed **Girls Talk!** as a program model to promote gender equity and to empower young women to act as agents of change in their communities, both nationally and globally. (201`)

Initiative To Empower Orphaned Youth

Throughout the world, hundreds of thousands of orphaned youth live in state institutions. When they are released at age 18, most of them do not possess the life skills or education necessary to lead healthy lives and many of them end up homeless, trafficked, exploited, or worse. (201)

Strategies To Help Adolescents Include:

- Research and assessments
- Projects
- Collaborations and networks
- Conferences
- Training (201)

United Nations Convention On The Rights Of The Child:

Non-governmental organizations have been instrumental in broadening international dialogue and expanding consensus for greater action. The **International Labor Organization** (ILO) and the **United Nations** (UN) are at the forefront in developing instruments to prevent child exploitation and forced labor. In 1959, the United Nations **Declaration on the Rights of the Child** proclaimed, "The child shall be protected against all forms of neglect, cruelty, and exploitation. The child shall not be subject to traffic in any form." The most significant development with regard to protection of children is the establishment of the United Nations Convention on the Rights of the Child in 1989, which outlines children's human rights in civil, political, economic, and cultural terms, and states the child's right to survival and development. (203)

Children's Rights Are Weak Due To Inadequate Law Enforcement:

The Convention on the Rights of the Child **Article 34** states, "The child has the right to be protected from all forms of sexual exploitation and sexual abuse. State officials should take all appropriate measures to prevent the persuasion or coercion of a child to engage in any unlawful sexual activity, the exploitation and use of children in prostitution or other unlawful practices, and the exploitative use of children in pornographic performances and materials". It requires that the laws in each country adopting the convention must see children as the subjects of rights, not as commodities. However, implementation of the convention at the national level has been weak due to inadequate law enforcement. Moreover, attention to children's rights in particular and human rights in general is limited in many countries. (204)

Prior to the founding of the United Nations, a number of treaties were adopted in an effort to combat forced labor, trafficking, financial gains from the prostitution of others, and other forms of exploitation. Many recent international treaties, instruments, and laws include direct references to the exploitation of children; others specify the obligations on the part of the State with regard to the treatment of children living in difficult circumstances (Annex 1). Further developments in international law are likely with the objective to create a binding instrument, which bans the most intolerable forms of child labor such as sexual exploitation of children. (205)

The World Congress Against Commercial Sexual Exploitation of Children, which took place in 1996, Sweden, was the first attempt to coordinate international cooperation and draw international attention to the problem. **The Declaration and Agenda for Action** calls for full implementation of the **Convention on the Rights of the Child**. It was stated "There is and can be no issue of choice, free will, or self-determination in a situation of sexual exploitation, precisely because sexual exploitation is a suppression of choice, eradication of free will, and destruction of self-determination." (206)

Projects Around the World:

Baltic States:

- Prevention, Investigation, & Repatriation of Victims of Human Trafficking in Latvia: This project provides training to encourage cooperation among law enforcement officials and NGO leaders in combating trafficking of young people in Latvia. Regional trafficking response teams have been established in three regions.
- Strengthening Social Service Provision to Victims of Human Trafficking in Latvia: This project strengthens social service provision to victims of human trafficking by assessing current services, creating partnerships between service providers, and a local shelter; and by ensuring that the shelter staff is properly trained to respond to victims' needs.

Africa:

- Project for the Prevention of Adolescent Trafficking, Tanzania: This project aims to increase the capacity of NGOs in the lake region of Tanzania to work with the government to ensure more effective implementation of laws dealing with the protection of female victims of violence and human trafficking.

Latin America:

- Community Response to Trafficking, Dominican Republic: This project aims to enhance ongoing efforts to combat trafficking in the Dominican Republic and to develop community-based responses to trafficking. This project also includes anti-trafficking awareness raising activities at the grassroots level.

Asia:

Taiwan Community Response to Trafficking Project: In collaboration with the **Taiwan Women's Rescue Foundation**, IOFA provided training on human trafficking, and facilitated the formation of anti-trafficking working groups by bringing together NGOs, community groups, law enforcement, and government officials to combat human trafficking in Taiwan. (201)

Recommendations By The International Community Focus On, But Are Not Limited To The Following:

- Strengthen multi-level international cooperation and collaboration between government and non-government sectors
- Improve the protection of children and their rights, and raise the awareness of children's rights
- Strengthen public information campaigns to target the demand side (sex exploiters)
- Strengthen and implement extraterritorial criminal laws (laws existing or taking place outside the territorial limits of a jurisdiction), extradition, and other measures to prosecute the sex exploiter of children, criminalize child pornography, including its possession, and register sex offenders
- Ensure effective law enforcement in both countries of origin and destination and facilitate the gathering of evidence, detection, and prosecution of sex exploiters by fostering cooperation between countries
- Distribute adequate resources and build up the capacity for preventive action against sexual exploitation of children
- Increase access to basic education, particularly with regard to the plight of the girl child and the inferior status assigned to women and children in many communities
- Conduct information campaigns on human sexuality and reproductive health
- Provide comprehensive services to support the child victims and their families and protect child victims from being penalized
- Develop alternative means of livelihood for child victims and their families to prevent further commercial sexual exploitation. (207)

There is an urgent need for effective global action, strengthened law enforcement, and law reform dealing with the commercial sexual exploitation of children. Appropriate, accessible, culturally appropriate, gender-sensitive services, including legal, social, medical, psychological, and other support measures are essential. Psychological, social, and medical interventions as well as long-term monitoring may be needed to treat the sex exploiter. (186)

Conclusion:

The commercial sexual exploitation of children involves coercion, violence, and forced labor and is a modern-day form of slavery. Inadequate societal systems to promote children's rights, or lack thereof, and are influential factors in exposing children to various forms of exploitation. The lack of protection for a woman's sexuality and the low value placed on women and girls by oppressive societal traditions puts young girls in a particularly vulnerable position. (207)

Many countries prefer to describe the problem of children involved in the sex sector as a problem brought in from other cultures. This may be an attempt to take attention off homeland policies, which cause the root of poverty, indifference to the welfare of children, and *marginalization. *Marginalization: being assigning to a place of insignificance, put out of sight or mind, considered unimportant, or a powerless position within a society or group.

The poor are most vulnerable to sexual exploitation. Moreover, the poor are not only defined in terms of lack of access to employment, goods, and services, but in addition are more specifically qualified through their lack of access to power. In this hierarchy, in both developed and developing countries, children are least important. (196)

The economic and social dependence on prostitution is strong in many developing countries. Although utter poverty has declined, social welfare is still largely absent and personal incomes are either very high or very low while child protection laws remain ineffective or non-existent. Sexually exploited children frequently are unable to access social welfare. It is crucial that legislators and policymakers adopt a clear position on children in the sex sector. A major hurdle is that legislators have avoided directly dealing with the issue as an economic problem, therefore, the logical and effective government policies and programs targeting the business are lacking. (207)

In view of the differences between child prostitution and adult prostitution, creating separate measures for each age group is recommended. Child sex workers should be treated as a much more serious problem because children are clearly more vulnerable and helpless against the established structures of the sex sector and much more likely to be victims of "debt bondage" and *vested stakes to exploiters. *vested: to be placed or given into the possession or discretion of some person or authority.

There are few doubts that the sexual exploitation of children results in serious, often life-long or life-threatening consequences for physical, psychological, and social development, including the threat of early pregnancy, maternal mortality, injury, retarded development, physical disabilities, and sexually transmitted diseases, including HIV/AIDS. At the community level, the commercial sexual exploitation of children represents an erosion of human values and rights.

When children lack a healthy environment, access to health care, education, recreation, and minimum standards of food, clothing, and shelter, they become particularly vulnerable to exploitation. The **Convention on the Rights of the Child** reaffirms that people under the age of 18 are entitled to full protection from all forms of commercial exploitation by adults. The commercial sexual exploitation of children is a fundamental violation of children's rights; the goal is to eradicate these practices and to ensure that children are given equal human rights. (197)

What Can I Do About Trafficking?

Learn To Recognize Victims Of Trafficking:

- Victims of trafficking perform labor against their will by force, fraud, or coercion. Any child under the age of 18, who is induced to perform a commercial sex act, is a victim of a severe form of trafficking, as a minor cannot consent.
- Victims may have experienced violence, sexual abuse, and/or psychological threats and may have legitimate fears for themselves and their families.
- Victims of trafficking may be from outside the United States and often will not have any immigration documents. Their captors may have confiscated their documents.
- Remember that it is very difficult to identify victims of trafficking, especially children. Children will rarely identify themselves as victims. Instinctively, they may not trust easily. This is often due to their sufferings. It should be noted; there is a strong possibility that their trafficker has coached them to answer questions in a certain way. They are young, vulnerable, and frightened of both their traffickers and the police. Most have no documents and are often told they will be deported and their families harmed if they try to escape. (187)

Treat Trafficking Victims With Compassion And Respect:

Remember, it does not matter how they entered the United States, whether they initially consented to being brought here for a job or school, or whether their current employment activity is illegal (such as prostitution). If at any time the person was deceived, coerced into forced labor, is being held against his or her will in some sort of debt bondage, or is being used as a laborer bound in servitude because of debt, she or he is a victim of trafficking. (187)

Appropriate Referrals:

- Call the **Trafficking in Persons Information and Referral Hotline** 888-373-7888 to help suspected victims access services in your area. (208)

- Call the **Trafficking in Persons and Worker Exploitation Task Force Complaint Line** 888-428-7581 to begin an investigation of a suspected case by federal law enforcement authorities. (209)
- If the victim is a minor, contact local child protection authorities in accordance with your state and county mandatory reporting laws, particularly if the child needs emergency care in a licensed foster home or facility.
- Find a reputable attorney to talk to the victim about legal immigration issues and ensure that his or her rights are protected. (187)

Educate Yourself And Others:

Learn about this sinister trade in human beings and then help spread the word. Become an advocate and raise awareness in your community.

Resources For Children:

Help Them Protect Themselves From Trafficking And Labor Exploitation:

- UNICEF Global Classroom: Teaching to Counter Trafficking
- ILO: Child Labor–An Information Kit for Teachers, Educators and their Organizations
- USDOL: Youth Rules (resources to teach children about labor laws in the United States)
- Youth Advocate Program International (YAPI), Course Curricula (modules on teaching children about commercial sexual exploitation and modern slavery)
- Legal Aid Foundation of Los Angeles, Three Tales of Slavery Comic Books (187)

Other Anti-Trafficking Programs:

- In Albania, **The Delta Force**, a rapid reaction unit to intercept traffickers is an organized crime unit, which has arrested child traffickers, including several public officials, and the **Office of Internal Control** within the Albanian police, which has investigated and arrested police officers for complicity in trafficking.
- In Romania, **the Southeast European Cooperative Initiative** (SECI) is a multi-lateral law enforcement effort involving fourteen countries in Southeastern Europe. To date, this initiative has had four successful operations resulting in the arrest and conviction of traffickers and the rescue and safe return of hundreds of young women and children. These operations are regional cooperative law enforcement efforts that entail 100% border checks, brothel and bar raids, and other concurrent multilateral and in-country law enforcement operations to break up trafficking rings and rescue victims. Another comparable initiative involving Georgia, Ukraine, Uzbekistan, Moldova, and Azerbaijan is also underway.
- The State Department's **Bureau of Population, Refugees, and Migration** funds a program run by the **International Organization on Migration** for a rescue effort for children trafficked to work in rural Ghanaian fishing villages. The International Organization on Migration assists fishermen in developing sustainable fisheries; the

fishermen in turn release the children to the International Organization on Migration to repatriate to their families.

- The State Department's **Office to Monitor and Combat Trafficking in Persons** provided funding to the **United Nations Crime Center** to produce, translate, and distribute a public service announcement on child trafficking and labor.
- The United States **Agency for International Development** supports the activities of a non-governmental organization in Tanzania to increase community awareness among children, parents, and police about trafficking and to improve strategies to combat child trafficking.
- The Office to Monitor and Combat Trafficking in Persons funded the establishment of a safe house/shelter for non-Thai and Hill Tribe women and children near Chiang Mai, Thailand.
- The State Department's **Bureau of International Narcotics and Law Enforcement Affairs** sponsored a border security project in Albania. Six Department of Justice advisors train officials and monitor port-of-entry operations at the airport and seaports.
- The State Department's **Bureau for Educational and Cultural Affairs** brings hundreds of International Visitors to the United States each year to learn about trafficking. International Visitors include government officials, non-governmental leaders, journalists and law enforcement officials. (210)

Keeping Children Out Of Harm's Way Is—Unfortunately—Not Always A Priority:

There is growing international acceptance of the need for more effective action and strengthened law enforcement in the countries of destination to which sex offenders come. Extra-territoriality laws on the part of the countries of origin are being implemented to penalize the conduct of their nationals who commit crimes against children in other countries. In both international and national law, the legal stance on the sale and trafficking in children, child prostitution, sexual exploitation of children, pedophilia, and child pornography are all violent crimes against children and are treated as such.

How effectively these duties are carried out depends on the extent to which the society regards the protection of children as important. The legal environment reflects the political environment, and unless a society gives priority to the protection of its children, the laws will not protect them. In reality, child victims are offered little or no protection as many laws suffer from weak enforcement. The consequences for the offender are few and the child victim is commonly overlooked. (211)

Who Is Responsible For Protecting Children?

To ensure that children benefit from the protection international conventions have been designed to give, practical indicators are needed, based on reliable statistical data relevant to regional, national, and local situations. Researchers argue that children's' rights and the responsibility of the government, community, and family towards its children should be the starting point in developing a framework for measurement and monitoring. (196)

<u>NOTES</u>

Chapter Nineteen

CHILD PORNOGRAPHY AND INTERNET DANGERS

Child Pornography—From Photographs To Sadistic Torture And Murder:

According to the National Coalition for the Protection of Children and Families, child pornography consists of photographs, videotapes, magazines, books, and films that depict children in sex acts, all of which are considered contraband and are illegal; including child nudity, simulated sex involving children and computer-animation depicting child porn. The very act of photographing a child in any sexual context is child sexual abuse. The internet has become an increasingly vast area where those involved in child pornography have found their niche. Although law enforcement has begun to police the internet, it still relies largely on a CyberHoodWatch to detect lawbreakers. (212)

Demand For Babies And Toddlers:

More babies and toddlers are appearing on the internet and the abuse is getting worse. It is more torturous and sadistic than it was before. The typical age of children is between 6 and 12, but the profile is getting younger. The demand for pornographic images of babies and toddlers is soaring. (213)

Who Possesses Child Pornography?

- Men, women, and children of all ages
- Rich and poor
- People from small towns and large cities
- Religious and non-religious (214)

The Effects Of Pornography And Sexual Messages

Many people think that pornography is just harmless fun and that it has no detrimental effects. However, it is virtually impossible not to be affected by pornography and the sexual messages that saturate our society today, legal or not. (212)

Shaping Harmful Attitudes And Relationships:

Research has shown that pornography and its messages are involved in shaping attitudes and encouraging behavior that can harm individual users and their families. Pornography is often viewed in secret, which creates deception within marriages that can lead to divorce. In addition, pornography promotes the appeal of adultery, prostitution, and unreal expectations that can result in dangerous promiscuous behavior. (212)

Young people growing up in our overly sexualized culture are being exposed to sexually explicit material on a daily basis through network television, movies, music, and the internet. Children are being subjected to sexual material and messages before they are mentally prepared to understand or evaluate what they are viewing. In addition, the majority of sex education is taking place in the media, not in the home, church, or school. (212)

False Messages Sent By Our Sexualized Culture:

FALSE: Sex acts (and sex desires) with anyone, under any circumstances, and in any form, is beneficial and has no negative consequences.

FALSE: Women have one value—to meet the sexual demands of men.

FALSE: Marriage and children are obstacles to sexual fulfillment.

FALSE: Everyone is involved in promiscuous sexual activity, infidelity, and premarital sex. (212)

Pornography Is Highly Addictive:

Not only is the pornography industry, as well as the mainstream media, filling consumers heads with these false beliefs and attitudes, but also studies have found that pornography can be highly addictive. In fact, Dr. Victor Cline, an expert on sexual addiction, found that there is a four-step progression among many who consume pornography. (212)

- **ADDICTION:** Pornography provides a powerful sexual stimulant or aphrodisiac effect, followed by sexual release, most often through masturbation.
- **ESCALATION:** Over time, addicts require more explicit and deviant material to meet their sexual "needs."
- **DESENSITIZATION:** What was first perceived as gross, shocking and disturbing, in time becomes common and acceptable.
- **ACTING OUT SEXUALLY:** There is an increasing tendency to act out behaviors viewed in pornography.

The National Council on Sexual Addiction estimates that 6 to 8% of Americans are sexual addicts.

Sex Crime Dangers In Our Communities:

Sexually oriented businesses, such as strip clubs and massage parlors, attract crime to communities. In addition, the general content of pornography supports abuse and the rape myth, that women enjoy forceful sex, and serves as a how-to for sex crimes, primarily the molestation of children. (215)

147

Land use studies by the **National Law Center for Children And Families** show evidence of the correlation between adult businesses and crime. For example, in Phoenix neighborhoods where these type businesses were located, the number of sex offenses was 506% greater than in areas without such businesses. The number of property crimes was 43% greater, and the number of violent crimes 4% greater.

Dr. Mary Anne Layden, Director of Education, University of Pennsylvania Health System, pointed out, "I have been treating sexual violence victims and perpetrators for 13 years. I have not treated a single case of sexual violence that did not involve pornography." (215)

Most will agree on the amount of harm caused by child pornography, which consists of photographs, videos, magazines, books, and films that show children engaged in sexual acts, all of which are illegal. All production of these materials is an illegal and permanent record of the abuse or exploitation of children. (212)

"Virtual" Child Porn Law Ruled Unconstitutional:

Material digitally-doctored to look like child pornography was also illegal, until a Supreme Court decision in April 2002 found the "virtual" child porn law unconstitutional. (212)

Basically, the law limits legal "virtual child pornography" to material that either doesn't depict explicit sexual acts (under Section 2) or isn't "obscene" (under Section 1). This law is written so that even if Section 2 were to be held unconstitutional, Section 1 could be left intact — and thus "obscene" virtual child pornography would remain prohibited even if the more explicit provision was found unconstitutional.

Congress later passed a new law, 2003's PROTECT Act. Part of that law prohibits certain, though not all, *types* of virtual child pornography, and another part specifically prohibits *obscene* virtual child pornography.
For more information go to http://judiciary.senate.gov/special/S151CONF.pdf

Child and adult pornography is frequently used by pedophiles to lure children. The typical child molester befriends the child, often through internet chat rooms, and, after building "trust," exposes the child to pornography. This is done in attempt to make the child think that this behavior is acceptable and to lure him or her to participate. The experience of exploitation and abuse becomes a lifelong struggle for the victim and leaves them with the fear that their photos are still out there.

Pornography And Sex Abusers:

Pornography is very influential in the actions of sex offenders and serial murders with 90% of the predators who molest children having had some type of involvement with pornography and using adult and child pornography to aid them in their molestations. (216)

- 86% of rapists studied admitted regular use of pornography.
- 57% admitted imitating pornographic scenes in the commission of sex crimes. (217)
- Rapists are 15 times more likely than non-offenders to have been exposed to hard-core pornography in childhood [average ages 6 to 10], and report an early age of "peak experience" with pornography. (218)
- In a national poll of mental health professionals, 254 psychotherapists reported in their clinical practices cases that pornography was found to be an instigator or contributor to a sex crime, personality disturbance, or antisocial act. (219)
- 87% of molesters of girls and 77% of molesters of boys studied in Ontario, Canada, admitted to regular use of hard-core pornography. (220)

Pornography, Especially Child Pornography, Is Used By Pedophiles For Three Reasons:

- To stimulate themselves
- To lower inhibitions and resistance to sexual activity in the intended child victims
- To teach a child how to perform the sexual activity with the adult (221)

Police say 40% of people charged with child pornography also sexually abuse children, but finding the predators and identifying the victims are daunting tasks. (222)

Law enforcement officials estimate there as many as 50,000 sexual predators online at any given moment. (223)

How Internet Pedophiles Protect Themselves:

Internet pedophiles have increasingly adopted counter-intelligence techniques to protect themselves from being traced. (224)

Startling Facts:

Usually, the sex crime setting does not involve violence and rarely do strangers pose online as children. (225)

- Only 5% of offenders concealed the fact that they were adults
- 80% of offenders were explicit about their intentions with the youth
- In 73% of crimes, youth go to meet the offender on multiple occasions for multiple sexual encounters. (225)
- 1 in 5 children who use computer chat rooms has been approached over the internet by pedophiles (226)
- 89% of sexual solicitations were made in either chat rooms or Instant Messages (IM)
- Approximately 13 million youth use Instant Messaging and 1 in 5 received sexual solicitation (227)
- 1 in 33 received aggressive sexual solicitations. They were asked to meet, called by phone, and/or were sent mail, money, or gifts (228)
- Only 25% of youth who received sexual solicitation told a parent. (228)

- Half of the teens who often communicate through the internet with someone they have not met in person and 1/3 of youth (ages 8-18) have talked about meeting someone they have only met through the internet (229)
- Nearly 1 in 8 youth discovered that someone they were communicating with online was an adult pretending to be much younger (229)
- 15% of "dual offenders" tried to victimize children; but instead solicited undercover investigators who posed as minors online. Overall 36% of dual offenders showed or gave child pornography to identified victims or to undercover investigators posing as minors online. (230)

Demand For Sex On The Internet:

- Sex is the #1 search topic on the internet (231)
- 60% of all website visits are sexual in nature (232)
- There are 1.3 million pornographic websites worldwide (233)

More Than Half Of Illegal Internet Sites Are In The United States:

- More than half of all illegal sites reported to the **Internet Watch Foundation** are hosted in the United States. Illegal sites in Russia more than doubled in 2002 from 286 to 706. (224)

- Pornographic web pages now top 260 million and are growing at an unprecedented rate. (233)

Annual Revenues Top $12 Billion Dollars From Internet Pornography:

- The internet pornography industry generates $12 billion dollars in annual revenue– that is more than the combined annual revenues of ABC, NBC, and CBS (234)

Commercial Pornography Sites:

- 74% display free teasers (porn images) on the homepage; often banner ads are used
- 66% did not include a warning of adult content
- 11% included such a warning, but did not have sexually explicit content on the homepage
- 25% prevented users from exiting the site (mouse-trapping)
- Only 3% required adult verification (235)

Porn Sites Visited By Multi-Millions Of Men And Women:

Example: More than 32 million individuals visited a porn site in September 2003. Nearly 22.8 million of them were male (71 %), while 9.4 million adult site visitors were female (29 %) (236)

Largest Group Of Viewers Are Children:

Children (ages 12 to 17) make up the largest percentage of viewers of internet pornography (237)

Mobil Phone Pornography:

- By the end of 2004, approximately 21 million 5 to 19 year-olds had wireless phones. (238)
- 1 in 10 young people (13%) report using a handheld device that connects to the internet (239)
- In 2005, worldwide revenue from mobile phone pornography rose to $1 billion, expected to triple within a few years. (240)
- 87% of university students polled had virtual sex using Instant Messenger, webcam, and telephone. (241)
- At over $13.3 billion, the 2006 revenues of the sex and porn industry in the U.S. are bigger than the NFL, NBA, and Major League Baseball combined. Worldwide sex industry sales for 2006 are reported to be 97 billion. To put this in perspective, Microsoft, who sells the operating system used in the majority of computers around the world, reported sales of 44.8 billion in 2006. (242)

Students Were Most At Risk For Cybersex Compulsions Due To:

- Increased access to computers
- More private leisure time
- Developmental stage characterized by increased sexual awareness and experimentation (243)

Both computer classes & colleges might need to recognize this increased vulnerability and institute new primary prevention strategies. (243)

Pornography Accessed In Schools And Libraries:

How It Can Be Controlled:

In the area of technology misuse, the internet is becoming an easy place where children can access adult pornography. The **Internet Online Summit** held in 1997 in Washington, D.C., revealed that 70% of children viewing pornography on the internet are doing so in public schools and libraries. Educators need to know the harm of pornography, the many facets of the issue, and what to do to help stop child pornography on the internet. (212)

Note: Controls implemented by CIPA below.

Educators Role:

Protecting Children Against The Devaluation Of Women And Children:

Pornography is a neglected problem in our society. It devalues women in particular; suggesting women are objects to use rather than valuable human beings. The same devaluation occurs when children are involved. Educators must not only teach against such disrespect, but also work to protect children from gaining access to internet pornography as the internet becomes more commonplace in schools. (212)

Children Being Neglected At Home May Fall Into A Trap:

Child pornography can be placed in the same category with other destructive habits and traps. Children who fall into the trap of becoming objects of pornography tend to have a need for love from an adult. This can be the result of being neglected at home by parents or having problems in school. Teachers can play a strong role in such situations by being a caring adult who is available to listen, increasing feelings of self-worth in troubled children. (212)

Since younger and younger children use the internet, teach them to avoid pornographic magazines and internet sites at an early age. Educators with internet access in their rooms and buildings must make it a priority to supervise children on the internet. Using filtering programs in schools has stirred up much debate from those who feel that filtering software keeps children out of sites that hold appropriate information, but may contain "inappropriate" words. They feel teachers should be able to teach children what to avoid without filtering these sites. Those who are pro-filtering believe that the filters do a good job in disallowing children into inappropriate sites. (212)

Adolescents who access the internet for sexual and reproductive health information are only minimally protected by pornography-blocking software. For example, only 5% of online health information was filtered out by pornography-blocking software when installed at moderate settings while blocking 90% of pornographic content. (244)

Freedom of the web would work well in secondary education, but some educators feel it is too big a risk that elementary children will run across pornographic sites. A single moment on one of these sites is all it takes to increase interest or start desensitization to such images. A combination of teaching and filtering is the recommendation at the elementary level. (245)

Having a teacher nearby and actively taking an interested in what the students are pursuing on the internet can effectively deter inappropriate access. Having computers situated in rooms where the screen content can be viewed by the teacher at all times is also a good classroom deterrent. (212)

Public Libraries And Access To Pornography:

Reports from over 450 public libraries include documentations over 2,062 incidents of internet pornography. Of those:

- 962 incidents of adults accessing porn

- 472 incidents of children accessing pornography
- 106 incidents of adults exposing children to porn
- 41 cases of child porn being accessed
- 5 attempts to molest children in libraries

A pedophile-monitoring group has confirmed that online pedophiles are telling each other to use public libraries to download child pornography. (246)

Public libraries have become a breeding ground for the sexual exploitation of children. (247)

Among Age Group 15 to 24 Internet Users:

- 67% support the law requiring internet filters at schools and libraries
- 2 out of 3 say being exposed to online pornography could have a serious impact on those under 18
- A majority (59%) think seeing pornography on the internet encourages young people to have sex before they are ready. (247)

What Kids Are Doing Online:

- More than 11 million teenagers regularly view pornography online (248)
- The majority of teenager's online use occurs at home, right after school, when working parents are not at home. (249)
- 31% of 7th to 12th grade students pretended to be older to access a website (246)
- Nearly 1/3 of 8 to 18 year-olds have a computer in their bedroom, and 1 in 5 have an internet connection (250)
- A study by the NOP, an international research group, found that of the four million youth, ages 7 to 17 who surf the net, 29% freely give out their home address and 14% freely give out their e-mail address (251)
- 44% of children polled have visited X-rated (sexual content) sites (252)
- 43% said they do not have rules about internet use in their homes (252)

While 75% Of Parents Believe They Know What Their Children View Online, The Truth About Kids' Internet Habits Are:

- 58% of teens say they have accessed an objectionable website
- 39% accessed offensive music
- 25% accessed sexual content
- 20% accessed violence (253)
- 1 in 4 kids participate in real time chat rooms. (254)
- 62% of parents of teenagers are unaware that their children have accessed objectionable websites (255)

Youth Online Privacy And Social Networking:

- 58% of teens don't think posting photos or other personal informational on social networking sites is unsafe
- About 49% are unconcerned that posting personal information online might negatively affect their future
- 64% post photos or videos of themselves
- 58% post information about where they live
- 70% of females post personal photos or videos of themselves
- 58% of males post personal photos or videos of themselves
- 8% have posted his or her cell phone number online

Teens That Have Online Profiles:

- Are generally more likely to say it is okay to give out certain pieces of personal information in offline situations than they are to have that information actually posted to their profile. (256)
- Have a greater tendency to say it is fine to share where they go to school, their IM screen name, e-mail address, last name, and cell phone number with someone they met at a party, when compared with the percentage who actually posts that information online.
- About 23% of teen profile creators say it would be easy for someone to find out who they are from the information posted to their profile
- 40% of teens with profiles online think that is would be hard for someone to find out who they are from their profile, but that they could eventually be found online
- 36% think it would be "very difficult" for someone to identify them from their online profile (256)
- 49% of high school students have posted personal information on their web pages that could assist a stranger to identify or locate them, such as name, age, or address. (257)

A Poll Conducted By The Girl Scout Research Institute Revealed:

- 30% of teenage girls said they had been sexually harassed in a chat room
- Only 7% told their parents about the harassment because they were worried that they would be banned from going online
- 86% of the girls polled said they could chat online without their parents' knowledge
- 57% could read their parents' e-mail
- 54% would explore a cyberspace relationship (258)

Youth Unintentionally Exposed To Pornography:

- Among teens online, 70% have accidentally come across pornography on the web (250)
- 9 out of 10 children (ages 8 to 16) have viewed pornography on the internet. In most cases, the sex sites were accessed unintentionally. This happens often when a

when a child, perhaps in the process of doing homework, uses a seemingly innocent sounding word to search for information or pictures. (259)

- In 26% of cases where youth accidentally stumbled into pornographic websites, the youth stated being exposed to another sex website when they were attempting to exit the initial website 260)

A survey conducted in 2000 of 1,501 U.S. children ages 10 to 17 showed that about 1 in 4 had unwanted exposure to images of nudity or sex acts. (261)

How Youth Are Reacting To Exposure To Pornography:

"Very upset" or "extremely upset" are the answers given by 23% of youth who admitted to being exposed to sexual content online. (260)

Less than 10% of sexual solicitations and only 3% of the unwanted sexual content exposures are reported to authorities, including law enforcement agencies or internet providers. (262)

Concerns For Parents:

The number one media concern for parents has shifted from television to the internet, with 85% of parents saying that it posed the greatest risk to their children among all forms of media. (263)

- 83% of parents say there is no excuse for not knowing enough about the internet to protect your kids or teens. (263)
- 81% of parents say that teens are not careful enough when giving out information online and 79% of online teens agree with their parents. (264)
- 80% of parents worry about sexual predators on the internet
- 77% of parents say they see the internet as an important tool that helps their kids learn
- 76% of parents say they would like to make the internet a safer place for kids
- 65% of all parents and 64% of all teens say that teens do things online that they wouldn't want their parents to know about. (265)

Pornographers Disguise Site Names to Include Words Like Disney, Barbie, Etc.:

Pornographers use "stealth" sites (cleverly disguised) with common brand names, including Disney, Barbie, ESPN, etc., to lure children. (266)

Parental Control Issues:

- 88% of parents think it's more important to know what their kids are doing online than to respect their kids' privacy (263)
- 87% of parents seek out information about their kids' internet use a few times a month. (263)
- 58% of parents use **Parents' Internet Monitoring Study**. (259)

- 42% of parents do not review the content of what their teenager(s) read and/or type in chat rooms or via instant messaging. June 2005. (259)

In a July 2000 survey, 34% of adults who have children participating in real time chat were most likely to use technology to monitor their internet time (254)

- 25% of kids (grades 7 to 12) with a computer at home, say it has a filter or parental controls (263)
- 23% of parents have rules about what their kids can do on the computer (263)
- Parents rely mostly on personal observation and setting guidelines for their children's Internet access.
- 1 in 2 parents do not use any blocking or filtering software. (254)

Parents Ignorant of Chat Lingo:

Teenagers use chat lingo to communicate in IM and parents do not know the meanings of some of the most commonly used phrases. (267)

- POS (parent over shoulder)
- P911 (parent alert)
- 95% of parents did not recognize common chat room lingo that teenagers use.
- 92% do not know A/S/L (age/sex/location) (267)
- 68% don't know what BRB means (be right back)
- 57% don't know what LOL means (laughing out loud)

Pornography's Progressive Pattern of Addiction

Dr. Victor Cline, a clinical psychologist at the University of Utah and a specialist in the area of sexual addictions, has observed a four-step syndrome common to his clients who have been involved with pornography. (268)

Step 1 - Addiction:

Once consumers of pornography are hooked, they keep coming back for more. The sexually graphic material provides the viewer with an exciting arousal effect, followed by sexual release, most often through masturbation. Pornography gives the viewer powerful imagery that can be recalled and elaborated on with the person's fantasy life. Despite negative consequences, most addicts are unable to rid themselves of their dependence on pornography. The addiction rules their lives.

Step 2 - Escalation:

Cline describes the second phase as an escalation effect. The pornography consumer, similar to the drug user, requires more and more stimulation to reach his or her "highs." In fact, some viewers prefer the powerful sexual imagery planted in their minds by exposure to pornography to sexual intercourse itself. This nearly always diminishes the viewer's capacity to love and express appropriate intimacy within relationships. (268)

Step 3 - Desensitization:

In this phase, material that was originally perceived as unthinkable, shocking, illegal, repulsive, or immoral, is now viewed as acceptable, and commonplace by the viewer of pornography. Regardless of the deviancy expressed, the viewer perceives the pornography and his or her use of it as legitimate.

Step 4 - Acting Out Sexually:

This last step describes an increased tendency to sexually act out the behaviors viewed in pornography, including promiscuity, voyeurism, exhibitionism, group sex, rape, sadomasochism, child molestation, and more. Clearly, this progressive pattern demonstrates how reality and fantasy become blurred for those who are entangled with pornography or when viewing is no longer enough. (268)

Early Emotional Wounding Is A Factor In Pornography Addiction:

Regarding the compulsive or addictive nature of pornography, Dr. Cline shares the following: "In over 26 years, I have treated approximately 350 males afflicted with sexual addictions (or sometimes referred to as sexual compulsions). In about 94% of the cases, I have found that pornography was a contributing factor or at least a direct causal agent in the acquiring of these sexual illnesses." (269)

Missing Children Often Appear on Porn Sites—Some Only 2, 3, or 4 Years-Old:

Approximately 20 new children appear on porn sites every month; many of these were kidnapped or sold into sex. In the last couple of years, authorities have seen young children, even babies on these illegal websites. (270)

Children are reported missing at the rate of 750,000 per year, 62,500 per month, 14,423, per week, 2,054 per day, and 85 per hour—that is 3 children every 2 minutes. (271)

Child Pornography Websites Are Growing In Numbers:

- From April to September 2000, 403 new child pornography sites were developed at a rate of 67 per month. (233)
- From February to July 2001, 1,391 new child pornography sites were developed at a rate of 231 per month for an increase of 345% at the rate of about 8 per day. (233)
- A 1999 U.S. Customs case discovered a child pornography website that, in its first three months, had nearly 150,000 hits and a download of 3.2 million images. (272)
- The number of internet child pornography images increased 1,500% since 1988. (273)
- Approximately 20% of all internet pornography involves children. (274)

According to researchers who monitored the internet over six weeks, 140,000 child pornography images were posted to the Internet during that time. Twenty children were estimated to have been abused for the first time and more than 1,000 images of each child were created for viewing. (275)

The U.S. Customs Service estimates that there are more than 100,000 websites offering child pornography. Revenue estimates for the industry range from $200 million to over $3 billion per year. These unlawful sexual images are purchased easily by shopping online. Subscribers typically use credit cards to pay a monthly fee of $30 to $50 to download photos and videos, or a one-time fee of a few dollars for single images. (276)

Arrests Increasing:

- Arrests for possessing and distributing child pornography have been climbing steadily, in part because federal agencies are devoting more resources to the issue. (261)
- In 1992, U.S. Customs recorded 57 arrests for possession of child pornography transported across borders, 48 indictments, and 69 convictions. By 2000, those numbers had grown to 320 arrests, 299 indictments, and 324 convictions. (261)
- Since 1992, the U.S. Customs Service has arrested more than 1,000 people on charges related to child pornography and has never lost a case that has gone through the judicial process. (261)

Arrests In The U.S. For The Possession Of Child Pornography:

Between 2000 And 2001:

- 83% had images of children ages 6 to 12
- 39% had images of children ages 3 to 5
- 19% had images of infants and toddlers under age 3

Who Possesses Child Pornography?

- Individuals whose income ranges from poverty to wealth
- Individuals whose level of education ranges from not finishing high school to post college degrees
- Those who come from cities, suburbs, small towns, and rural areas
- Some are well-known, well thought of in their communities, and/or have high-profile jobs
- Some seem isolated and appear to be obsessed with the internet, and/or have long criminal histories (277)

Between July 1, 2000, and June 30, 2001,

Of An Estimated 1,713 Arrested:

- Mostly Male
- 91% were white

- 86% were older than 25
- 41% had never married
- 38% were either married or living with partners
- 21% were separated, divorced, or widowed
- Most were unmarried at the time of their crime
- Only 3% were younger than 18 (277)

Of Those:

- 83% had pornographic images of prepubescent children
- 80% had images graphically depicting sexual penetration
- Approximately 1 in 5 had images depicting sexual violence to children such as bondage, rape, and torture
- 39% had child-pornography videos with motion and sound. (277)
- Law enforcement found that 48% had more than 100 graphic still images, and 14% had 1,000 or more graphic images. (277)
- 40% were dual offenders who sexually victimized children and possessed child pornography, with both crimes discovered in the same investigation. An additional 15% were dual offenders who attempted to victimize children by soliciting undercover investigators who posed online as minors. (277)

How Old Were Children In These Images?

According to investigators who handled the cases of estimated arrestees, most had images of children who had not yet reached puberty.

- 83% had images of children ages 6 to 12
- 39% had images of children ages 3 to 5
- 19% had images of toddlers or infants younger than age 3
- 62% had pictures primarily of girls
- 14% had pictures primarily of boys
- 15% had pictures showing boys and girls in equal numbers (277)

How Graphic Are The Images?

According to investigators who handle these cases, most had graphic images explicitly showing sexual acts by or on children.

- 92% had images of minors focusing on genitals or showing explicit sexual activity
- 80% had pictures showing the sexual penetration of a child, including oral sex
- 71% possessed images showing sexual contact between an adult and a minor, such as adults and minors each touching the other's genitals or breasts
- 21% had child pornography depicting violence such as bondage, rape, or torture and most of those involved images of children who were gagged, bound, blindfolded, or otherwise enduring sadistic sex

- 79% also had what might be termed "soft core" images of nude or semi-nude minors, but only 1% possessed such images alone. (277)

Efforts To Stop Child Pornography And Internet Dangers:

Passed into_law on December 7, 2007, a new bill demands Internet Service Providers (ISPs) report online child exploitation.

SAFE Act of 2007:

To modernize and expand the reporting requirements relating to child pornography, to expand cooperation in combating child pornography, and for other purposes, be it enacted by the Senate and House of Representatives of the United States of America in Congress assembled. This Act may be cited as the "**Securing Adolescents from Exploitation-Online Act of 2007**" or the "**SAFE Act of 2007.**"

Public Opinion:

- 8 out of 10 Americans believe federal laws against internet obscenity should be vigorously enforced
- 90% of women support vigorous enforcement of federal laws against Internet obscenity.
- 72% of men support vigorous enforcement of federal laws against internet obscenity
- 7 out of 10 Americans say they do not believe these laws are currently being vigorously enforced (278)

Children's Internet Protection Act (CIPA):

The Children's Internet Protection Act (CIPA) is a federal law enacted by Congress in December 2000, to address concerns about access to offensive content over the internet on school and library computers. CIPA imposes certain types of requirements on any school or library that receives funding support for internet access or internal connections from the "E-rate" program, a program that makes certain technology more affordable for eligible schools and libraries. In early 2001, the **Federal Communications Commission** (FCC) issued rules implementing CIPA. (279)

What CIPA Requires:

- Schools and libraries may not receive the discounts offered by the E-Rate program unless they certify that they have an internet safety policy and technology protection measures in place. An internet safety policy must include technology protection measures to block or filter internet access to pictures that are obscene, are child pornography, or are harmful to minors.
- Schools subject to CIPA are required to adopt and enforce a policy to monitor online activities of minors.

- Schools and libraries subject to CIPA are required to adopt and implement a policy addressing access by minors to inappropriate matter on the internet.
- This includes safety and security of minors when using electronic mail, chat rooms, and other forms of direct electronic communications, unauthorized access including "hacking" and other unlawful activities by minors online, unauthorized disclosure, use, and dissemination of personal information regarding minors, and restricting minors' access to materials harmful to them.
- Schools and libraries are required to certify that they have their safety policies and technology in place before receiving E-rate funding.
- CIPA does not affect E-rate funding for schools and libraries receiving discounts only for telecommunications, such as telephone service.
- An authorized person may disable the blocking or filtering measure during any use by an adult to enable access for bona fide research or other lawful purposes.
- CIPA does not require the tracking of Internet use by minors or adults. (279)

Child Pornography Protection Act (CPPA):

The Child Online Protection Act Commission, a congressionally appointed panel, is mandated by the Child Online Protection Act, which was approved by Congress in October 1998. The primary purpose of the Commission is to "identify technological or other methods that will help reduce access by minors to material that is harmful to minors on the internet."

The Commission released its final report to Congress on Friday, October 20, 2000. CPPA was enacted to close a loophole in the nation's child pornography laws. The loophole would have allowed pedophiles to use new technologies to create computer generated child pornography, which could have been legal to possess, distribute, and produce, if the government could not identify or prove that the child depicted in the pornography was an actual child.

CPPA supporters argue that both real and computer generated images of child pornography are used in the commission of child sexual molestation and are equally inciting to pedophiles and seductive to child victims.

Child Online Protection Act (COPA):

COPA made it a crime for commercial websites to make pornographic material that is harmful to minors available to juveniles. The purpose of COPA is to protect children from instant access to pornographic "teaser images" on porn syndicate web pages. This legislation requires pornographers to take a credit card number, adult verification number, or access code to restrict children's access to pornographic pictures and allow access to consenting adults. (279)

The report advised Congress that it could take steps to protect children online by dedicating more resources to the prosecution of internet obscenity and child pornography. The report also identified a number of technologies that may satisfy the affirmative defense requirements. One of the suggestions supported by all members of the Commission was the recommendation to educate America's parents about what measures are available for protecting children online. (279)

Since its enactment in 1996, CPPA has been challenged in federal court by the pornography industry and the ACLU. The **United States Supreme Court** heard arguments on October 30, 2001 to decide whether the Act is constitutional. (280)

Child Protection And Sexual Predator Punishment Act Of 1998:

This law increases protection for children from sexual predators, with two central provisions:

- Internet Service Providers (ISPs) are required to report evidence of child pornography and abuse violations to law enforcement
- A "zero-tolerance" policy toward the possession of child pornography. The possession law allows prosecution for illegal possession of any item of child pornography. (281)

Our children are at a higher risk for internet crimes than most parents realize. Do not be one of the uninformed. Understand the scope of the problem, facts, and figures to better identify the online dangers, as well as the positive benefits, of childhood internet activity.

Communications Decency Act Of 1996 (CDA):

CDA was the first legislative effort to protect children from pornography on the internet. Although the United States Supreme Court struck the indecency provisions of the CDA in ACLU vs. Reno, the obscenity amendments survived, resulting in an important victory for the protection of children and families online.

Legal Organizations That Fight For The Protection Of Children And Against The Dangers Of Online Pornography And Sexual Predators:

The National Law Center for Children and Families a nonprofit organization whose mission is focused on the protection of children and families from the harmful effect of illegal pornography by assisting in law enforcement and law improvement.

The American Center for Law and Justice a nonprofit public interest law firm and educational organization dedicated to the promotion of pro-liberty, pro-life, and pro-family causes.

There are agencies set up for reporting child pornography and who encourage the public to be part of the "cyberhood watch" on the internet. Educators are legally bound to report child abuse of any form and have an important responsibility to report internet child pornography.

- National Center for Missing and Exploited Children Cyber Tipline
- PedoWatch
- The Child Protection Society (212)

Internet Safety Tips To Teach Children:

- Do not give out personal information such as your address, telephone number, parents' work address and telephone number, or the name and location of your school without parental permission.
- Tell your parents immediately if you come across any information that makes you feel uncomfortable.
- Never agree to get together with anyone you meet online without first checking with your parents. If your parents agree to the meeting, be sure that it is in a public place, and bring a parent along.
- Never send anyone your picture or anything else without first checking with your parents.
- Do not respond to any messages that are mean or in any way make you feel uncomfortable. It is not your fault if you get a message like that. If you do, tell your parents right away so they can contact the online service.
- Talk to your parents so they can set up rules for going online. You and your parents can decide on the time of day that you can be online, the length of time and appropriate websites to visit.
- Do not access other websites or break these rules without parental permission.
- Never give out your password to anyone other than your parent or guardian.
- Only add friends to your site if you know them personally.
- Never respond to harassment or rude comments posted on your profile. Delete any unwanted messages or friends who continuously leave inappropriate comments. Report these comments to the networking site if they violate that site's terms of service.
- Remember that posting information about your friends could put them at risk. Protect your friends by not posting any names, passwords, ages, phone numbers, school names, or locations. Refrain from making or posting plans and activities on your site.
- Consider going through your blog and profile and removing information that could put you at risk. Remember, anyone has access to your blog and profile, not just people you know.
- Check the privacy settings of the social networking sites that you use. Set it so that only friends you approve can view your profile and no one can be your friend unless you approve them. (212)

NOTES

Chapter Twenty

SEX OFFENDER TREATMENT...IS THERE A CURE?

MYTH: Treatment for sex offenders is ineffective. (282)

FACT: Treatment programs can contribute to community safety because sex offenders who attend and cooperate with the conditions of the program are less likely to re-offend than those who reject intervention. (282)

The majority of sex offender treatment programs in the United States and Canada now use a combination of cognitive-behavioral treatment and re-offending prevention, designed to help sex offenders maintain behavioral changes by anticipating and coping with the problem of re-offending setbacks. Treatment that specifically deals with sexual offending generally involves group and/or individual therapy focused on becoming aware of the feelings of the victim and learning how to show compassion.

Cognitive Restructuring, Relating To Conscious Intellectual Activity:

- Thinking
- Reasoning
- Remembering
- Learning about the sexual abuse cycle
- Re-offending prevention planning
- Anger management and assertiveness training
- Social and interpersonal skills development
- Changing abnormal sexual arousal patterns (282)

Different Types Of Offenders Typically Respond To Different Treatment Methods:

With varying rates of success, treatment effectiveness can depend on several factors:

- The type of sexual offender (incest, multiple offender, rapist, etc.)
- The type of treatment being used (cognitive-behavioral, relapse prevention, psycho-educational, psychodynamic, use of medications, etc.)
- The method used to administer the treatment
- How well the community probation and parole departments work together when supervising the offender

Pedophiles, A Different Class Of Child Molester:

According to Dr. C. River Smith and Heidi J. Raynor at **All About Counseling**, whether or not a child sexual molester can be rehabilitated depends on what type of child molester they are. Incest offenders are not clinically termed as a pedophile. Pedophiles are a different class of child molesters, and are considered sexual addicts. In spite of their best efforts, a pedophile will abuse children as long as there is opportunity. Some pedophiles have to drive out of their way just to avoid the temptation of children they might otherwise meet. (283)

The type of child molester most resistant to treatment is a fixed pedophile. Unlike other types of offenders, they primarily abuse children who are non-family members. There is only a small percent of fixed pedophiles who responded to treatment. In general, this is not the case with incest perpetrators. Smith and Raynor believe that most people who abuse will probably be able to stop if they are held accountable, punished appropriately, and are given the proper kind of therapeutic treatment.

Do Abusers Feel Remorse?

Many abusers feel guilty. However, for the pedophile, the guilt means very little; it does not prevent them from re-offending as they are obsessed with children and act in addictive ways. In looking at effective treatment, empathy training that instills in the abuser an understanding of the child's pain and point of view of the sexual offense is one of the key pieces in helping an abuser to stop abusing. (283)

Several Studies Show This Type Of Treatment Program To Be Highly Effective:

- Those that are sex offense-specific (284)
- Those that are extensive in nature (285)
- And when the offender can be observed carefully (286)

According to statistics on the effectiveness of treatment, 8% of offenders who participated in treatment programs did not re-offend. Considering the devastating impact these offenses have on the victims, any reduction in the re-offense rates of sex offenders is significant.

Research also demonstrates that sex offenders who fail to complete treatment programs are at increased risk for both sexual and non-sexual re-offending. (282)

MYTH: The cost of treating and managing sex offenders in the community is too high. They belong behind bars. (282)

FACT: One year of intensive supervision and treatment in the community can cost $5,000 to $15,000 per offender, depending on the type of treatment. The average cost for incarcerating an offender is significantly higher at approximately $22,000 per year, not including treatment costs. (282)

Supervised Release Including Proper Treatment Could Prevent Further Abuse:

According to Lotke, 1996, without the option of supervised release including proper treatment, the vast majority of incarcerated sex offenders would serve their maximum sentences and return to the community without having had effective treatment while incarcerated—nor would they be on probation or parole with supervision controls to effectively manage their sexually abusive behavior. Managing those offenders who are agreeable to treatment and to being supervised intensively in the community following an appropriate term of incarceration can serve to prevent future victimization while saving taxpayers substantial imprisonment costs. (282)

Medication And Behavioral Therapy:

- Hormones such as medroxyprogesterone acetate and cyproterone acetate decrease the level of circulating testosterone, thereby reducing sex drive and aggression. These hormones reduce the frequency of erections, sexual fantasies, and sexual behaviors including masturbation and intercourse. Hormones are typically used in conjunction with behavioral and cognitive treatments involving conscious intellectual activity such as thinking, reasoning, or remembering. Antidepressants such as fluoxetine have also successfully decreased sex drive but have not effectively targeted sexual fantasies. (287)
- Aversive conditioning is behavior modification involving the use of negative stimuli to reduce or eliminate an inappropriate behavior.
- Covert sensitization has the patient relaxing and visualizing scenes of abnormal, deviant sexual behavior followed by imagining a negative event such as getting his penis stuck in the zipper of his pants.
- Assisted aversive conditioning is similar to covert sensitization except that the negative event is actual and not imagined, such as a foul odor being sprayed in the air by the therapist. The goal is for the patient to associate the abnormal, behavior with the foul odor. Aversive behavioral reversal is commonly referred to as "shame therapy. " The concept here is to humiliate the offender into ceasing the deviant sexual behavior; for example, by having the offender watch videotapes of the crime with the goal being that the experience will be distasteful and offensive to the sexual abuser. (287)

Positive Conditioning Approaches:

There are positive conditioning approaches that involve training the offenders in social skills and teaching them to use other, more appropriate behaviors. Reconditioning, for example, is giving the patient immediate feedback, which may help him change his behavior. For instance, a person might be hooked to a biofeedback machine that is connected to a light; he is taught to use self-control by keeping the light within a specific range of color while he is exposed to sexually stimulating material. (287)

Cognitive Therapies:

Cognitive therapies such as restructuring cognitive distortions and empathy training include correcting a pedophile's misconception that the child wishes to be involved in the sexual activity. A pedophile observing a young girl wearing shorts may wrongly think, *She wants me.* Empathy training involves helping the offender to identify with the victim, see the offense from the child's point of view, and understand the harm he could cause by the molestation. (287)

Prison Therapy:

Some sex-offender treatment occurs in prison, often as group therapy. "The therapist and peers try to break down the denial that typically exists," says Fred Berlin, who has studied the treatment of sex offenders for many years at Johns Hopkins University. The group therapy helps the offender face the fact   that he or she is in denial of the crime they have committed against a child and why rationalizing this behavior is wrong.

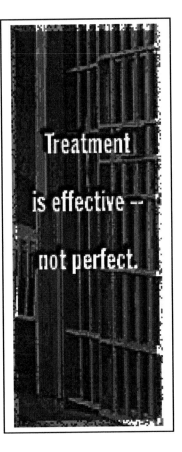

Berlin explains that denial can run deep. In an environment where it is okay to speak openly about the struggles with unacceptable cravings and sexual relationships with children, therapeutic confrontation is often effective in breaking down the walls of denial. (288)

A pedophile says, "I fondled a young boy. He was clearly aroused and seemed to be enjoying it." The therapist may tell the offender, "You cannot get into the mind of a young person and see the confusion and pain this will cause." Berlin says, "When offenders experience a craving that clouds their sensitivity, they cannot objectively see the consequences of their behavior."

Relapse Prevention Therapy:

In viewing pedophilia as a strong craving, therapists have adopted the technique of relapse prevention used in the treatment of addiction to alcohol and other drugs. One goal is to have the offender identify the emotions that they experience just before a relapse, such as depression, anger, intoxication, marital conflict, or other stresses. Offenders list additional warning signs and share them with other offenders so that they can watch for them, such as spending time with children, or long periods of isolation. They discuss lifestyle changes, such as not living or working around children, can prevent relapse. (288)

Treatment based on psychoanalytic introspection is an examination of one's own thoughts and feelings. It is important to help offenders understand the root of their problems. Knuchman focuses on teaching the men that their problem is greater than just sexual contact with the victim. It has to do with how they manage their lives and how they meet not just their sexual needs, but all their other needs as well. For many of them, sexual contact with a child is a way to feel competent, powerful, and in control of his life. (289)

<u>*Risk Factors To Consider*</u>:

- What are the issues associated with this offense?
- What was going on in the person's life at the time of the offense?
- What kind of stress was he experiencing?
- Where did it happen?
- What made it a safe place to commit the offense?
- What are the victim's characteristics: size, age, sex, and availability?

<u>*Castration*</u>:

For the more dangerous pedophiles, chemical or surgical castration may be the most effective treatment in controlling sexual impulses. Surgical castration is the removal of the testes that produces the male sex hormone testosterone. When coupled with monitoring of hormone levels, castration is a drastic but effective solution to sexual offenses. In European studies on castration from the 1940s and 1950s, re-offending rates were under 10%, showing that castration is probably the most effective treatment for certain kinds of sex offenders. (288)

Castration is more likely to be done chemically, usually by injecting a slow time-release drug that neutralizes testosterone, thus, lowering the sex drive. "Although the drugs are expensive and may produce dangerous side effects like severe weight gain or thinning of the bones, it brings real relief to pedophiles who should remain celibate. Simply lowering the sex drive makes sense", says Berlin, who has prescribed testosterone reducers for more than 150 people, of which only a handful were required to do so by a court order.

Berlin concludes, "Eliminating the sex drive may alter one's sexual identity, but such drastic treatment must be balanced against the reality of being a pedophile. Pedophilia is a horrible condition that nobody would ever want to have. The offenders that I have worked with have come to appreciate the fact that they don't have to live in society constantly looking over their shoulder. For many, finding something like castration that helps them to be in control is good news, not bad."

<u>*State Laws On Chemical And Surgical Castration*</u>:

<u>*Eight States That Allow Chemical Or Surgical Castration Of Sex Offenders*</u>:

- California
- Florida
- Georgia
- Louisiana
- Montana
- Oregon
- Texas
- Wisconsin

<u>*States That Allow Treatment As Punishment For Certain Sexual Offenses*</u>:

- California
- Florida
- Georgia
- Louisiana
- Montana
- Oregon
- Wisconsin

Florida, like California, makes treatment mandatory for repeat offenders. In each of these states, treatment is a condition for release from custody and the process generally begins before the offender is released. In Louisiana, treatment is a condition for reduced sentences. (288)

<u>*States Where Castration Laws Only Apply To Offenders Convicted Of Sex Offenses Against Minors*</u>:

- California
- Georgia
- Louisiana
- Montana
- Wisconsin

California, Florida, and Louisiana allow offenders who must undergo treatment to decide between surgical or chemical castration. Texas is the only state that currently allows certain repeat offenders to undergo surgical castration without a treatment option.

<u>*Arguments For Castration*</u>:

- Those who are in favor of castration argue that it is justified and appropriate treatment. It controls their irresistible urges to rape and/or molest. Sex offenders can be released into society without endangering the public.

<u>*Arguments Against Castration*</u>:

- There are side effects to chemical castration such as life threatening blood clots and serious allergic reactions.
- Some have argued unsuccessfully that forced castration violates the protection against cruel and unusual punishment guaranteed by the Eighth Amendment to the U. S. Constitution.

Since the mid-1990s states have allowed, and in certain instances required, castration as a way of penalizing sexual offenders or as a condition of their release from custody. (290)

How Do We Know If Treatment Is Working?

While most treatments for mental disease help the patient, treatment for pedophilia is primarily designed to protect society. Therefore, treatment can be evaluated by asking one simple question: Is the offender harming more children? (288)

According to Grossman, the question may sound simple, but the answer is not that easy. Child sexual abuse is illegal and shameful. Special problems exist with sex offender research. It is difficult to know if a pedophile has re-offended unless there is an arrest or conviction record. "After all," says Grossman, "you cannot just ask the offender if he has molested other children and expect an honest answer. We do know that approximately 97% of sexual offenses are never reported to police, and only a few are ever convicted."

There Are Several Factors That Make Treatment Research Difficult:

- Who was treated?
- Who were the ones most likely and least likely to re-offend?
- Who would most likely benefit by the treatment?
    - a. First offenders?
    - b. Hard-core offenders?
- Exactly what treatment was used?
- Was the treatment done in or out of prison?
- Was castration used?
- Was the success measured? How?
- Did the offender commit again? Sex crime or other crime?
- Was a comparison group randomly chosen from:
    - a. Similar offenders?
    - b. Men who refused treatment?
    - c. Men who did not complete treatment?
- How long was the follow-up?

Re-Offending Statistics:

According to Hanson and Bussiere in 1998, persons who commit sex offenses fall into several different categories. As a result, research has identified significant differences in re-offense patterns from one category of offenders to another.

Looking At Reconviction Rates Alone, One Large-Scale Analysis Reported The Following Differences:

- Child molesters had a 13% reconviction rate for sexual offenses and a 37% reconviction rate for new, non-sex offenses over a five-year period.
- Rapists had a 19% reconviction rate for sexual offenses and a 46% reconviction rate for new, non-sexual offenses over a five-year period. (282)

Certain Characteristics Also Distinguish The Rate Of Re-Offending:

- The gender of the victim
- The relation to the offender
- Offenders who had non-family female victims had a re-offending rate of 18%
- Offenders who had non-family male victims re-offended at a rate of 35%.
- Incest offenders had a re-offending rate of approximately 9% (282)
- Use of alcohol and difficulty forming intimate relationships with adult women increase the chance of re-offending in men convicted of pedophilia and later released. (287)
- Men who prefer boys are approximately twice as likely to re-offend as those who prefer girls. (287)

Prentky and Burgess found it difficult to determine a reliable estimate of recidivism for child molesters given the limited number of observed studies. They used the findings of Marshall and Barbaree, who in 1988 estimated the re-offence rate (as measured by further convictions) as 25% for treated offenders and 40% for untreated offenders.

Prentky and Burgess reported that this was reasonably consistent with other studies. They did warn that child molesters comprise such a diverse group that it is not accurate to make broad statements, which pertain to all offenders.

Only 10% Of Sexual Abuse Is Reported By Victims:

It must, however, be taken into consideration that it is difficult to attain accurate statistics on the number of re-offenders of sex crimes based on official criminal justice system information since only 10% of sexual abuse is reported by the victims. (282)

Examining The Research:

Researchers examined 43 previous studies that compared 5,078 treated sex offenders and 4,376 untreated sex offenders. The treatment given was cognitive-behavioral therapy with an average follow-up time of 46 months, (3 years, 1 month). (288)

Results:

- 12.3% of treated men re-offended
- 16.8% of untreated men re-offended

The difference, which the study authors called a "small advantage," was statistically significant, meaning it probably did not happen by chance, but rather because the treatment was effective. (289)

Follow-up Studies Show That Offenders May Not Be Quick To Re-Offend:

In a 1991 study, only 7.4 % of 406 pedophiles committed further sexual crimes over a five-year follow-up period. Some repeat offenders were not included, but it disproved the common misconception that offenders would be quick to re-offend. (291)

Experts Say, "Treatment Must Continue":

Regardless of the confusing results, many in the field of sex offender management believe we must continue to try treatment. According to Grossman, large studies show that the rate of re-offending drops approximately 30% with treatment. She comments that, "higher rates would be better, but we treat diseases with higher setback rates than that." (289)

Most Pressing Question:

Treatments results help answer the most pressing question about pedophiles; how do we know they can safely be released? (289)

Plaud describes the answer to that question as a professional judgment based on the probability that with treatment the rate of re-offending will drop. He agrees that the risk will never be zero and sees it as a balance between what we know and can measure while taking into consideration that important research data and civil liberties tend to be uncertain and changeable.

Some Sex Offenders Can Be Treated Successfully, But Some Cannot:

Plaud's findings show that most sex offenders are not predatory and violent, but are people familiar to the victim such as a family member or a friend who does not use violence, although this crime does involves touching and fondling. Then there are psychopathic, pedophilic monsters who will likely re-offend, hurt, or kill a child. Offenders who benefit from treatment rarely have a violent nature and studies show treatment is effective for certain types of offenders. According to Berlin, although there are some sex offenders who cannot be treated successfully he believes there are those who can come through programs successfully and not re-offend again. (289)

ADOLESCENT MALE SEX OFFENDERS CHALLENGE THERAPIST'S SKILL

By Joyce F. Lakey, M.S., L.C.S.W.

Counseling adolescent male sex offenders is a job for a skilled therapist as these youth are typically as cunning and deceitful as the adult sex offenders they learned to mimic. At first, most of them are defiant, difficult to manage and not responsive to treatment because they are painfully aware that treatment implies change—change is difficult. (292)

An adolescent sex offender may be defined as a youth, between puberty and the legal age of adulthood (age 17 in most states), who commits any sexual interaction with a person of any age against the victim's will, without knowing, consent, or in an aggressive, exploitative, or threatening manner. For instance, a 14-year-old boy who forces himself on an elderly, intellectually handicapped neighbor for his own sexual pleasure is legally considered a sex offender as much as a 16-year-old who manipulates a six-year-old brother or sister into consensual mutual fondling.

The type of counseling and treatment used can be determined by recognizing certain characteristics that are typical of adolescent male sex offenders concerning the most important aspects of their misbehavior, namely, the way they think about themselves and others, their understanding of how to behave, and their attitudes toward responsibility.

Some Of The Characteristics Typical Of Adolescent Sex Offenders Include:

- Obsessive thoughts about sex
- Feelings of inadequacy masked by arrogance and self-confidence
- A need for adventure which is usually opportunistic and frequently illegal
- An urgency for power and control
- An immature conscience, if any
- Poor social skills
- They may have been emotionally, physically, or sexually abused (292)

Other Contributing Factors That May Or May Not Exist:

- Having a transient and or dysfunctional family
- Poor school performance
- Poverty
- Lack of role models
- Use of alcohol and drugs

Psychiatric Diagnoses For Adolescent Male Sexual Offenders Include:

- Conduct disorder
- Poor impulse control
- Antisocial behavior
- Aggression

- Dysthymia, a mood disorder characterized by chronic mildly depressed or irritable mood often accompanied by other symptoms such as eating and sleeping disturbances, fatigue, and poor self-esteem
- Depression
- A tendency towards personality and affective disorders

One or several of these are always combined with cognitive distortions that enable the offender to perceive their world much differently than their non-offending peers. (292)

Thinking Errors:

Of 52 Cognitive Distortions (Thinking Errors), Three Relate to This Study. (293)

1. Adolescent sex offenders behave morally and accept personal accountability only if it serves their purpose. Therefore, they think that lying, cheating, and blaming others are legitimate ways to defend their inappropriate behaviors. For example, "If my mother hadn't allowed my sister to run around the house in her underwear, I wouldn't have molested her." Typically, they refuse responsibility for their choices, and they might deliberately seek negative attention in their hunger for recognition.

2. Adolescent sex offenders consider themselves uniquely above having to obey the rules of society. In fact, they feel they can make their own rules. They take pride in being different from others and must display their need to be in control. They tend to think that they possess much more knowledge and expertise than they actually do which causes them to make immature and impulsive decisions based on rumor, misinformation, and myths.

3. Adolescent sex offenders' exhibit twisted morality values. For example, they typically believe that it is better not to be caught than it is not to perpetrate in the first place. For them the "Golden Rule," is to do unto others before they do unto you. They are extremely sensitive and bitter about pain that others caused them, but lack remorse and empathy about the pain they cause others. (292)

The Basics Of Treating The Male Adolescent Sex Offender:

Preventing Re-Offending:

To prevent the male adolescent sex offender from re-offending, the therapist must first slow down his thinking process in order to help him to identify and correct his thinking errors. Treatment must supply the adolescent with appropriate information about sexuality, relationships, values, and morality. The youth must be encouraged to consciously incorporate these new guiding principles within him through learning and interaction with others, with a goal to achieve increasingly more appropriate behavior. Counseling should build up a moral base that will gradually lead to the adolescent having a conscience. Social skills must be sharpened to bring him up to his proper age level; empathy, remorse, and new coping skills must be developed while studying his offense cycle and finding ways to prevent him from re-offending. (292)

Cycle Of Abuse And Accountability:

Many other needs of adolescent sex offenders become evident throughout treatment, including addressing the abuse some of the offenders themselves experienced in childhood. Research suggests that the best possible treatment occurs in a structured environment through weekly individual counseling and several group therapy sessions. Reasonable consequences must be established as disciplinary action with constant repetition of lessons in morality and reminders of the results of breaking the law. In essence, the youth must learn to take responsibility for his own behavior and make a connection between his inappropriate actions and learning by them.

Willingness To Change:

According to Lakey, adolescent sex offenders can change if they wish to do so. If they choose not to change, they endanger all of society.

Joyce F. Lakey completed 12 years of studies while working with

adolescent male sex offenders in a residential setting.

She has presented workshops on treatment and continues to write professional articles.

Joyce F. Lakey may be contacted at 3121 Oak Street. Terre Haute, Indiana, 47803

(812) 232-6656 ~ www.childresearch.net/Resource/News/1999/9903.HTM,

NOTES

Chapter Twenty One

NORMALIZATION AND LEGALIZATION OF PEDOPHILIA...CAN IT HAPPEN?

Which Sexual Preference Will Achieve Protected Status Next?

Pedophiles Making Progress Toward Normalization:

Pedophiles have found certain sociology and university staff members who support adult/child sex by calling them "subcultures" instead of perversions. They are working toward normalizing and legalizing these behaviors in the realm of psychiatry and thus, within world culture. (294)

Children Targeted Into Perverted Lifestyles:

Because of the widespread use and availability of the internet, many sexually confused and troubled individuals are finding mutual support in forums and chat rooms. They are reinforcing their mental illnesses instead of finding the help they need to overcome these sexual perversions. Activists in the U.S. and other countries have targeted children to recruit into these lifestyles. (294)

Age Of Consent Efforts:

Ontario, Canada has already reduced the age of consent to 14 for both heterosexuals and homosexuals. In May 1995, the **Ontario Court of Appeals** lowered the age of consent for anal sex to 14. It was concluded that the Ontario sodomy law denied men under 18 a "basic form of sexual expression." (295)

In March 1995, judges ruled that Ontario's anal sex law was unconstitutional because it set a higher age of consent for anal sex than for other sex acts. In September 1995, the court in Ontario made 14 the age of consent for all sex acts. A university researcher described the campaign to normalize pedophilia saying, "Changes in morality do not occur overnight; they seep into society, often silently, like flood waters into a basement. Personal behavior that was once shameful and abominable somehow becomes acceptable, tolerable, and even praiseworthy... I am referring to the quiet campaign to make pedophilia acceptable, if not respectable."

In Holland, the age of sexual consent is now 12, unless the preteen complains to the authorities about the sexual encounter. **The Dutch Association for the Integration of Homosexuality** (DAIH) takes credit for helping to change the laws in Holland. They lobbied successfully for the elimination of a 1971 law prohibiting sexual contact between those older than 21 and those younger than 21. The laws were amended in 1987 and again in 1991. The current law allows sex between a child and adult if the parents of the child approve.

At a conference in the Netherlands, where teenage delegates lobbied for the right of teens and children as young as 10 to have sexual pleasure and sexual freedom, approximately 130 youths from 111 countries signed the sexual rights document. They also demanded the right to abortion on demand without parental consent or knowledge.

Dutch Court Approves Pedophile Political Party:

Observers around the world were stunned by the announcement that a group of self-professed pedophiles in the Netherlands was seeking to form a political party. The party, which has only three known members, seeks to lower the age of sexual consent from 16 to 12. They want to legalize child pornography and sex with animals. They argue that preventions only make children "curious" and seek to overturn all sexual taboos that are left in Dutch society.

A Dutch judge wrote in the ruling, "Freedom of expression, including the freedom to set up a political party, can be seen as the basis for a democratic society, and it is the right of the voter to judge the appeal of political parties." (296)

Pedophile Organizations Claim Genuine Concern For Children:

Small groups of highly organized child molesters who are determined to change public opinion operate worldwide through pedophile organizations whose members claim genuine concern for the welfare of children. Their belief is that sex with children is harmless and some even claim that sexual relations are healthy for children. The goals of these groups include decriminalizing child molestation and lowering the age of consent. They argue that laws prohibiting sexual relations with children are based on mistaken ideas that adult/child sexual relations are harmful to the child, and that sex with kids is healthy and beneficial for them. They deny, however, that their members practice sex with children. (297)

The Intention Of Pedophile Organizations:

The overall intention of these various organizations is to legalize sexual relations between adults and children. They want to break down the social discrimination that pedophiles face. They maintain that pedophilia, or as NAMBLA calls it, inter-generational sex, is a sexual orientation or preference just like homosexuality or heterosexuality. Age, they say, should not be a barrier to "consensual" sex between children and adults. (298)

Pedophile Organizations—Who They Are And How They Get Started:

North American Man Boy Love Association (NAMBLA) was formed in 1978 in Boston and held its first national conference in the same year. Over 200 people from 15 states and 3 Canadian provinces attended. The conference grew out of a defense committee that was formed for 24 men accused of operating a "boy prostitution" ring involving children in foster homes. They argued that the men were motivated by love not money. NAMBLA promotes pedophilia as a lifestyle helping to defend men accused of child sexual assault and lobbying against laws that prohibit adults from having sex with children and adolescents. In a newsletter, they asked for cash donations for a New England man who fled the country after his conviction of assault with intent to rape a child less than 16 years of age.

They hold marches and conferences, like the one they have in New York in June each year, and strive to educate the public on the compassionate nature of man/boy relationships. (298)

Woman's Counterpart Of NAMBLA

The counterpart of NAMBLA is **North American Woman Girl Love Association**; and another, NAWBLA, **North American Woman Boy Love Association** promotes sex between young boys and older women.

Man Girl Love Association Website Closed By FBI:

Namgla.net, a website for the North American Man Girl Love Association, was shut down by the FBI as part of the **Innocent Images National Initiative** targeting child pornography networks that operate globally via the internet. The announcement was made by the Assistant Director in charge of the FBI in Los Angeles in conjunction with FBI field offices around the country and foreign law enforcement agencies overseas. This website serviced an international community of online predators where thousands of graphic images of sexually abused children could be shared. (299)

Group Motto 'Sex By Age 8 Or It's Too Late':

They also believe in child/child and child/adult bisexuality starting at ages 4, 5, and 6 if protected with contraceptives. But while they advocate legalizing sex with children, they do not practice it. Their claim is, "No one can come into our society who has ever had sex with children." This is very difficult to believe, especially when you consider their motto, 'Sex by age 8 or it's too late'. (298)

Various groups promote holidays intended to spread understanding and acceptance of pedophilia for example, The International Boy Love Day or IBLD. (300)

Questioning The Assumption Of Harm:

One of the greatest barriers these groups have in their efforts to decriminalize sex between adults and children are the many studies demonstrating a consistent association between child sexual abuse and negative outcomes. Advocates of pedophilia have attempted to change these barriers in a variety of ways. They often blame the negative outcomes on parents or professionals who seek to prevent or intervene in incestuous relationships. (300)

Pedophile Organizations And Political Activism To Advance Their Cause:

Pedophile organizations argue that taking political action "is ultimately one of the most important activities we as child lovers can engage in. On a personal level, self-acceptance is a key factor, but if we are ever to advance our cause on a greater scale, political action is necessary. Being convinced ourselves that we are right is simply not sufficient. We must take our message to the rest of society." (300)

Laws And Pedophile Organizations:

Enforcing the law on pedophile activist groups is very difficult because they often operate underground and because they deal largely in child pornography, the laws against that issue are the most commonly used legislation to fight these associations. (298)

Young children are not legally capable to consent to sexual activity because they are too young to make knowledgeable decisions. The argument that they are old enough is a self-serving pedophile attempt to legalize their behavior. Pedophile organizations seek to do away with laws that are in place to protect young people such as laws against sexual assault and against any kind of sexual activity between an adult and a child.

Pedophile organizations may attempt to use their constitutional rights as a justification for their efforts for example, the freedom of beliefs, opinions, and freedom of speech. However, these rights have limitations, and the abuse of children is one of those limitations.

Arguments Against Pedophile Organizations—Victims Committing Suicide:

The existence of these organizations not only provides justification for pedophiles to satisfy their desires, but they also present a real danger to all children by making future offenses more likely. In a court case involving a pedophile who was a choir director, the court was told that two of the child victims had committed suicide as a result of the sexual abuse. If child/adult sex is not harmful to the children, why is there such a high suicide rate among the victims? The effects of child sexual abuse are devastating and many of the victims never fully recover. The notion that sex with children is healthy for children is entirely false. (298)

While there are organized sexual predators whose activities cause public outrage, it is the millions of individual sexual predators worldwide with every day actions that are a far greater threat to the safety of our children. It is impossible to be with our children every moment; therefore, it is imperative that we teach them to recognize and evade the lures used for generations by sexual predators of every kind. During the 2002 **White House Conference on Missing, Exploited, and Runaway Children**, Ken Wooden told

President Bush, "If predators are using the lures, shouldn't we be teaching our children these lures?" (297)

While the average child molester does not belong to a pedophile organization, we would be foolish not to take seriously any group whose members are committed to sexual activity with children. Indeed, pedophiles are often difficult to detect and can be found in the most unlikely of places. Both adults and children must have the tools to recognize and avoid potentially abusive individuals or situations. (297)

NOTES

Chapter Twenty Two

THE LAW

- Over 69% of sex offenders in our prisons victimized a child (302)
- 60% of convicted sex offenders are on parole or probation (302)
- Only 1 to 10% of victims ever tell. Boys report far less than girls do (301)

Adam Walsh Child Protection And Safety Act Of 2006:

This bill contains provisions from two crime bills: **H.R. 4472, the Children's Safety and Violent Crime Reduction Act** of 2006, which passed the House, and **S. 1086**, which the Senate passed by unanimous consent on May 4, 2006. (303)

This Bill Is Beneficial In Many Ways:

- It created a **National Sex Offender Registry** with uniform standards for the registration of sex offenders, including a lifetime registration requirement for the most serious offenders and it establishes strong federal penalties for sex offenders who fail to register.
- By creating a national sex offender registry, the Act enables child protective service officials in all 50 states to share information and more effectively investigate child abuse cases.
- The bill also imposes enhanced penalties for the most serious crimes against children, as well as mandatory minimum penalties for re-offenders.

It is named for Adam Walsh (son of John and Revé Walsh) who was kidnapped and murdered 25 years ago when he was only six years old. (303)

Background:

This legislation was proposed as a wide-ranging effort to oppose the persistent problem of violent and sexual crimes against children. Recently, public attention has been focused on several tragic attacks in which young children have been murdered, kidnapped, and sexually assaulted by sex offenders and career criminals.

The Act recognizes, by name, some of those children, as their stories helped provide the movement for this powerful legislation. Among those children recognized in the bill: Jacob Wetterling, Megan Nicole Kanka, Jessica Lunsford, Jetseta Gage (a 10-year-old girl who was abducted and murdered by a registered sex offender) and siblings Dylan Groene (who was murdered) and his sister, Shasta Groene (8 and 9 years old, respectively, who were kidnapped from their bedroom and sexually molested by a convicted sex offender out of jail on release from a pending molestation criminal case. The bill is named for Adam Walsh (who was abducted from a mall during a shopping trip with his mother and later found murdered). (303)

While all 50 states have sex offender registries, the information contained in those registries is not always shared. A national registry will give law enforcement at all levels access to information that will allow them to more effectively track sex offenders. (304)

Sex Offender Registration Laws Are Necessary:

- Sex offenders pose a high risk of re-offending after release from custody.
- Protecting the public from sex offenders is a primary governmental interest.
- The privacy interests of persons convicted of sex offenses are less important than the government's interest in public safety.
- Release of certain information about sex offenders to public agencies and the public will assist in protecting the public safety. (303)

Community Notification Also:

- Assists law enforcement in investigations
- Establishes legal grounds to hold known offenders
- Deters sex offenders from committing new offenses
- Offers citizens information they can use to protect children from victimization

Title I - Sex Offender Registration And Notification Act:

Bill Provisions: Title I establishes the National Sex Offender Registry. The national registry will include the following information for each sex offender: Name, address, employment, vehicle identification information, fingerprints, a DNA sample, complete criminal history, a recent photo, and other information. (303)

The public will not have access to the detailed National Sex Offender Registry; instead, a national public website will be available that will include relevant information about sex offenders. The public website will permit recovery of information by a single inquiry for any given zip code or geographic radius. In addition to a central national public website, each individual jurisdiction is required to establish its own Internet registry, which shall be accessible to the public.

The Act mandates that a sex offender shall register and keep the registration current in each jurisdiction where he resides, is an employee, and is a student.

Initial registration shall be completed in the jurisdiction where the conviction took place, and any later updates shall be completed in-person, in the offender's jurisdiction of residence.

Under the Act, sex offenders are required to register prior to their release from prison, or within three days of being sentenced if there is no term of imprisonment. Thereafter, sex offenders must verify their information in person at regular intervals, depending on the severity of the sex offense they committed. This severity is determined by the sex offender's placement in a three-tier system.

- The least serious offenders are placed in Tier I, are required to appear in person once a year, and remain on the registry for 15 years.

- Tier II offenders must appear in person every six months and remain on the registry for 25 years.
- The most serious offenders, placed in Tier III, remain on the registry for life and are required to appear in person every three months to verify their information.

Pursuant to this Act, any sex offender who knowingly fails to register or update his information faces up to ten years in prison. If an unregistered sex offender commits a crime of violence, he will receive a five-year mandatory prison sentence, in addition to any other sentence imposed. (303)

The Act requires the Department of Justice to create and distribute software to jurisdictions to establish and operate uniform registries and Internet sites. The software will allow for immediate information sharing among jurisdictions, internet access by the public, and communication to certain community notification to participants who choose to opt-in to receiving notice. (303)

Title II - Federal Criminal Law Enhancements Needed To Protect Children From Sexual Attacks And Other Violent Crimes:

The Act creates a number of increased penalties for federal sex offenses and violent crimes against children. Offenses for which penalties are increased:

- Sexual abuse
- Child sex trafficking
- Coercion or enticement to engage in criminal sexual activity or cause child prostitution
- Additionally, the Act creates new penalties for the sale of date rape drugs via the internet.

Increased Penalties For Existing Offenses:

- 30 years to life or death for the murder of a child
- A 30 year mandatory minimum for raping a child
- A 10 year mandatory minimum for child sex trafficking or prostitution

Statute Of Limitations:

Title II also suspends the statute of limitations for all federal felony offenses of sexual abuse, sex trafficking, or child pornography. (303)

The Act also extends several of the guarantees of the 2004 Crime Victims' Rights Act (CVRA) to federal habeas corpus review of state criminal convictions. Because such cases involve federal courts (but state prosecutors), this extension is limited to those provisions of CVRA that are enforced by a court (Congress cannot compel state prosecutors to enforce a federal statute). The victims' rights extended by this Act to federal habeas proceedings are: the right to be present at proceedings; the right to be heard at proceedings involving release, plea, sentencing, or parole; the right to proceedings free from unreasonable delay; and the right to be treated with fairness and with respect for the victim's dignity and privacy.

Title III - Civil Commitment Of Dangerous Sex Offenders:

The Act provides for civil commitment (defined in the bill, and involves secure civil confinement with appropriate care and treatment) procedures for sex offenders who, while incarcerated, show that they cannot conform their behavior once released. This title authorizes grants to states to operate civil commitment programs for sexually dangerous persons. Additionally, it authorizes civil commitment of certain sex offenders who are dangerous to others due to serious mental illness, abnormality, or disorder.

Title IV - Immigration Law Reforms To Prevent Sex Offenders From Abusing Children:

This title provides that any alien convicted of the federal crime of failing to register as a sex offender is deportable. Additionally, the Act provides that a citizen convicted of a specified offense against a minor is not eligible to petition for a family-based visa. That bar, however, may be waived if the Secretary of Homeland Security determines that the citizen poses no risk to the alien with respect to whom the petition is filed. (303)

Title V - Child Pornography Prevention:

This title strengthens existing pornography record-keeping and labeling requirements for persons who produce materials containing simulated sexual conduct. The purpose of these provisions is to ensure universal age verification and record keeping in order to protect children and teenagers from being exploited by pornographers. Under the Act, these records may be inspected on demand by the Department of Justice. (303)

Title VI - Grants, Studies, And Programs For Children And Community Safety:

The Act provides for a number of pilot programs, grants, and studies to address child and community safety issues. Such programs include a pilot program for the electronic monitoring of sex offenders; funding for **Big Brothers and Big Sisters**; and grants to allow parents to obtain fingerprint records for their children. (303)

The Act also instructs the **Department of Health and Human Services** to create a national registry of persons who have been found to have abused or neglected a child. The information will be gathered from state databases of child abuse or neglect. It will be made available to state child protective services and law-enforcement agencies for purposes of carrying out their responsibilities under the law to protect children from abuse and neglect. The national database will allow states to track the history of parents and guardians who are suspected of abusing their children. When child-abusing parents come to the attention of authorities (for example, when teachers begin to ask about bruises), these parents often will move to a different jurisdiction. A national database will give the state to which these parents move the ability to know the parents' history. It will let a child-protective-services worker know, for example, whether he should prioritize investigation of a particular case because the parent has been found to have committed substantiated cases of abuse in the past in other states. Such a database also will allow a state that is evaluating a prospective foster parent or adoptive parent to learn about past incidents of child abuse that the person has committed in other states. (303)

Title VII - Internet Safety Act:

This title creates new penalties for child exploitation enterprises defined as a violation of at least one in a list of detailed sex crimes against children as part of a series of felony violations constituting three or more separate incidents and more than one victim, and committed in performance with three or more other persons providing a mandatory minimum sentence of 20 years imprisonment for that offense. The title also adds a mandatory 10-year enhancement for registered sex offenders who commit one in a list of federal felonies involving a minor.

Additionally, this title creates a new crime for embedding words or digital images into the source code of a website with the intent to deceive a person into viewing obscenity. The internet safety provisions also enhance federal prosecution resources needed for the investigation and prosecution of child sex offenses. Those enhancements include funding the hiring of at least 200 additional assistant United States attorneys, the addition of at least 10 **Internet Crimes Against Children** (ICAC) Task Forces, and the addition of 45 forensic examiners within the **Regional Computer Forensic Laboratories and Cyber Crimes Center**. Additionally, the internet safety provisions expand the civil remedy available to children who have been sexually abused or exploited.

Operation Predator:

The administration launched **Operation Predator** to help law enforcement track down and arrest foreign pedophiles, human traffickers, sex tourists, and internet pornographers who prey on our children. (303)

Project Safe Childhood:

The Department of Justice launched **Project Safe Childhood** to help Federal, State, and local law enforcement investigate and prosecute crimes against children that are facilitated by the internet and other electronic communications. (303)

Sex-Offender Registration:

- In the United States, there are various laws requiring the registration of sex offenders with state, law-enforcement agencies.
- Each state determines the criteria for registration and notification, which is the means by which law enforcement disperses information to the public.
- The laws and acts listed below were used by each state to develop their own state, sex-offender registration and notification laws. (303)

18 U.S.C. 4042 - Duties of the Bureau of Prisons:

This statute requires the federal **Bureau of Prisons**, upon release of a designated sex offender from prison or upon such an offender's sentence to probation, to provide notice to:

- The chief, law-enforcement officer of the state and local jurisdiction in which the offender will reside. (303)
- The state or local agency responsible for the receipt and maintenance of sex-offender registration information in the state or local jurisdiction in which the offender will reside. (303)

IMPORTANT INFORMATION:

State Laws And Registration Information

To find more information about the laws in your specific state and information about your state's sex offender registry, contact your state or local law enforcement agency. (303)

Worldwide Laws:

Worldwide laws against child sexual abuse/Legislation of INTERPOL interpol.int/Public/Children/SexualAbuse/NationalLaws/Default.asp (303)

Sex Offender Registries:

The **National Alert Registry** has combined all of the states sex offender registries into one national sex offender's database. Now you can do one search using one database and find registered sex offenders from all over the nation at registeredoffenderslist.org

The National Alert Registry's nationwide database is updated immediately when new information on registered sex offenders is available. As soon as new sex offenders register in your zip code, a RED ALERT sex offender notification can be sent to you. (303)

National Alert Registry:

Protect your children by identifying registered sex offenders in your area: registeredoffenderslist.org/blog/sex-offenders/child-molestation-statistics/

Federal Laws

18 U.S.C. 1466a – Obscene Visual Representations Of The Sexual Abuse Of Children:

Attempts or conspiracies to knowingly produce, distribute, receive, or possess with the intent to distribute a visual depiction of any kind, including a drawing, cartoon, sculpture, or painting that depicts a minor engaging in sexually explicit conduct and is obscene, or depicts an image that is, or appears to be, of a minor engaging in graphic bestiality, sadistic or masochistic abuse, or sexual intercourse, including genital-genital, oral-genital, anal-genital, or oral-anal, whether between persons of the same or opposite sex. Such depiction lacks serious literary, artistic, political, or scientific value are forbidden: (303)

- Any communication involved in or made in furtherance of the offense is communicated or transported by the mail, or in interstate or foreign commerce by any means, including by computer, or any means or instrumentality of interstate or foreign commerce is otherwise used in committing or in furtherance of the commission of the offense
- Any communication involved in or made in furtherance of the offense contemplates the transmission or transportation of a visual depiction by the mail, or in interstate or foreign commerce by any means, including by computer
- Any person travels or is transported in interstate or foreign commerce in the course of the commission or in furtherance of the commission of the offense
- Any visual depiction involved in the offense has been mailed, shipped, or transported in interstate or foreign commerce by any means, including by computer, or was produced using materials that have been mailed, shipped, or transported in interstate or foreign commerce by any means, including by computer; or the offense is committed in the special maritime and territorial jurisdiction of the United States or in any territory or possession of the United States. (303)

18 U.S.C. 2251 – Sexual Exploitation Of Children:

It is forbidden for any person to employ, use, persuade, induce, entice, or coerce any minor to engage or assist any other person to engage in, or to transport any minor in interstate or foreign commerce with the intent that the minor engage in any sexually explicit conduct if such person knows or has reason to know that such visual depiction was produced using materials that have been mailed, shipped, or transported in interstate or foreign commerce by any means, including by computer, or if such visual depiction has actually been transported in interstate or foreign commerce or mailed. (303)

It is forbidden for any parent, legal guardian, or person having custody or control of a minor to knowingly permit such minor to engage or assist any other person to engage in sexually explicit conduct for the purpose of producing any visual depiction of such conduct if the parent, legal guardian, or person knows or has reason to know that such visual depiction will be transported in interstate or foreign commerce or mailed if that visual depiction was produced using materials that have been mailed, shipped, or transported in interstate or foreign commerce by any means, including by computer, or if such visual depiction has actually been transported in interstate or foreign commerce or mailed.

It is forbidden for any person to knowingly make, print, publish, or cause to be made, printed, or published, any notice or advertisement seeking or offering:

- To receive, exchange, buy, produce, display, distribute, or reproduce, any visual depiction, if the production of such visual depiction involves the use of a minor engaging in sexually explicit conduct and such visual depiction is of such conduct.

- To participate in any act of sexually explicit conduct by or with any minor for the purpose of producing a visual depiction of such conduct, if such person knows or has reason to know that such notice or advertisement is or will be transported in interstate or foreign commerce by any means including by computer or mail. (303)

18 U.S.C. 2252 – Material Involving The Sexual Exploitation Of Minors:

It is forbidden for any person to knowingly transport or ship in interstate or foreign commerce by any means, including by computer or through the mail, any visual depiction if the producing of such visual depiction involves the use of a minor engaging in sexually explicit conduct and such visual depiction is of such conduct.

It is forbidden for any person to knowingly receive or distribute any visual depiction that has been mailed, shipped, or transported in interstate or foreign commerce, or which contains materials that have been so mailed, shipped, or transported, by any means, including by computer, or reproduce any visual depiction for distribution in interstate or foreign commerce by any means, including by computer or through the mail, if the producing of such visual depiction involves the use of a minor engaging in sexually explicit conduct and such visual depiction is of such conduct.

It is forbidden to knowingly sell or possess with the intent to sell any visual depiction that has been mailed, shipped, or transported in interstate or foreign commerce, or which was produced using materials that have been so mailed, shipped, or transported, by any means, including computer, if the producing of such visual depiction involves the use of a minor engaging in sexually explicit conduct, and such visual depiction is of such conduct.

18 U.S.C. 2252a – Material Constituting Or Containing Child Pornography

It is forbidden for any person to knowingly mail, transport, or ship in interstate or foreign commerce, by any means, including by computer, any child pornography; to receive or distribute any child pornography that has been mailed, shipped, or transported in interstate or foreign commerce, by any means, including by computer any material that contains child pornography, to advertise, promote, present, distribute, or solicit through the mail, or in interstate or foreign commerce, by any means, including by computer, any material or purported material in a manner that reflects the belief, or that is intended to cause another to believe, that the material or purported material is or contains:

- An obscene visual depiction of a minor engaging in sexually explicit conduct
- A visual depiction of a minor engaging in sexually explicit conduct
- Reproduces any child pornography for distribution through the mails, or in interstate or foreign commerce by any means, including by computer
- Sell or possess with the intent to sell any child pornography
- Possess any book, magazine, periodical, film, videotape, computer disk, or any other material that contains an image of child pornography

- Distribute, offer, send, or provide to a minor any visual depiction, including any photograph, film, video, picture, or computer generated image or picture, whether made or produced by electronic, mechanical, or other means, where such visual depiction is, or appears to be, of a minor engaging in sexually explicit conduct that has been mailed, shipped, or transported in interstate or foreign commerce by any means, including by computer
- Anything that was produced using materials that have been mailed, shipped, or transported in interstate or foreign commerce by any means, including by computer; or if such distribution, offer, sending, or provision is accomplished using the mails or by transmitting or causing to be transmitted any wire communication in interstate or foreign commerce, including by computer, for the purpose of inducing or persuading a minor to participate in any activity that is illegal.

18 U.S.C. 2256 – "Child Pornography" Defined:

Child pornography is defined as any visual depiction, including any photograph, film, video, or computer or computer-generated image or picture, whether made or produced by electronic, mechanical, or other means, of sexually explicit conduct, where

- The production of such visual depiction involves the use of a minor engaging in sexually explicit conduct;
- Such visual depiction is a digital image, computer image, or computer-generated image that is, or is indistinguishable from, that of a minor engaging in sexually explicit conduct; or such visual depiction has been created, adapted, or modified to appear that an identifiable minor is engaging in sexually explicit conduct.

42 U.S.C. 13032 – Reporting Of Child Pornography By Electronic Communication Service Providers:

Whoever, while providing an electronic communication service or a remote computing service to the public through a facility or means of interstate or foreign commerce, obtains knowledge of facts or circumstances from which a violation of certain offenses involving child pornography is apparent, must report those facts or circumstances to the CyberTipline at the National Center for Missing and Exploited Children as soon as is reasonably possible.

State Laws:

State governments have taken a number of steps to prevent the sexual exploitation of children. Today every state, as well as the District of Columbia, has enacted statutes that specifically address this problem. At this time, all states impose criminal liability on producers and distributors. (303)

FOR INFORMATION REGARDING YOUR STATE LAWS,

PLEASE CONTACT THE FOLLOWING AGENCIES:

National Association of Counsel For Children
Suite 340
1825 Marion Street
Denver, CO 80218-1125
Toll-Free: 1-888-828-NACC
Telephone: 303-864-5320
Fax: 303-864-5351
www.naccchildlaw.org

The National Center for Prosecution of Child Abuse
American Prosecutors Research Institute
Suite 510
99 Canal Center Plaza
Alexandria, VA 22314-1588
Telephone: 703-549-4253
Fax: 703-836-3195
www.ndaa-apri.org

The National Clearinghouse on Child Abuse and Neglect Information
330 C Street, SW
Washington, DC 20447-0001
Toll-Free: 1-800-FYI-3366
Telephone: 703-385-7565
Fax: 703-385-3206
E-mail: nccanch@calib.com
www.calib.com/nccanch

National Conference of State Legislatures
7700 East First Place
Denver, CO 80230-7143
Telephone: 303-364-7700
Fax: 303-364-7800
www.ncsl.org

END NOTE: The term "child pornography," because it implies conventional pornography with child subjects, is an inappropriate term to describe the true nature and extent of sexually exploitive images of child victims. Use of this term should not imply that children consented to the sexual acts depicted in these photographs; however, it is the term most readily recognized by the public to describe this form of child sexual exploitation. It is used to refer to illegal pictorial material involving children under the standards developed by statute, case law, and law enforcement agency protocols. It is hoped that a more accurate term will be recognized, understood, and accepted for use in the near future. (305)

The Center for Effective Public Policy is a partner with the NCJFCJ to develop and implement a groundbreaking judicial educational training initiative on the management of juvenile sex offenders. (306)

Reporting Child Sexual Abuse, Investigative Procedures:

When child sexual abuse is suspected, call your local child protective services, such as the **Department of Family and Children Services,** to report your suspicions. (307)

You do not have to give your name, but even if you choose to identify yourself, the report is still kept strictly confidential.

The department of **Child Protective Services** in your area works closely with the local police or sheriff's office to protect children and to investigate the alleged sexual abuse.

Mandated Reporters:

Mandated reporters are professionals who may work with children in the course of their professional duties. There are seven groups of mandated reporters as defined in the ANCRA, Sec.4: (308)

Medical personnel such as physicians, dentists, LPNs, RNs, medical social workers, emergency medical technicians, nurse practitioners, chiropractors, hospital administrators, etc. are mandated reporters.

School personnel such as administrators, certified and non-certified staff, superintendents, teachers, principals, school counselors, school nurses, school social workers, assistant principals, teacher's aides, truant officers, school psychologists, secretaries, etc. are mandated reporters.

If a school board member knows an allegation of abuse, the school board as a governing body or the individual member has the authority to direct the superintendent of the school district, or other equivalent school administrator, to report the abuse as required by the **Abused and Neglected Child Reporting Act**.

Social Services and mental health personnel including, social workers, psychologists, domestic violence personnel, substance abuse treatment personnel, staff of state agencies dealing with children such as Department of Human Services, Department of Public Aid, Department of Public Health, Department of Corrections, and Department of Children and Family Services are mandated reporters.

Law enforcement personnel such as employees of the court, parole or probation officers, emergency services staff, police, state attorneys and staff, juvenile officers, coroners, medical examiners, etc. are mandated reporters.

Childcare personnel including all staff at overnight, day care, pre-school or nursery school facilities, recreational program personnel, foster parents, etc. are mandated reporters.

Members of the clergy and all staff workers that have reasonable cause to believe a child known to him or her in a professional capacity may be an abused child is mandated to report this to the appropriate law enforcement agencies.

Who Else Is A Mandated Reporter?

It should be noted that the protection of children is the responsibility of the entire community and that the law provides that anyone with any reasonable cause to believe a child known to him or her may be an abused child shall report this to the appropriate law enforcement agencies or help lines. (308)

(ANCRA Sec.4)
Call the DCFS Hotline at 1-800-252-2873 or 1-800-25-ABUSE.

As professionals who work with children, mandated reporters are assumed to be in the best position to recognize and report child abuse and neglect as soon as possible. Mandated reporters are the state's early warning system to identify probable abuse early enough to avoid serious and long-term damage to a child.

The state's primary goal is to protect the child and, whenever possible, to stabilize and preserve the family so that it may remain intact.

The **Abused and Neglected Child Reporting Act** places several requirements on you as a mandated reporter:

- You are required to report suspected child abuse or neglect immediately
- Privileged communication between professional and client is not grounds for failure to report
- Willful failure to report suspected incidents of child abuse or neglect is a misdemeanor (first violation) or a class 4 felony (second or subsequent violation)
- Professionals may be subject to penalties by their regulatory boards. A member of the clergy may claim the privilege under Section 8-803 of the Code of Civil Procedure
- You may have to testify regarding any incident you report if the case becomes the subject of legal or judicial action
- State law protects the identity of all mandated reporters, and you are given immunity from legal liability as a result of reports you make in good faith
- Reports must be confirmed in writing to the local investigation unit within 48 hours of the hotline call. Forms may be obtained from the local DCFS office or you may duplicate and use the forms in Appendix D of this manual. (308)

Sexual Abuse Defined:

Sexual Abuse occurs when a person responsible for the child's welfare commits any of the following acts:

- Sexually transmitted diseases are by DCFS definition "diseases which were acquired originally as a result of sexual penetration or conduct with an individual who was afflicted"
- Sexual penetration includes any contact between the sex organ of one person and the sex organ, mouth, or anus of another person. Typical acts include vaginal, oral, and anal sex.
- Sexual exploitation is defined by DCFS as "sexual use of a child for sexual arousal, gratification, advantage, or profit"
- This includes such acts as explicit verbal enticements, child pornography, self-masturbation in the child's presence, and forcing a child to watch sex acts
- Sexual molestation is defined by DCFS as "sexual conduct with a child when such contact, touching, or interaction is used for arousal or gratification of sexual needs or desires". Examples include fondling a child or having the child touch the perpetrator sexually (DCFS Procedures 300.Appendix B)

For both physical and sexual abuse, parents and caretakers are charged with the responsibility to take reasonable steps to stop abuse. If they do not, they may be charged with abuse themselves. (ANCRA Sec.3)

In considering whether there is reasonable cause to make a report, there are some issues that are important for mandated reporters to consider in deciding whether to report an incident as suspected abuse or neglect. While it is not the function of the mandated reporter to investigate, enough information must be obtained to determine if a hotline call is needed.

- Did you observe evidence that some damage was done to the child? In physical abuse, this is most often some physical evidence of harm: a bruise, a fracture, or cuts
- Information from the victim about a specific incident of molestation, penetration, or exploitation
- With neglect, there are concrete observations of a failure to provide for physical needs
- What communication has the child provided? Is the information consistent and plausible with what you have observed?
- If the explanation comes from someone other than the child, how credible and/or complete is this information?
- Since the signs of sexual abuse can be uncertain, if a child tells you he or she is being abused by a caretaker or person responsible for the child's welfare, report it
- Have there been past incidents, which in retrospect may have been suspicious?

Child Victim Is Questioned By Trained Staff:

At some point during the investigation of child sexual abuse allegations, the child victim is questioned by trained staff using a technique called a forensic interview.

Forensic interviewing establishes a child-centered, truth-seeking atmosphere. The interview is structured to determine the truth rather than create evidence. A child is permitted and encouraged to relate an event or series of events in a non-judgmental setting. The child is allowed to expand upon his or her interpretation of events without the interviewer placing suggestions in the child's mind. Pertinent information gained through a forensic interview will enable the interviewer to make a legally competent judgment regarding the allegations. This truth seeking focus results in better outcomes for the child, family, and legal system in these critical situations. (309)

This interview is videotaped so that the child will not necessarily have to repeat the details of the abuse again, and again.

The video is admissible in a court of law with the understanding that the child may be called to testify on the stand at the request of either the defense or the prosecuting attorney. The jury, however, will not be told which attorney requested the testimony of the child in the courtroom, but only that the court petitioned the child to testify. (310)

The way children are questioned and the court proceedings vary from state to state and from county to county.

Juvenile Sex Offenders Being Tried As Adults:

On the other side of the coin the laws against child sexual abuse are becoming more and more severe and juvenile offenders are being tried and sentenced as adults. (311)

Fairness For Prisoners' Families: A Guide To Understanding HB 1059,

The Georgia Sex Offender Legislation Brief Summary Of HB 1059:

- Establishes mandatory sentence of 25 to 50 years in prison for kidnapping if the victim is less than 14 years old; for rape, regardless of the age of the victim; for aggravated sodomy, aggravated child molestation, aggravated sexual battery; and for incest if the victim is less than age 14
- Creates crimes of aggravated assault with intent to rape a child less than 14 years old with a 25- to 50-year prison sentence; and aiding, abetting, or harboring a sex offender, with a sentence of 5 to 20 years in prison
- Includes "Romeo and Juliet" provisions that make certain sex crimes a misdemeanor if the victim is 14 or 15 and the defendant no more than three years older to allow for youthful indiscretions between willing teenage partners
- Requires that anyone convicted of a serious violent felony (murder, felony murder, armed robbery, kidnapping, rape, aggravated child molestation, aggravated sodomy, aggravated sexual battery) and sentenced to life in prison and serve a minimum of 30 years in prison before consideration for parole, sixteen years more than current law
- Any sex offender deemed a sexually dangerous predator by the **Sexual Offender Registration Review Board** would have to wear a global positioning satellite electronic monitor for the rest of his or her life

Prohibits registered sex offenders from living, working, or loitering within 1,000 feet of any childcare facility, church, school, or area where minors congregate. It also makes it illegal for child sex offenders or sexually dangerous predators to loiter in those areas. (311)

Concerns About HB 1059:

HB 1059 Is Not A Step Forward:

- This bill does not provide for a treatment or rehabilitation for those convicted of sex offense
- It does not provide for any resources or services for survivors of sexual assaults
- The mandatory minimum sentencing results in the loss of discretion for both judges and the prosecutors
- This law will only continue to compound the problems facing Georgia citizens, such as the over-inflated prison budget that depletes funds from more worthy programs like education and will pack Georgia's prisons and jails, leading to horrendous conditions inside the state facilities
- The 1000 feet restrictions will not enhance monitoring of people convicted of sex offenses nor increase public safety
- Proposed Section 42-1-15 on page 34, lines 14-30, prevents a person from residing within 1000 feet of any childcare facility, church, school, or area where minors congregate. An "area where minors congregate" is defined to include any public or private park, any playground, and astoundingly all bus stops or "other places established for the public to congregate and wait for public transportation." (Page 19, lines 33 through 34, and page 20, lines 1 through 2)
- Studies of similar provisions in other states prove that this requirement will effectively prohibit a sex offender from living or working in any urban area. The only places they will be able to live are isolated, poorly monitored areas.
- Other states who have passed similar laws have found that these measures lead to convicted sex offenders living in clusters, far from treatment centers and their jobs. There are few places that meet the 1000 feet restriction.

Additionally, in Iowa, authorities cannot find twice as many sex offenders since a similar state law went into effect banning offenders from living near childcare centers and schools. According to new statistics obtained by the Iowa Department of Public Safety, 298 of more than 6,000 sex offenders statewide were:

- Unaccounted for by law enforcement vs. 142 on June 1, 2005
- These restrictions cut off offenders from jobs, housing, transportation, treatment and other support that enhance their chances for successful rehabilitation

Juvenile Offenders:

Juvenile offenders present major challenges to the justice system. The role of the court and probation are key elements to successful interventions and outcomes. The **National Council of Juvenile and Family Court Judges** (NCJFCJ) is involved in ongoing efforts to develop guidelines for judges and juvenile probation officers in the management of juvenile sex offenders, as well as training both groups to improve the effectiveness of the process. (312)

The Center for Effective Public Policy is a nonprofit organization first incorporated in Pennsylvania in 1981 with its main office in Silver Spring, Maryland, and satellite offices in Hatboro, Pennsylvania; Columbia, Missouri; Jefferson City, Missouri; Columbia, South Carolina; and San Francisco, California. The center's staff members have diverse qualifications and backgrounds in criminal justice, organizational development, nonprofit management, training, human services research, and policy development. The center has provided specific assistance to courts, state and local governments, corrections agencies, nonprofit organizations, the faith-based community, and private philanthropic foundations in three primary areas:

Program Design, Training, And Organizational Development:

- Designing and conducting national, regional, and local conferences and meetings involving state and local policymakers from the judicial, legislative, and executive branches of government
- Designing and conducting national, regional, and local specialized training workshops for policymakers, including judges, sentencing commission members, legislators, and paroling authorities, and for the staff of these and other organizations
- Facilitating key meetings of state and county policy teams, task forces, and parole boards.
- Providing facilitation, expertise in communication skills, and management training to key staff in courts, state and local corrections agencies, and private and public organizations (312)

Research, Training, And Technical Assistance:

- Assisting both agencies and systems to explain and describe current practice
- Identifying and analyzing problems, conducting organizational needs assessments, and carrying out recommended changes.
- Conducting research, including research design, literature reviews, instrument design, data collection, data analysis, and the synthesis necessary to support policy development.
- Publishing scholarly papers, surveys, directories, and documentation of lessons learned related to the center's efforts
- Designing and delivering training events for diverse audiences to support skill development, implementation of best practices, and to facilitate system change
- Making presentations at national professional meetings and conferences
- Serving as a clearinghouse of current developments and emerging innovations in intermediate sanctions, parole and probation violation/revocation decision-making, parole release decision-making, sex offender management, domestic and sexual violence, community justice, criminal justice planning, and corrections population management for jurisdictions and for other national projects and organizations

Support To Policy Change Activities:

- Providing assessments of the public policy environment that favor or hinder policy change
- Providing substantive assistance to policymakers in correctional and public policy analysis and policy development
- Conducting proposal review, on site assessment, and site selection of states and counties seeking participation in national projects in which the center has been involved.
- Engaging in national assessments of current practices and policies and articulating future trends and innovations in criminal justice

The center has provided these services through its administration and operation of numerous major national projects, technical assistance contracts with individual jurisdictions, and training and research projects. (312)

History Of The Law Against Child Sexual Abuse:

The Jacob Wetterling Act:

In October 1989, 11-year-old Jacob Wetterling was abducted near his home in St. Joseph, Minnesota by a masked man at gunpoint. Police later learned that halfway houses in St. Joseph also housed released sex offenders. In 1989, Minnesota law enforcement had no widespread lists of sex offenders to aid their efforts in solving the case. (Only a handful of states, including Alabama, Arizona, California, Florida, Nevada, and Ohio, had such tools at the time.) Jacob's parents, through the formation of the **Jacob Wetterling Foundation**, helped push Minnesota policymakers to change this situation by enacting sex offender registration in 1991. Several states followed suit in establishing their own registration system. According to the Department of Justice (DOJ), 39 states had some form of sex offender registration in place by 1994. As the issue gained momentum nationally, Congress passed the Jacob Wetterling Crimes Against Children and Sex Offender Registration Act as part of the Violent Crime Control and Law Enforcement Act of 1994 (commonly referenced as the 1994 Crime Bill). The legislation, signed into law by President Clinton on September 13, 1994, mandates that each state create specific programs to register persons convicted of a criminal offense against a minor or a sexually violent offense. (313)

Megan's Law:

Around the time of the final passage of the Jacob Wetterling Act, another hole in the criminal justice system, lack of community awareness of the presence of a convicted sex offender, was exposed by the case of 7-year-old Megan Kanka. On a mid-summer evening in 1994, Megan's parents reported to the police that their daughter was missing from their neighborhood in Hamilton Township, New Jersey. After conducting a door-to-door search of the surrounding houses, police began to focus their investigation on a residence where three convicted sex offenders lived, located across the street from the Kankas. One of the men, Jesse Timmendequas, later confessed to the rape and murder of Megan Kanka. Determined to prevent similar occurrences, Megan's parents spearheaded a campaign to enact legislation in New Jersey providing for community notification when sex offenders are released into a particular neighborhood. Their efforts proved fruitful and the state enacted Megan's Law in 1995. As with the Jacob Wetterling Act, Congress caught on to state action and passed a federal version of Megan's Law the following year. (Similar legislation was offered as an amendment to the 1994 Crime Bill but was rejected by members of Congress.) (313)

Tracking And Identification Act Of 1996:

Federal lawmakers continued to build upon the foundation of the Jacob Wetterling Act by enacting the Pam Lychner Sexual Offender Tracking and Identification Act of 1996. Senator Phil Gramm (R-Texas) and Senator Joseph Biden (D-Delaware) authored this proposal, named in memory of a victim's rights activist who died in the infamous TWA Flight 800 crash off the coast of Long Island, New York, to create a national database of convicted sex offenders that would track sex offenders as they move from state to state, and cover for states not in compliance with The Jacob Wetterling Act. In arguing for the bill on the Senate floor, Senator Biden addressed non-compliance with sex offender registration mandates, "If any states fail to act, we cannot allow there to be a black hole where sexual predators can hide and are then lost to all states." (313)

The Legislation:

The Jacob Wetterling Act is Subtitle A of Title XVII of the 1994 Crime Bill. Provisions of the act require persons convicted of a criminal offense against a minor or a sexually violent offense and persons deemed to be sexually violent predators to register a current address with state law enforcement. As defined by this act, sexually violent offenses include aggravated sexual abuse and sexual abuse, which are legal terms used in U.S. code signifying rape. The act lists various acts that are considered criminal offenses against a minor, but ultimately discretion is left to the states. The act describes a sexually violent predator as one who is inflicted with a mental abnormality or personality disorder that makes the person likely to engage in predatory sexually violent crimes. (313)

Further provisions require state registration programs to inform released convicts under this act of their duty to register and keep law enforcement informed of any address changes and to obtain fingerprints and a photograph of such convicts. State law enforcement agencies are also required to enter relevant information on a released convict into an appropriate record system, notify law enforcement having jurisdiction where such convict expects to reside, transmit the conviction data and fingerprints to the Federal Bureau of Investigation (FBI), and verify the released convict's address on each anniversary of the person's initial registration date. Criminals under this act must continue to register for 10 years after the date of their release from prison. Finally, the legislation mandates that the data collected for its purposes remain undisclosed except among law enforcement and government agencies under certain circumstances. (This was later changed by the enactment of Megan's Law as stated below).

The Jacob Wetterling Act gives states great leeway in executing a sex offender registration program. Beyond meeting the minimum requirements stated above, each state's program may differ greatly, reflecting the specific concerns of state lawmakers. States are given 3 to 5 years from the 1994 enrollment to implement the legislation.

Megan's Law amends the Jacob Wetterling Act of the 1994 Crime Bill. The legislation strikes provisions of the Crime Bill that prohibit disclosure of sex offender registry information and replaces it with language allowing the release of information for any purpose permitted under the laws of the State. The last part of this is crucial: the law gives states the power to determine what kind and how much of the information is disclosed to whom and for what purpose. States may go as far as giving unregulated public access to sex offender information by publishing it on a state-funded website or a state may choose not to disclose any of the information at all. Another inconsistency is whether states choose to release data on all types of sex offenders or just on "high-risk" criminals. Of course, as states pass different laws, legal action may succeed in limiting some degree of disclosure allowed.

Community Notification:

Megan's Law allows each State the discretion to establish criteria for disclosure, but compels them to make private and personal information on registered sex offenders available to the public. (313)

The Pam Lychner Act:

The Pam Lychner Act steps up the provisions of the Jacob Wetterling Act, which requires state law enforcement to pass on sex offender data and fingerprints to the FBI, by establishing at the FBI a national database of released sex offenders to track their whereabouts and movement. Stipulations mandate that persons convicted of sexual offenses in states that do not have a minimally sufficient registration program register a current address, fingerprints, and current photograph with the FBI. Additionally, the legislation amends the Jacob Wetterling Act by changing the length of state registration requirement from 10 years to 10 years or life, depending on the number of prior convictions and the type of crime committed. (313)

AMBER Alert:

On January 13, 1996, 9-year-old Amber Hagerman was riding her bicycle in Arlington, Texas, when a neighbor heard her scream. The neighbor saw a man pull Amber off her bike, throw her into the front seat of his pickup truck, and drive away at a high rate of speed. The neighbor called police and provided a description of the suspect and his vehicle. Arlington Police and the FBI interviewed other neighbors and searched for the suspect and vehicle. Local radio and television stations covered the story in their regular newcasts. Four days later Amber's body was found in a drainage ditch four miles away. Her kidnapping and murder remain unsolved. (313)

The AMBER Alert Program, named for Amber Hagerman, is a voluntary partnership between law enforcement agencies, broadcasters, and transportation agencies to activate an urgent bulletin in the most serious child abduction cases. Broadcasters use the **Emergency Alert System** (EAS) to air a description of the abducted child and suspected abductor. This is the same concept used during severe weather emergencies. The goal of an AMBER Alert is to instantly call an entire community to assist in the search for and safe recovery of the child. (313)

The PROTECT Act:

In 2003, President Bush signed the PROTECT Act that expanded the use of AMBER Alerts, making grants available to all 50 States so law enforcement can quickly alert the public about missing children and their abductors. (313)

National And State AMBER Alert Information

National Coordination—on April 30, 2003, President George W. Bush signed the Prosecutorial Remedies and Other Tools to end the Exploitation of Children Today (PROTECT) Act of 2003 into law. (313)

For question and answer fact sheets for all 50 states and the District of Columbia on Megan's Law legislation requiring registration and notification of sex offenders: www.klaaskids.org/pg-legmeg.htm

Building on the steps already taken by the Bush Administration to support AMBER Alert programs, this Act classified the national coordination of state and local AMBER Alert programs, including the development of guidance for issuance and distribution of AMBER Alerts and the appointment of a national AMBER Alert coordinator.

In anticipation of the passage of this national legislation, on October 2, 2002, Attorney General John Ashcroft appointed the Assistant Attorney General for the Office of Justice Programs to serve as national AMBER Alert coordinator.

For more information about the national coordination of the AMBER Plan, visit the U.S. Department of Justice Office of Justice Program's AMBER Plan website.

State Legislation:

In the fall of 2001, the **National Center for Missing & Exploited Children** (NCMEC) launched a campaign to encourage the development of AMBER Alert plans across the country. The success of the program has led to the creation of more than 100 known plans nationwide. NCMEC's goal is to offer technical assistance and training, in connection with the U.S. Department of Justice, to all AMBER Alert plans throughout the country. (313)

International AMBER Alert:

Introduction and Overview:

This database compiles and organizes laws pertinent to **America's Missing: Broadcast Emergency Response** (AMBER Alert). Its contents are designed to provide a primary constitutional resource for individuals, agencies, and jurisdictions seeking a better understanding of what the law permits and what the law requires of multiple agency personnel in AMBER Alert situations. (314)

The contents of the AMBER Alert legal database are organized around the basic set of issues likely to arise in emergencies that involve multiple agency personnel, the public, and the media: data collection policies, data broadcasting practices, the Memorandum of Understanding (MoU), and liability. International agreements, federal laws, and state laws are set forth in each of the relevant areas.

The database is intended to be informational only. The reader should be able to determine with relative ease the state of the law in his or her jurisdiction as well as any requirements imposed by federal or international law. The AMBER Alert legal database is designed as a resource to aid state officials in drafting legislation that will support essential AMBER Alert functions of agency personnel in those states that do not have proper support and mandate. A brief review of the contents of the database should also permit a policymaker or researcher to make comparisons and contrasts of the various state laws.

Finally, the AMBER Alert legal database is designed to compliment AMBER Alert training and technical assistance programs. Program managers and instructors will be able to focus their training efforts more specifically to the legal conditions of the participants by briefly reviewing the existing law. Future updates will address emerging legal issues, providing additional resources, particularly with reference to the AMBER Alert and other Department of Justice and Office of Juvenile Justice and Delinquency Prevention skill-based training modules. (315)

For more information, see Chapter Eighteen, Efforts To Stop Trafficking In Children And Child Prostitution.

NOTES

Chapter Twenty Three

SAFETY TIPS ON HOW TO TALK ABOUT SEXUAL ABUSE TO CHILDREN AND ADVICE FOR PROFESSIONALS WHO WORK WITH CHILDREN

Child Sexual Abuse Prevention Programs:

Prevention programs may differ in terms of their content, style, method of presentation, age of the child for which the program is designed, and the training and background of the trainer. But most emphasize a common set of concepts.

Most Prevention Programs Include The Following Concepts:

Body Ownership:

Children have a right to control who touches their body and where they are touched.

Touching Ranges:

Teach children the difference between touching that is "okay" and "not okay" and the progression from "good" to "confusing" to "bad" touch.

Secrets:

There are some kinds of secrets that should be shared, and children need to tell a responsible adult if they are touched inappropriately. They need to know that they are not being a tattletale.

Intuition:

Children should be taught the importance of trusting and acting on their own feelings when a touch or action makes them feel uncomfortable.

Assertiveness Skills:

Children should be taught that they have the right to say NO to an adult who makes them feel uncomfortable, the right to use self-defense techniques and the importance of getting away from an offending person.

Support Systems:

Support systems should be established to help children who have been abused. (316)

Talking To Your Children About Sexual Abuse:

No one wants to tell children about sexual abuse. However, if you do not, your child may learn about it from a child molester.

The following safety tips were provided by educators, counselors, police, sheriff deputies, parents, youth leaders, child and adolescent psychologists, and other professionals and caregivers who work with and care about children of all ages.

Avoid Scary Details.

Use language that is honest and age appropriate. (317)

Speak Openly About Safety Issues Involving Sexual Abuse.

Children will be less likely to come to you if you seem uneasy about the issue of sex or sexual abuse. If they feel you are comfortable discussing the subject matter, they may be more willing to listen to you. (317)

Get To Know Your Children Well:

Show interest in your children's everyday activities and always be attentive to their fears and concerns. Listen to them when they talk to you giving them quality time, all of the time.

Take The Time To "Visit" With Your Children:

Ask them about their day and during the conversation note any unusual requests or demands that anyone has put upon them. Look for sexually explicit language and gestures. Be as casual as possible while talking and listening. If you detect that something is wrong and you show panic, they will notice it and become uncomfortable, causing them to withdraw from further conversation.

Be Sensitive To Their Fears:

Be suspicious if your child goes out of their way to avoid a person. (317)

Take The Time To Get Involved In Your Children's Activities.

It is much less likely that a molester will single out your child if you are an attentive parent. Be particularly watchful of coaches and other youth leaders who are not married and who do not have children of their own. Their intentions are probably good, but this could be a red flag.

Listen To Your Children Or The Child Molester Will.

Pedophiles target children who appear to be neglected or lonely as a tactic to gain their confidence but their true motive is to use children for their own sexual gratification.

Who Does Your Child Know And Trust?

Get to know the people who are involved with your child who are in a position of trust, even a relative or close friend. Be aware of adults or older children who spend a large amount of their time with your child. (317)

Get To Know The Trusted Adults In Your Child's Life.

This includes friends, teachers, coaches, relatives, clergymen, nursery workers, and stepparents, to name a few. Anyone can be a pedophile; but, be sure you have good reason before accusing someone of this devastating crime. Be cautious, but not responsible for ruining the life of a person who genuinely cares about children and who is innocent of any wrongdoing.

When Choosing Someone For Childcare:

Be cautious of teenagers as well as adults. It is in their pre-to-mid-teen years that many pedophiles commonly experience their first sexual encounters with children. Statistically, almost half of convicted child sexual molesters are juveniles. (317)

Know Where Your Children Are And They Are Who With, At All Times:

Never take a chance, with anyone. When your child is in someone else's home for any length of time, even in the home of a close friend or a relative, call periodically and speak to them on the phone. You can usually tell by their tone of voice if anything is wrong.

Teach Them To Never Get Into A Car Or Go Into Someone's Home
Without First Gaining Your Permission:

Children should be instructed not to get into anyone's car or go into anyone's house unless they have special permission from Mom, Dad, babysitter, or whoever is responsible for taking care of them. Tell them to always let you know where they are going, where they will be playing while outside and to come to you first if they are asked to go into someone's home or leave the area where they are supposed to be playing.

Teach Them Not To Talk To Anyone Who Asks For Directions:

Children should know that if someone in a car stops and asks them for directions, they should not answer, but turn and run away. Adults and teenagers do not usually ask children for directions. Explain that this person may be trying to get them into their car. If this happens, they should come straight home and tell Mom or Dad. It is very important they know, before danger strikes, to never, ever talk to any strangers and not to get into an automobile with anyone, even someone they know, without your permission.

Teach Them Not To Help Strangers Who Say They Are Looking For Something:

Children should know that this might be a trick. Adults that ask children to help them find things they have lost such as jewelry, money, a puppy, etc. should be told that they have to go and ask their parent's permission first; even if it is someone they know that asks them to get into a car or to enter their home to help them find something.

Know When, Where, And Who:

Always know whom your children are going with, where they are going, how to get in touch with them, and when to expect them back. Be sure you know that you can trust the person they are going with. Their safety depends on your care and protection.

Never Allow Your Children To Go Door To Door Alone, Selling Items Or For Any Reason:

There could be a pedophile residing near you, even in your own neighborhood. Your child's well-being is worth your time to go along.

Never Leave Young Children Unattended, Anywhere:

Do not allow children to wander around in a store, restaurant, or any other public place. Pedophiles and abductors look for children who are by themselves in places like play areas, malls, and game areas. They keep watch for children who are home alone after school. There are evil people who are paid substantial amounts of money to abduct children for the purpose of trafficking, child pornography, and child prostitution. Abductors have snatched children away who were unattended or who wandered away from their parents while in stores or other public places. They were then brought into the restroom, drugged, dressed in different clothing, and easily carried out of the store unnoticed. Such bizarre happenings warrant strict attention and care of children. Certainly, reasonable discipline given young children who wander off is much better than the possibility of losing them forever. Safety harnesses are a great way to keep up with small children.

Never Let A Child Under The Age Of 10 Go To The Restroom Alone:

Little boys have gone into men's public bathrooms and fallen victim to pedophiles. Public bathrooms are a prime place for molesters to attack children who are unattended. If your child is 10 or older, stand outside the restroom door and instruct the child to answer you when you ask, "Are you OK?" Have a code word the child can say to let you know if he or she is in possible danger.

SECRET CODE:

Many children are lured by strangers, and also by people who they are familiar with, who might say they have been sent by a parent to get them. "Come with me," they will say, "Your Mom (or Dad) has been in an accident and needs you."

Abductors dressed as police officers or ambulance drivers get away with this kind of masquerade far too easily. To prevent this from happening, make up a secret code with your children. Choose a code like "funny face," "butterfly," or any other pet word or phrase that will be easy for them to remember, The rule should be that they are not to go anywhere with anyone, unless that person knows the SECRET CODE.

Home Alone:

If a child will be at home alone, teach him or her that if someone comes to the door, do not answer it; not even for someone they may recognize. Tell them to be very quiet until they go away. Let them know that if they don't follow this rule they might let someone in who is there to harm them. Tell them to never, ever let anyone in when they are by themselves unless that person knows the SECRET CODE.

Use The Buddy System:

Teach your children to never play outside or go bike riding alone. Using the Buddy System, have them find at least one or two friends. Tell them, "If you cannot find playmates, then play inside until you can find someone else to play with. If you are walking alone and an adult or a teenager starts talking to you, get away from him or her as quickly as possible and come straight home. Remember that you must never get into a car or go off with anyone, not even a friend, unless you have permission. Be sure to TELL a trusted adult if anyone bothers you."

Role Plays:

Children understand action better than words. To include sexual abuse prevention in their daily live, practice by acting out some of the things that can happen with "role plays." (317)

Common Lures Used To Entice Children:

One of the most common lures pedophiles use to gain the affection and trust of children is to give gifts and money. Using this tactic, children are enticed to visit "The Friendly Enemy" often. With the friendship well established, the sexual assault will begin to develop. Therefore, be guarded about gift giving. The best way to handle the situation is to instruct children to not accept gifts and money unless they have permission. Take note of people who give excessively. If anyone does give a gift, always diplomatically examine the motive. It could be a very kind, innocent gesture, or it could be a red flag. Always supervise the receiving of gifts and money.

How to Warn Children About Common Lures:

Give your children examples of things that someone might use to get them to keep sexual abuse a secret. For example: candy, money, special privileges, threats, fear of loss, separation, or punishment, etc. (317)

WARN CHILDREN IN THIS WAY; say to them, "I know that you love to receive gifts and money, but sometimes when certain grownups or teenagers give a lot of gifts, it might be because they want you to do something that you don't want to do. If anyone offers you a gift or money, do not accept it; first come and tell me about it. When you obey this rule you will be rewarded." (Rewarding your child with an inexpensive gift or some treats may keep them from being tempted to accept gifts and money secretly.)

Pets Used As Lures:

Most children love pets, especially kittens and puppies. Child molesters commonly take advantage of this fact and use this lure to entice unsuspecting children into a nearby automobile, into their home, or other shelter.

WARN CHILDREN IN THIS WAY; say to them, "If anyone comes up to you, even someone you know, and says they have some puppies or kittens or any other kind of pet to show you, do not go with them. Some adults or teenagers will tell you this and try to get you to go with them into a car or house or other building; and they may not be very nice people. If someone says they have a pet to show you, just say NO. Then, run home and tell Mom or Dad what happened. If you know the person who has the pet, Mom or Dad will go with you to see it. Never go alone with anyone without permission. Some people who seem nice may not be nice at all and you must be careful."

Picture Taking:

Children are used to being photographed, but taking pictures of children is a characteristic trait of pedophiles. Photos taken in secret can lead to child pornography and sexual assault. Alert your children about not letting people take pictures of them without your knowledge. If your child tells you that anyone has taken a picture of him or her, always contact that person and ask for a copy of the photo for your album. That way you will be able to detect if anything is suspicious. If someone has innocently taken pictures of your child, they will be glad to share them with you. Be tactful, but always question the motives.

WARN CHILDREN IN THIS WAY; say to them, "Don't let anyone take your picture unless they have our permission; having your school pictures taken is okay, and taking pictures at birthday parties and times like that might be alright. But if someone does take your picture, please make sure you tell Mom or Dad right away."

Keeping Secrets:

Children have fun at keeping secrets. However, it is in keeping the SECRET of having being sexually molested that victims are so devastated, even into adulthood. The SECRET your child keeps may be the one that is concealing sexual abuse.

WARN CHILDREN IN THIS WAY; say to them, "If anyone, especially an adult or a teenager, tells you to keep a SECRET of any kind, it is important to tell one other person what the secret is. You can trust Mom or Dad, or you can tell some other adult you know you can trust, like your favorite teacher or a grandparent. Some secrets are fun and safe to keep. Some secrets are not fun and safe to keep. Whomever you choose to share a secret with will help you know if you should keep the secret or not."

Overnight Trips:

Overnight trips with youth leaders and other adults or teens are something to be planned carefully. Consider going as a chaperon. If you cannot go with your child, arrange to talk to them every day they are away from you. Make sure that you know whom your child spends the night with and whom the parents are. When they arrive home, have a thorough, but relaxed, conversation about the events of the sleepover. Listen for anything unusual or questionable that may have taken place.

Permission to Call:

Let your children know that if they are away from home and become frightened or uneasy, for any reason, they may use a phone to call home without having permission from anyone. Make sure your children know their phone number and how to call long distance collect. From a regular phone and a pay phone, teach them how to call 1-800-COLLECT. Consider giving your child a cell phone to use in case of emergency.

Teach your children how to use 911: Use role-play. Contact your local police department and ask them if they have special equipment available to help teach children how to use 911.

Phone codes: Teach children how to use the caller ID, consider a RING CODE such as; ring...hang up...ring...hang up...ring and wait for an answer. Instruct them to answer the phone only when they hear the RING CODE. Everyone else can leave a message or call back later.

Support network: Make absolutely sure that the phone numbers of the people in your children's "support network" (people your children know they can contact in an emergency) are by the telephone or in a place where your child has easy access.
(317)

212

Know Where Registered Sex Offenders Live:

Make it a point to know where registered sex offenders live in your community. Tell your children to avoid these people at all costs and to tell you if he or she tries to make contact with them. (317)

- Stay away from sex offenders homes! Teach your child: DON'T harass or visit any sex offender's home or yard; DO tell a safe adult if anyone acts inappropriately towards them (such as creepy, too friendly, threatening, offering gifts in a secret way, or touching them). DO run, scream, and get away if someone is bothering them; DON'T keep secrets; DON'T assist strangers; DON'T take rides from strangers, DON'T go places alone.
- Parents: DO ask questions and DO talk about any uncomfortable feelings they have or experiences with people who cause these feelings.

Education Is Essential:

Because the risk of child sexual molestation is an epidemic, children MUST be properly educated about all the parts of their body. The subject needs to be handled carefully and in a calm, relaxed atmosphere. If children are made to feel uncomfortable or ashamed about the private parts of their bodies, the chances are extremely high—if they have been or ever are sexually abused—the feelings of guilt and shame will keep them from telling anyone what has happened to them. Therefore, in speaking to children about their right to privacy, be certain to help them realize how special they are and that they have the right to say NO if anyone tries to touch their bodies inappropriately. (317)

- Ask questions and talk about any uncomfortable feelings children have experienced. Understand the interactions with people who may have contributed to these feelings.
- Use proper or semi-proper names for body parts: (penis and vagina) with phrases such as "private parts are private and special."
- Instruct your children that if anyone touches them or tries to see their private parts, tries to get them to touch or look at another person's private parts, shows them pictures of or tries to take pictures of their private parts, talks to them about sex, walks in on them in the bathroom or does anything that makes them feel uncomfortable to immediately tell you or a "support network" person.
- Tell your children that, some children and adults have "touching problems." These people can make "secret touching" look accidental (such as tickling or wrestling) and they should still tell you even if they think (or were told) it was an accident.
- Explain that touching problems are like stealing or lying and that the people who have these kinds of problems need special help so they won't continue to have problems or get into trouble. Don't describe it as a sickness.
- Be sure to reinforce that touching other people's private parts is NOT OK for ANY children and it is NOT OK for ANY ONE, adults or other children, to do this. Tell them that you do not want them to do "secret touching" with anyone, no matter who they are. Explain that you will NOT be mad at them if they do come and tell you this has happened, even if it has been happening a lot. The important thing is to tell someone so it can be stopped.

- Educate your children about bad kinds of secrets. Tell your children that some people try to trick kids into keeping the touching a secret. Tell your children, "If someone tells you to keep a secret, be sure to share it with a trusted adult to see if it is a **Safe Secret** to keep."

How To Handle Suspicion Of Sexual Abuse:

If you suspect a child has been abused, inquire in a non-threatening way. Assure them—they are not, nor will they be, in any kind of trouble; emphasizing that they are not at fault. Banish their imagined fears by telling them you will always love them no matter what they tell you. Continue to reinforce this. You may need to be patient until they are ready to tell you. DO NOT pressure them as a child may take being pressured as a sign of being in trouble. (317)

Reassure:

Tell them that they don't have to keep secrets. Many times shame will keep children silent.

Reinforce:

Begin at the earliest age possible, as this will help you and your child to be comfortable with these topics. Have open communication about these topics regularly with your child.

Trust Your Instincts:

If you believe abuse is going on, act on that belief. You know your child and you know when their behavior changes.

How To Say It:

A little humor helps break the tension when discussing a delicate subject with a child.

Safety Tips provided by educators, counselors, police, sheriff deputies, parents, youth leaders, child and adolescent psychologists, and other professionals and care-givers who work with and care about children 1999-2007.

Teaching Children About The Parts Of The Body:

- Every part of your body has a name and a use. Your head is very important; it is where you keep your ears, your nose, your eyes, and your lips. Your mouth is good for eating tasty foods and for asking for a new toy. But if you feel uncomfortable about a person trying to kiss you or put something in your mouth, it is perfectly all right to say NO!
- Children should not allow anyone to touch their private body parts. That kind of touching and kissing is okay someday when you grow up and are married. Married people show their love for each other by holding, touching, and kissing. When you are grown, it will be okay. But this is not right for you now.
- Your arms and hands do so many important things, it is hard to name them all. When you meet someone and wish to be polite, it is nice to shake hands with him or her. Shaking hands is okay. But some other parts of your body are private, like your breasts. Little boys and grown men don't necessarily have to keep their breasts covered, like when they are wearing a bathing suit or a pair of shorts. Little girls should always keep their breasts covered because girls are very special in that way. Still, no one has the right to touch little boy's or little girl's breasts. This is a private part of your body. If anyone ever tries to touch you there in a way that frightens you or makes you feel bad, you have the right to say, NO!
- Another part of your body that is very private is here (point). This is called your genitals. On a girl, that body part is called a vagina and on a boy, it is called a penis. We all know that we keep this part of our bodies covered up. No one has the right to touch you there in a way that frightens you or makes you feel like you have a knot in your stomach. If that ever happens, you have the right to say NO!
- When you are a child, no one has the right to touch your breasts or your genitals except when Mom or Dad helps you get clean or when the doctor needs to give you a check-up; then Mom or Dad or someone who really cares about you can be with you in the room, and that's okay.
- You are very special, so if anyone ever touches your private body parts and asks you to touch their private parts, use your legs and feet to run away. Then use your mouth to TELL your Mom or Dad, your teacher, or another grownup you love what just happened. You have the right to say NO to someone like that.

A number of convicted pedophiles interviewed for research admitted that children who resisted their advances often escaped seduction and sexual abuse.

215

Teach Children How to Resist Sexual Advances:

- I know that children like to make noise, so if anyone tries to harm you in any way, you have permission to scream and holler, kick, and do whatever you have to in order to defend yourself. No one should ever try to hold you and keep you from getting away. No one should ever try to force you into a car, a house, or any other building. If you are at a nursery, a baby sitter's, or the home of a friend or relative, they should never try to get you into a room alone with them and try to touch your private body parts or make you touch their private body parts. They should not try to get you to do anything that frightens you or makes you feel unhappy.

THE FRIENDLY ENEMY SERIES:

ADULT, CHILDREN, AND ADOLESCENT WORKBOOKS
Teach Our Youth How To Protect Themselves Against Sexual Abuse And Exploitation

Programs That Work:

Many innovative and child-friendly sexual abuse prevention programs have been designed and implemented in recent years. These programs and follow-ups help determine the long-term effectiveness of such initiatives. (318)

Teaching About Secrecy:

Programs that teach about secret touching are very effective since sexual abuse always involves secrecy. (318)

Recognition Of Inappropriate Touch:

Young children who were taught to use their feelings to decide whether a touch was appropriate or inappropriate were less able to distinguish this for themselves than children who were taught to follow a body safety rule. "It is not okay for a bigger person to touch or look at my private parts (unless I need help, like if my private parts are hurt or sick). When taught to use a safety rule as the primary decision-making tool, children do demonstrate the ability to recognize unsafe situations. (318)

Teach How To Resist Inappropriate Touch:

Children learn best through active participation. It is not enough to tell children to say NO and go TELL, they need the opportunity to practice those behaviors. Through role-playing, children get a chance to develop assertiveness skills and practice saying NO to an adult. (318)

Reassure Children That Abuse Is Not Their Fault:

This concept needs to be repeated often throughout the program. Young children's self-absorption gives them the tendency to blame themselves. (318)

Teach Children The Proper Names Of Body Parts:

Perpetrators of sexual abuse count on children being taught that it is inappropriate to talk about sex. By talking to children about genitals and age appropriate sexual matters in a respectful manner, we stop giving them the idea that all these things are secret and not to be talked about. (318)

Parental Support Plays A Key Role In Prevention:

The impact of school-based curriculum depends on the support of parents, including permitting their children to participate in the programs, explaining the program concepts to their children, correcting any misunderstandings they may have about sexual abuse and helping the children to apply their new knowledge to their daily life. (318)

It is important to teach children skills to protect themselves. However, we must acknowledge the power imbalance between children and adults and the need for adults to be vigilant and assume the primary protection for children. Putting the responsibility on children for their own protection has sometimes resulted in the community blaming children for not stopping the abuse, particularly if they had been taught prevention programs. Parents need to be given the message of the vital role they must play in listening to, educating, and advocating on behalf of their children in an adult world.

In Review:

Safety Tips—Repeat These Often To Children:

- Never accept candy or gifts from a stranger
- Never go anywhere with a stranger, even if it sounds like fun. Predators can lure children with questions such as, "Can you help me find my lost puppy?", or "Do you want to see some cute kittens in my car?" Remember, adults you don't know should never ask you to do things for them
- Run away and scream if someone follows you or tries to force you into a car
- Say NO to anyone who tries to make you do something wrong or touchs you in places that are private
- Always tell a trusted adult if a stranger asks you personal questions, exposes him or herself to you, takes pictures of you, or makes you feel uneasy in any way
- It's OK to tell, even if the person made you promise not to, or threatened you in some way
- Always ask permission before you leave the house, yard, play area, or to go into someone's home

Practice These Often:

- Make sure younger children know their name, address, phone number including area code, and who to call in case of an emergency
- Review with your child how to use 911
- Discuss what to do if they get lost in a public place or store. Most places have emergency procedures for handling lost children. Remind your children that they should never go to the parking lot to look for you. Instruct your children to ask a cashier for help or stand near the registers or front of the building away from the doors
- Point out the homes of safe friends around the neighborhood where your children can go in case of trouble
- Be sure your children know in whose car they may ride and in whose they may not. Teach them to move away from any car that pulls up beside them, even if that person looks lost or confused
- Develop secret code words for your children and remind them never to tell anyone the code word or to go with anyone who doesn't know the code word
- Teach your children never to ride with anyone they don't know, or with anyone they do know, without your permission
- If your children are old enough to stay home alone, make sure they keep the doors locked and never tell anyone who knocks or calls they are home alone; not even people they know (319)

Recommendations For Program Design:

Prevention programs must take into account the overall well being of the children and individual developmental needs and abilities.

Program content and method of presentation must not be unduly frightening to children. They must be developmentally appropriate. Programs aimed at preschool and kindergarten children should be very specific, concrete, and include behavioral rehearsals that allow children to learn self-protective behaviors through role-playing. It is important for them to practice and discover what works and what does not work.

Training of parents and caregivers is needed to insure the maintenance of training effects is followed properly and to detect and respond to any long-term adverse effects, should they develop.

Finally, evaluation of the effects of the training must be part of every prevention program. Efforts should also be made to talk with children during training and for consistent follow-ups to determine how much of the content they have learned, what they have retained, and whether any adverse side effects may have occurred. An example could be increased anxiety.

Center for Early Education Development (CEED) provides information regarding young children (birth to age 8), including children with special needs, in the areas of education, child care, child development, and family education. CEED activities include research, training, and publications geared toward improving professional practices, supporting parents, and informing policy development. For more information: cehd.umn.edu/ceed (316)

Protecting Your Teens:

Educate Them About Date Rape Drugs:

Victims have had drugs unsuspectingly slipped into their drinks for the purpose of reducing their resistance to sexual advances. Once the individual is drugged and incapacitated, they are then sexually assaulted. Left in a helpless or unconscious state, they cannot escape, resist, or call for help. (320)

It is also not unusual for teens and college students to mix these drugs purposefully with alcohol to get a faster and better "high." This can be fatal; it is a deadly combination. NEVER mix any drugs with alcohol!

Effects Of Date Rape Drugs:

Some of the most common drugs in use are: GHB (gamma hydroxybutyric acid), Rohypnol (flunitrazepam), and Ketamine (ketamine hydrochloride) (321)

Physical Effects:

Nausea, vision problems, slurred speech, drunk feeling, dizziness, seizures, convulsions, all or partial blackouts, sleepiness, difficultly with motor movements, loss of muscle control, tremors, sweating, vomiting, slow heart rate, aggressive or violent behavior, problems breathing, coma, and death.

Mental Effects:

Dream-like state, confusion, hallucinations, lost sense of time and identity, distorted perception of sight and sound, feeling out of control, out of body experience, coma, numbness, partial or complete amnesia.

Anyone given any form of date rape drugs may experience only one, a few, or all of these symptoms during the period when the drug is taking effect. (321)

- Immediate reporting makes it easier to detect date rape drugs in the body
- These drugs usually leave your body quickly
- Never accept drinks that may have been dosed
- Be responsible for your own drink
- Do not take part in "dosing" other people. This is a felony!

Contact: 1-800-994-WOMAN www.ksu.edu/womenscenter/ and www.4woman.gov/faq/rohypnol.htm NWHIC, a service of the U.S. Department of Health and Human Services Office on Women's Health

<u>*Facilitated Rape Is A Felony:*</u>

<u>*Partying Smart*</u>

Despite the advantage date rape drugs and alcohol may give to a would-be attacker, there are things you can do to lower your risk of becoming a victim of drug-facilitated rape. Most of us are afraid of the stranger rapist who is going to jump out of the alley or who is waiting for us in our apartment. The startling reality is that 84% of women who are raped know their rapist. One of the best things you can do is to stay aware of your surroundings, particularly at parties, bars, and clubs. (321)

<u>*Safe Drinking Tips:*</u>

- Do not leave beverages unattended
- Do not accept any beverages, including alcohol, from someone else
- At a bar or club, accept drinks only from the bartender or server
- At parties, do not accept open container drinks from anyone. Don't take a drink from a punch bowl
- Don't drink beverages that you did not open yourself
- Don't share or exchange drinks with anyone
- If you realize that your drink has been left unattended, discard it
- Don't drink anything that has an unusual taste or appearance (salty taste, excessive foam, unexplained residue)
- Drink moderately so that you can keep your wits about you
- Drink slowly, rather than gulping your beverage, so that if it has been drugged you may have more time to become aware of it
- Hold the drink with your hand covering the opening while your attention is diverted, for example when you're in conversation
- If you must leave your drink, such as while dancing or using the restroom, get a new one when you return (321)

<u>*Why Be So Suspicious?*</u>

Many date rape drugs dissolve easily in juice, coffee, carbonated, and alcoholic beverages. Most are colorless, odorless, and tasteless when dissolved in any liquid. The effects of these drugs are enhanced when mixed with alcohol!
GHB is usually found in liquid form that is colorless and odorless, and has no taste when mixed in a drink or even water! Sometimes there is a salty aftertaste, depending on how it was produced.

<u>*Meeting New People:*</u>

- Stay away from people who are not respectful of you or your personal space
- Stay away from people who think "if you are drunk, you should know what to expect"
- Stay away from people who are violent and/or insulting

- Avoid men who show no respect for women. If a man does not respect women as a group, he may not respect your wishes privately
- Always listen to your gut feeling
- Forget about being a nice person if you feel threatened or pushed (321)

Use THE BUDDY SYSTEM—It Works:

- Stay with trusted friends. "Trusted" means 100%, without a doubt, "know your parent would approve" trust
- In advance of attending a club or party, make plans to check on each other often and before leaving the event. Make sure you communicate
- If you start to feel strange or unusually intoxicated, seek help from a friend at once. A stranger who offers to help you or escort you from the event could be someone who's slipped you a drug and plans to do you harm
- Be alert to the behavior of friends and ask them to watch out for you. Anyone extremely intoxicated after consuming only a small amount of alcohol may be in danger (321)

Why Be So Cautious?

Many date rape drugs take effect after only 20 to 30 minutes, and the effects may last as long as 8 to 12 hours. When combined with alcohol, Rohypnol causes severe disorientation and produces blackout periods that are typically 8 to 12 hours long. The victim may or may not appear "awake" during this time.

Date Rape Drugs Are Easily Acquired:

Rohypnol is sold legally as a sleeping aid in Europe and Mexico, but it is not approved for manufacture or sale in the United States. In 1996, the **Food and Drug Administration** and the **Drug Enforcement Administration** banned its importation. Nevertheless, smugglers bring it into the country, where it is commonly used as a club drug among high school students, college students, and other young adults. Other names are roofies, roches, and the forget pill. (321)

If You've Been Assaulted:

The psychological trauma caused by sexual assault can be severe and long lasting, or may temporarily affect your mood, concentration, academics, relationships, or physiology.

What To Do After A Sexual Assault

It is best to get medical attention immediately. After an assault, it is vitally important to receive a medical exam and to consult a nurse or doctor about health issues, even if there are no visible wounds. If you feel you may have been drugged, urine should be COLLECTED IMMEDIATELY.

Call The Police:

Date rape drugs can disappear quickly from the body. Help prevent further assaults: take the perpetrator to court, seek justice, press charges, or go on record with your assault. The sooner you talk to the police the better. Evidence is lost as time goes by. You may want to have an advocate with you. (321)

Get Support From Other People:
Some rape victims feel that if they avoid talking about the assault, they will be able to forget about what happened to them. Most survivors who try this approach eventually realize that they need to deal with the assault. Their unresolved feelings and fears hold them back from enjoying their lives and participating fully in relationships. Talking about the assault can help relieve some of the control it has over you and help you begin the process of recovery. Therapy provides a safe, private place to deal with your feelings and concerns. It also can be helpful to talk about your reactions with friends and family members who are supportive and understanding.

Talk With A Counselor:

Many sexual assault victims find that therapy is a healing and empowering experience. A person trained to assist sexual assault victims will understand the unique concerns you have and know ways to help you cope with the physical and emotional effects of the assault. The right counselor can also help you deal with the reactions of family members and friends. Most rape crisis centers offer free services to sexual assault victims. Actual comments from survivors:

- *Therapy saved my life.*
- *I'm stronger than he is.*
- *I wasn't going to be his victim forever.*

Report The Crime:

Always report this crime to the proper authorities. You owe it to yourself and the abuser's "next victim."

Consider Legal Action:

Obtain referrals to attorneys experienced in this area.

Remember:

The healthy, competent, and wise individual seeks assistance! Getting help after being assaulted is a sign that a real and lasting healing process has begun.

Rape Facilitated By Drugs Is Increasing:

Sadly, these drugs can be fatal. (321)

ABDUCTION PREVENTION AND INTERVENTION:

Approximately 2,100 missing children reports are filed each day. Cases could be solved more easily if parents were able to provide the following information about their child: (319)

- Height
- Weight
- Eye color
- A good quality, recent photo
- Any distinguishing marks
- Accurate description of what they were wearing when they disappeared

Keep Information Up Dated:

- Make sure custody papers are in order
- Have ID photos taken of your children every 6 months, and have your children fingerprinted. Many local police departments sponsor fingerprinting programs— check for them in your town
- Keep your children's medical and dental records up to date

Preventative Precautions:

- Make online safety a priority. The internet is a great tool, but it is also a perfect place for predators to stalk children. Be aware of your children's internet activities and chat room friends, and remind them never to give out personal information. Avoid posting identifying information or photos of your children online
- Set boundaries for places your children go. Supervise them in places like malls, movie theaters, parks, public bathrooms, or while fundraising door to door

- Never leave children alone in a car or stroller, even for a minute
- Choose caregivers, babysitters, day care providers, and nannies carefully; be sure to check their references
- If you've arranged for someone to pick up your children from school or child care, discuss the arrangements beforehand with your children and with the school or child-care center
- Avoid dressing your children in clothing with their names on it. Children tend to trust adults who know their names

If Your Child Has Been Abducted:

Because the first few hours are the most critical in missing child cases, it is important to provide officials with information about your child immediately. Have a recent picture of your child and know the time and location you last saw your child and what your child was wearing.

You may also ask that your child be entered into the systems that can offer information and support during the search for your child:

National Crime and Information Center (NCIC) (304) 625-2000

Child Protection Education of America (866) USA-CHILD

The National Center for Missing and Exploited Children (800) 843-5678

After notifying the authorities, try to stay calm. You'll be able to remember details about your child's disappearance more easily if you remain rational and logical. (319)

Know The Rules:

Abduction And Kidnapping Prevention Tips For Parents And Guardians:

High-profile abductions of children, although a rare occurrence, have left many families frightened and unsure about how best to protect their children. According to a study conducted by the Washington State Attorney General's Office for the U.S. Department of Justice Office of Juvenile Justice and Delinquency Prevention, in 57% of the cases, the victims of child abduction murder are victims of opportunity. (322)

The Tips Noted Below Will Help Families Lessen The Opportunity For Abduction And Kidnapping And Better Safeguard Their Children:

- Teach your children to run away from danger, never toward it. Danger is anyone or anything that invades their personal space. If someone tries to grab them, tell them to make a scene; loudly yelling that this person is not my father/mother/guardian, etc. and to make every effort to get away by kicking, screaming, and resisting. Their safety is more important than being polite

- Teach your children that if they are ever followed in a vehicle to turn around and run in the other direction to you or another trusted adult
- Never let your children go places alone, and always supervise your young children or make sure there is a trusted adult present to supervise them if you cannot. Make sure your older children always take a friend when they go anywhere
- Know where your children are and whom they are with, at all times. Remind children never, ever to take anything from, or respond in any way, to anyone who approaches them whom they do not know. Teach them to run away as quickly as they can to you or another trusted adult
- Discuss security issues with your children so they will understand the need for precautions. Advise your older children about steps they may take for further safeguards. Know your children's friends and their families. Pay attention to your children and listen to them. If you do not, someone else will. And others may have ulterior motives for befriending your children
- Consider installing an alarm system in your home with a monitoring feature. Make sure your home is secured with deadbolt locks, and ensure landscaping does not provide places for people to hide. Check other access points such as gates, and make sure they have been secured. Consider installing exterior lighting around your home. Make sure your home is fully secured before you go to sleep and items such as ladders have been stored inside. Prepare a plan to vacate your home in case of any emergency. This should include but is not limited to a fire. Have a plan if an intruder tries or gets into your home
- Make your children part of securing your home. If you have installed an alarm system, demonstrate it to your children and show them how to make sure doors and windows are locked. This will not only help calm their fears but will also help make them part of your "safety plan" at home
- Have a list of family members who could be contacted in case of an emergency. Designate a family member or close associate who would be able to fill the role of advisor in case of an emergency
- Be alert to and aware of your surroundings. Know the "escape routes" and plan what you would do in different emergencies. Practice "what if" scenarios so you will be well prepared. Know the location of local hospitals and best routes to take to reach them. Know how to reach the nearest local law enforcement agency or sub-station
- Know your employees and co-workers. Do background screening and reference checks on everyone who works at your home, particularly those individuals who care for your children. Their knowledge of your family is extensive so make sure you have an equal understanding of whom they are
- Consider varying your daily routines and habits. Do not take the same routes or go at the same time on your regular errands. If you take your children to school, change that route as well
- Take steps to secure personal information about yourself. Consider getting a post office box and registering everything there including your vehicles and drivers' licenses. Have personal bills sent to your place of work or the post office box. Be discreet about your possessions and family's personal habits and information

- Report any suspicious person or activities to law enforcement. If you feel you or your children have been targeted or are being stalked, immediately report this information to law enforcement authorities. Do not wait.
- Remember you are your best resource for better safeguarding your family. Do not become unconcerned about personal security issues. (322)

Working With Children?—Tips For Careful Conduct:---Protecting Yourself

- If you work with children, in any capacity, know in advance what you can do to protect yourself from being accused of child sexual abuse
- Use a hands-off policy with children in your care and keep a respectable distance, physically, socially, and emotionally
- Sexual conversation is considered sexual molestation, be sure that you speak with discretion
- Never go into a room alone with a child and close the door behind you. Always have another person present who is the same gender as the child
- When talking or interacting with a child, sit at a desk or in chairs or stand facing each other with at least an arm's distance between you, keep your arms crossed, and do not touch the child
- If a child hugs you, gently move away from the child without frightening them or being too obvious as to make them feel rejected; tell them you have a little cold and that you don't want to spread germs. We who love children want to hug them back, but with pedophilia on the rise, we must protect ourselves as well as the children. We can make up for the lack of physical contact by using words of encouragement, positive reinforcement, and genuine concern
- Avoid being alone with any child; encourage parent/guardian participation. Invite family members to visit whenever they like. Make yourself available to the family during the time you are with the children in your care
- Do not associate with children outside of your volunteer or professional realm. Personal involvement may leave you suspect. Know your boundaries and keep them
- Always dress modestly when working with children, keeping a professional check on your appearance and demeanor. Your personal life is your business, but when you are in a position of working with children, your reputation and integrity is more important than being stylish
- Avoid over complimenting children about anything
- Never tell children that you love them or show favoritism. Smile, tell them that you care about them, and be encouraging, letting them know that they are special in this world and that they were born with a purpose. Congratulate them on their achievements and encourage them to follow through with their goals and dreams, but don't over-do
- Be careful not to give a child or their parents gifts of money or goods. That too can be misinterpreted as luring a child into a harmful relationship. If you know that a child

or the parents are in need, give your donation to the school or other organization that is accustomed to giving and let them distribute your gift. Insist that the donation remain anonymous

- Always report any unusual incident, no matter how unimportant it may seem at the time. It could be a red flag indicating that something is wrong in the life of a child
- If a child should confide in you about abuse of any type by anyone, always inform the police immediately. Do not promise a child that you will keep silent. Assure them that you will do all that you can to help them, but that this must be reported so that they can be protected. If you do not report abuse to the authorities, you can be fined and/or imprisoned (323)

Always be on the alert and report your suspicions of child sexual abuse in a timely manner for the protection of the alleged victim. However, be careful that you have reasonable cause before you take the chance of ruining the reputation of an innocent person. Then act quickly. You are not required to give authorities your name. Either way, your report will remain confidential.

National Child Abuse Hotline (800) 344-6000

By reading this book, you have become an important part of preventing sexual abuse, exploitation, abduction, and trafficking of children.

<u>NOTES</u>

APPENDIX

THE HISTORY OF CHILD SEXUAL ABUSE

There is no universal definition of child sexual abuse. However, a central characteristic of any abuse is the dominant position of an adult that allows him or her to force or coerce a child into sexual activity. (324)

Related Terms:

Pederasty: 1. Greek, "paiderastes", literally, "lover of boys", from paid-ped- + erastes lover, from erasthai-to love 2. Anal intercourse especially with a boy. Miriam-Webster's 11th. Collegiate Dictionary

Pederast: "One who practices anal intercourse, especially with a boy." Miriam-Webster's 11th. Collegiate Dictionary

Incest: 1. Sexual intercourse between persons so closely related that law forbids them to marry. 2. The statutory (law against) the crime of such a relationship. Miriam-Webster's 11th. Collegiate Dictionary

The history of child sexual abuse proves that it is ancient and worldwide. The statistics prove also, that it is now, and has always been of epidemic proportion. You will note that from one period of history to another, adults having sex with youth is considered "acceptable" by some and "unacceptable" by others. Today, that same statement is true. It has been called everything from honorable to demonic and has been described as everything from mentoring, to sadistic mutilation, to molestation. Author's Note

In ancient times, the Greeks and the Romans practiced pederasty. According to Athenaeus in the Deipnosophists, the Celts also preferred young boys in spite of the beauty of their women. It is said that they had a boy on one side and a woman on the other. (325)

The Greek and Roman child lived his or her earliest years in an atmosphere of sexual abuse. The rape of young girls was common, as is reflected in the scenes of many Greek comedies of little girls being raped, considered to be amusing. Greek, Roman, Indian, and Chinese doctors reported that female children rarely have *hymens, indicating penetration of the vagina. *hymen: a fold of mucous membrane partly closing the orifice of the vagina. (326)

Boys, too, were regularly handed over by their parents to neighboring men to be raped. Plutarch has a long essay on the best kind of person a father could give his son to for ^buggering. The common notion that this occurred only at adolescence is quite mistaken. It began around age seven, continued for several years, and ended by puberty, when the boy's facial and pubic hairs began to appear. Child brothels, rent-a-boy services, and sex slavery flourished in every city in ancient times. Children were so subject to sexual use by the men around them that schools were (by law) prohibited from staying open past sundown. Slaves were assigned to children to protect them against sexual attack from random strangers and their teachers. Petronius especially loved depicting adults feeling the immature genitals of boys, and Tiberius, was said by Seutonius, to have taught children in the tenders of years, which he called his little fishes, to play between his legs while he was in his bath. Those which had not yet been weaned, but were strong and hearty, he taught **fellatio. *buggering: to commit sodomy with. **fellatio: oral stimulation of the penis. (326)

Practices continued in the middle ages with the buggering of boys even in monasteries, continuing to be widespread and even accepted by society. By the time boys were in their teens, they were so addicted to violent sex that they sometimes formed adolescent-raping gangs that grabbed and raped any girls or young women they could find unprotected. This occurred to such an extent that these gangs would have raped the majority of women in some cities at some time in their lives.

GREECE: Love Conquers Al Caravaggio 1602 - 1603; Oil on canvas; Staatliche Museen, Berlin, Painted for a patron who veiled the work, for greater effect upon the eventual viewers. Love embodied by a wanton boy, triumphs over all human endeavors: war, science, music, and government.

In ancient Greece, pederastic relationships between an adolescent boy and an adult man outside of the boy's immediate family was considered an educational experience in moral values, as well as sexual instruction. (327)

As a more sophisticated and cosmopolitan society evolved in Rome and in Greece, pederasty lost its appeal as a recognized part of education. However, their emperors engaged in "male love," most of which was of a pederastic nature. Of the first fifteen emperors, it was believed that Claudius was the only one who practiced "normal" sex with women. (339)

At the Palaestra, Youth, holding a net shopping bag filled with walnuts as a love gift, draws close to a man who reaches out to fondle him; Attic red-figure plate 530-430 BCE; Ashmolean Museum, Oxford.

Pederastic art usually shows the man standing, grasping the boy's chin with one hand, and reaching to fondle his genitals with the other. Recent research has unearthed art in which there was in fact reciprocation of desire and other historians assert that it is a modern fairy tale that the younger was never aroused. (328)

POST-ISLAMIC PERSIA: Louis Crompton claims boy-love flourished spectacularly in Post-Islamic Persia, where art and literature also made frequent use of pederastic topics that celebrate the love of the wine boy, as do the paintings and drawings of artists such as Reza Abbasi, 1565 –1635. Western travelers reported that at Abbas' court, sometime between 1627 and 1629, they saw evidence of homosexual practices. Male houses of prostitution amrad khaneh, "houses of the beardless, "were legally recognized and paid taxes. (329)

In medieval Islamic civilization, pederastic relations were so readily accepted in upper class circles that there was often little or no effort to conceal their existence. (330)

CENTRAL ASIA: Baccha dancing boy in Samarkand.
Traditional dancers and sex workers in Central Asia.
Photo ca. 1905–1915.

In central Asia, the practice of pederasty is believed to have long been widespread, and remains a part of the culture. Though no longer widely practiced, boy marriages with adult men nevertheless still occur.

In the aftermath of the US-Afghan war, western mainstream media reported on patterns of adult/adolescent male relationships, documented in Kandahar in Afghanistan." Sir Richard Burton, Kama Sutra: the Hindu art of lovemaking, intro. Pathan proverb, also reported in similar forms from the Arab countries, Iran and North Africa. (331)

JAPAN: Trust between a man and a youth, Miyagawa Issho, ca. 1750; Panel from a series of ten on a shunga -style painted hand scroll (kakemono-e); sumi, color and gofun on silk. Private collection.

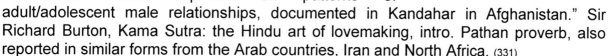

A man named Kukai, also known as Kobo Daishi was the founder of a practice known as shudo, the "Way of the Young." Though the term shudo first appeared in 1485, it is preceded in the Japanese homosexual tradition by the love relationships between Buddhist *bonzes and their **acolytes, who were known as chigo, which was popular among the religious community and the samurai society from the medieval period on. It eventually infiltrated all of society. Monks often had relationships with chigo, which is recorded in literary works known as chigo monogatari. It lost its popularity around the end of the 19th century, parallel to the growing European influence. *bonzes: Buddhist monks. **acolytes: one who assists a member of the clergy. (332)

Historically, Japan has been one of the most *endogamous societies in the world, preferring incestuous marriages with siblings, cousins, uncles with nieces and aunts with nephews, to the extent that genetics experts have discovered that the incestuous inbreeding has affected the size and health of Japanese people . Even today, there are rural areas in Japan where fathers marry their daughters when the mother has died or is incapacitated, in accordance with **feudal family traditions. Other recent surveys on sexual activities report memories of sexual abuse that are higher in Japan than comparable American studies, and "hot lines" of sexual abuse report mother/son incest in almost a third of the calls. Reportedly, the mother tells her teenage son that it is not good to masturbate, that it will lower his I.Q. and offers him to use her body to have sex. She also tells him that he cannot study effectively if he does not have sex or that she doesn't want him to get into trouble with a girl, to have sex with her instead. *endogamous: marriage within a specific group as required by custom or law. **feudal: of, relating to, or having the characteristics of a medieval fee. (326)

Childhood in contemporary Japan, although somewhat more western than that of other eastern nations, still includes masturbation by mothers "to put their children to sleep." Parents often, while having intercourse, have their children in bed with them, physically embracing the child. Co-sleeping frequently continues until the child is 10 or 15 years old; a recent Japanese study reports that daughters sleep with their fathers over 20% of the time after age sixteen. (326)

Pederastic relationships were commonly considered fashionable when wealthy men chose a boy who was from a poor family. In Japan, it was a position of admiration for a man of high position to transcend class distinction and develop a devoted relationship with a boy from the lower class. (330)

NORTH AMERICA: In the Koniagas of Kodiak Island and the Thinkleets, the most distasteful practice is that of grooming male concubines. A Kodiak mother will select her most handsome and most promising boy, dress and rear him as a girl, teach him only domestic duties doing women's work, associate him with women and girls to make him *effeminate. Later at the age of 10 or 15, he is married to a wealthy man who considers his young companion a great gain. These male concubines are called Achnutschik or Schopans. This practice continues today. *effeminate: having feminine qualities untypical of a man. (333)

This same tradition of male concubines is found in Nutka Sound and the Aleutian Islands, but not to the same extent as amongst the Koniagas. These young men have their beards carefully plucked out as soon as their facial hair begins to grow and their chins are tattooed like those of women. In California, the first missionaries found the same practice, the youths being called Joya. Male concubines are currently abundant worldwide. (334)

ALBANIA: In Albania, young men between the ages of 17 and 24 seduced boys between the ages of 12 and 16. This occurred as late as the mid 1800s. In literature, this type of love is called ashik, meaning "the beloved." A geg, which is a northern clansman, married at the age of 24 or 25, and usually, but not always, gave up boy love. (335)

ITALY: According to the detailed analysis of court records in Florence in the fifteenth century, Michael Rocke reported that the majority of local males were officially incriminated at least once during their lifetimes for engaging in homosexual relations with boys. (326)

Since courts were reluctant to try any but the most violent cases of boy rape many pederasts were never incriminated in court; and since pederasts past and present usually rape dozens of boys each, these early court statistics, more than anything else in history, reveal that pederasty is universal. If the majority of men were hauled into court for cases in connection with their pederasty, the number of boys actually being raped must have been nearly everyone.

SIENA: Pederasty was so accepted in medieval times that parents continued handing over their boys for sexual use to friends and others from whom they expected favors. Bernardino of Siena condemned parents as "pimps" of their own sons, saying that the fathers, who were pederasts themselves, were the ones most responsible for the abuse of their sons by taking money or gifts from their rapists. (326)

Boys were so likely to be raped that they could hardly walk down the street without being approached by a sodomite. The situation was so extreme that Bernardino urged mothers to send their girls out instead as they were not in danger among such men. The mothers also participated in the seduction of their sons. When a boy started to mature sexually, she gave him a bedroom to himself on the ground floor, with a separate entrance and every convenience so that he could do whatever he pleased and bring home whomever he liked.

KOREA: In 1893, a French physician, Paul Michaut, described Korea as a country where pederasty is common among the greater majority of the population and is practiced publicly in the street without the least condemnation as being unacceptable or evil. He associated its prevalence with that of syphilis, which was very common, noting that, those who are not infected are the exception. (336)

CHINA: The Way of the Academicians from Hua Ying Chin Chen (Variegated Positions of the Flower Battle) China, Ming dynasty (1368–1644)

Like so many early civilizations, ancient China institutionalized the pederasty of boys, with child *concubines, the castration of small boys so they could be used sexually as **eunuchs, the marriage of young brides with a number of brothers, widespread boy and girl prostitution and the regular sexual use of child servants and slaves. Under the popular ancient sim pua system of marriage, parents would adopt a girl during infancy, bring her up as a sister to their son and then force them into a marriage that must be considered incestuous in every way except genetically. Alternatively, they could adopt a son to marry his sister. Sexual use of adopted girls was said to be common. Parents would send their boys to aristocratic households for sexual use and if he was volunteered as a eunuch, his parents would have the boy's genitals cut off, and then carry them around in a jar. In some areas, male marriage to boys was so popular that there are records of sacrifices to patron gods of pederasty. *concubines: mistresses. **eunuch: a castrated man or boy. (326)

Man boy marriages lasting for a set period of time, after which the younger partner would find a wife, often with the help of the older one, appear to have been part of the culture in the province of Fijian in pre-modern times. The marriages were said to have been celebrated by the two families in traditional fashion, including the ritual "nine cups of tea." The popularity of these pederastic relationships in Fijian, where they even had a patron god, Hu Tianbao, gave rise to one of the more mild expressions for same-sex love in China, "The Southern Custom." Men's sexual interest in youths was also reflected in prostitution, with young male sex workers fetching higher prices than their female counterparts do, as recently as the beginning of the twentieth century. (337)

Foot Binding Fetish:

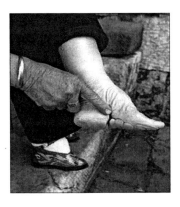

The Chinese universal practice of foot binding was also for sexual purposes, with a girl undergoing extremely painful crushing of the bones of her feet for years in order that men could "make love" to her big toe as a *fetish, a penis-substitute. *fetish: an object or bodily part whose real or fantasized presence is psychologically necessary for sexual gratification and that is an object of fixation to the extent that it may interfere with complete sexual expression.

The deformed foot became the focus of the man's perversion and of his sexual excitement during intercourse becoming an essential foreplay to the sex act. Handling it excited and stimulated him. The ways of grasping the foot in one's palms was profuse and varied; kissing, inserting the foot in his mouth, nibbling it or chewing it vigorously escalated the man to heights of ecstasy. He would then adoringly place it against his cheeks, chest, knees, or penis. Thus, even sex with a female could simulate homosexual intercourse for Chinese males.

Although Chinese literature has many descriptions of the screams of little girls whose feet were being crushed, it is not recorded as to whether they fully understood the sexual purpose of their mutilation. However, since they shared the family bed with their parents and presumably observed the father playing sexually with the mother's feet, it is likely that the sexual aim of the painful mutilation was apparent to the child. (326)

Other Common Mutilation Of Children:

The custom of *clitoridectomy, which is not part of any religious doctrine, goes back at least to pre-dynastic Egyptian times; even mummies were found to be missing their genitals. Presently, many Middle Eastern and African countries continue to practice circumcision of girls. A recent survey of Egyptian girls and women showed 97% of uneducated families and 66% of educated families still practice clitoridectomy, and the practice is not decreasing. Hosken says "more female children are mutilated today than throughout history" and estimates that there are presently 74 million mutilated females in countries where documentation exists. *clitoridectomy: cutting away of all or part of the clitoris, a small organ on a woman's genital area. (326)

Often the girl's *labia are cut off in addition to the clitoris and the remaining flesh is sewn together, leaving only a small opening for urination. The vagina must, of course, be cut open before intercourse. Men usually do not want to marry women with intact clitorises, believing they will be "oversexed" and betray them. It is the custom in some countries on the wedding night for the husband to be the one to cut his bride's vagina open with a knife, and then have repeated intercourse to prevent it from closing again. *labia: any of the folds at the margin of the vulva. (326)

Giving birth is also very difficult as they are cut further to allow the baby to pass through. The vaginal area is then re-sewn after the baby is born, for the purpose of giving the men more pleasure during intercourse, and has to be cut open for each successive birth. During all of these mutilations the girls undergo excruciating pain, usually hemorrhage, often suffer from tetanus, blood poisoning, chronic urinary tract infections and infertility, frequently pass out from the shock since no anesthetic is used and sometimes die of complications.

Sadly, the excuse given for clitoridectomy is that little girls are believed to be so oversexed by nature, that it is necessary "to release them from their bondage to sex" and "to stop them from masturbating." Someone actually said, "Little girls would fall off their bicycles because of sexual over stimulation if their clitorises were not cut off." Since the operation usually makes the girl frigid, it can be said that the mutilation does indeed reduces the sexual pleasure.

The following is a statement given by an Egyptian woman of her memory of how this happened to her after being used sexually by the men in her family during her early childhood.

I was six years old that night, as I lay in my bed, warm and peaceful. I felt something move under the blankets, something like a huge hand. Another hand was clapped over my mouth to prevent me from screaming.

They carried me to the bathroom. I remember a rasping metallic sound which reminded me of the butcher when he used to sharpen his knife. My blood froze in my veins as my thighs were pulled wide apart and I saw the knife as it was heading straight down towards my throat. Then suddenly the sharp metallic edge seemed to drop between my thighs and there cut off a piece of flesh from my body.

I screamed with pain despite the tight hand held over my mouth, for the pain was not just a pain, it was like a searing flame that went through my whole body. After a few moments, I saw a red pool of blood around my hips. I did not know what they had cut off from my body, and I did not try to find out. I just wept, and called out to my mother for help. But the worst shock of all was when I looked around and found her standing by my side. Yes, it was my mother, in flesh and blood, right in the midst of these strangers, talking to them and smiling with them.

The mutilation of children's genitals is such an important aspect of life in certain human cultures that whole religions and state systems have been founded upon the practice. Yet when scholars attempt to explain why almost everyone since the beginning of recorded history has massively assaulted the genitals of their children, they persistently deny that it is a sexual perversion or that those who do it ever mean any harm to the children. (326)

The Rape And Killing Of Children To Cure Adult Diseases:

Children's bodies were thought to be particularly useful in curing disease. The belief was that whatever the physical illness, a child could be used to "absorb the poison" that was responsible. For instance, when someone wanted to be cured of leprosy, they would kill a child and wash their body in its blood. When someone wanted to find out if a house whose previous occupants had died of plague was still infected or not, they rented some children to live in it for several weeks to see if they would die; rather like the use of canaries in mines to detect poisonous gas. When someone was impotent, depressed, or had venereal disease, doctors prescribed having intercourse with a child. (This is happening today in Africa with the epidemic of AIDS). (326)

As late as the end of the nineteenth century, men who were brought into custody for having raped young girls were let go because they believed that they were curing themselves of venereal disease. Raping virgins was particularly effective for impotence and depression; as one medical book put it, "breaking a maiden's seal is one of the best antidotes for one's ills." Clubbing her unceasingly, until she faints is a great remedy for man's depression. It cures all impotence. Then, of course, when a parent had a disease, they always had their children handy to absorb the poison. Thus, British doctors in the nineteenth century regularly found when visiting men who had venereal disease that their children also had the same disease, on their mouth, anus, or genitals.

Opposition To Pederasty:

Pederasty was being opposed at the same time that it was being practiced, both within the cultures and outside the cultures where it existed. In Greece, a few of its cities prohibited pederasty, and in others, such as Sparta, only chaste, non-sexual relationships were permitted. (326)

In the beginning of the fifteenth century, more violent pederasty disputes began to be handled by the courts. The huge number of cases prosecuted revealed that every place where boys gathered, from schools and monasteries to taverns and pastry shops, was like a "school of sodomy" where pederasts gathered to violate boys.

As parents began to change their ideas of how they should treat their children, they became more and more reluctant to hand over their boys for use by pederasts. They began monitoring tutors to see that they were not pederasts, and reformers began to warn caregivers that servants very often take liberties with a younger child that they would not risk with a young man.

Some suggested that public houses of female prostitution should be encouraged as the best way to keep men away from the boys. The rape of boys in British public schools, with the full knowledge, involvement and even the approval of their elders, nevertheless continued into the twentieth century where every older boy and even teachers had a younger boy as their *bitch to use sexually. *bitch: the crude name for a male who is used by another male to perform sexually as sodomy.

The Judaeo-Christian faiths also condemned sodomy, although their definition of sodomy was defined in various terms. Later, Islam, and later still, the Bahai Faith made public the terms of a proposed law against pederasty. The second century preacher, Clement of Alexandria, used pederasty as a strong disapproval of Greek religion by stating, "For your gods did not abstain even from boys. One loved Hylas, another Hyacinthus, another Pelops, another Chrysippus, another Ganymedes. These are the gods your wives are to worship! (338)

As a method of imposing Christianity as a state religion, the early Christian Roman emperors did away with pederasty, along with other openly sexual practices of the Greco-Roman religion and culture. Violators were dealt with harshly. The law code of Visigoth's king Chindasuinth called for both partners to be castrated immediately, to go before the bishop of the diocese where the deed was committed and to be placed in solitary confinement in a prison. These punishments were often linked to the penance given after the Sacrament of Confession. In Rome, since the time of Theodosius in 390, the punishment was burning at the stake. (326)

The Catholic Church, working through the inquisition courts as well as through the civil judicial court, used every means at its disposal to fight what it considered to be the "corruption of sodomy." Men were fined or jailed and boys were flogged. The harshest punishments, such as burning at the stake, were usually reserved for violent crimes and crimes committed against the very young.

The rise of Christianity led to the suppression of pederasty by the Byzantine emperors, as it was one of the main issues of a typical pagan culture. The church fathers saw pederasty as being in conflict with biblical teaching. Such teaching includes references to the Old Testament, in which Leviticus called for the death penalty for a number of sexual sins including crude sexual relations between men. The New Testament teachings of Paul also speak against these things and even speech about pederasty was suppressed as stated, "Conversation about deeds of wickedness is appropriately termed filthy, shameful speaking, as talk about adultery and pederasty and the like" and was to be put to silence. (338)

Reform Efforts:

In the eighteenth century, childrearing reformers began trying to bring this open sexual abuse under control. Now, the child was the one being punished for touching his or her genitals by being threatened with clitoridectomy, *infibulation, circumcision, and various types of body cages and other genital restraint devices. These terrorizing warnings and surgical interventions only began to die out at the end of the nineteenth century, after two hundred years of brutal and unnecessary assault on children's bodies and psyches just for touching themselves. Despite the reformers efforts, progress was slow and of little effect. *infibulation: extreme female genital mutilation involving complete cutting away of the clitoris and most of the labia majora, followed by stitching to close up most of the vagina. (326)

During the nineteenth century reformers tried to bring the rest of society into the fight against child sexual abuse by legislation designed to prevent outright battering and sexual abuse of children, which of course still continued in the majority of families. However, those who tried to oppose buggering and beating boys in schools were opposed by parents who claimed that, "It didn't hurt us, and it won't hurt them either." Those who tried to pass child labor legislation to reduce horrendous working conditions and hours were labeled Communists, and those who thought that children should be reared with kindness were considered impractical visionaries.

This evolution of parent-child relations, according to Lloyd deMause, is a source of historical change, lying in the ability of present and future generations of parents to face up to their own childhood traumas and work through their anxieties in a slightly better way than has been done in the past. It is in this sense, says deMause, that history is like psychotherapy, which also heals through revisiting one's childhood traumas and dealing with past anxieties. If the parent, historically the mother, is given even the slightest support by society, the evolution of child rearing progresses to a higher level. With that, changes in past behavior are formed and history begins to move in new, innovative directions.

What's Happening Today:

The time of denying that sexual seduction is extremely traumatic for children appears to have ended. Studies on the effects of childhood sexual abuse reveal that the damage done is far more severe than anyone imagined. The flood of books and articles documenting the emotional problems of victims both in childhood and in later life has to be read in detail to appreciate the profound sense of betrayal and the terrifying fears felt by children who have been molested. Even single incidents have the power to permanently ravage the lives of victims. (326)

In recent decades, it has become acceptable to defend children against sexual attack; but only in the most *psychogenically advanced nations have the rates of sexual abuse of children dropped to only half of the children born. The tradition of pederasty continues to the present day in certain areas of Afghanistan, the Middle East, North Africa, and Melanesia. *psychogenic: originating in the mind or in mental or emotional conflict.

AMERICA: In America the most accurate scientific studies, based on lengthy interviews, report that 30% of men and 40% of women remember having been sexually molested during childhood (molestation being defined as actual genital contact, not just exposure). About half of these are reports of incest involve family members. The other half were with non-family members. In at least 80% of the cases, it was a caretaker. These experiences of seduction are not just pieced together from fragmented memories, but are remembered in detail and not likely to have been fantasies. They usually took place over an extended period and have been confirmed by follow-up reliability studies in 83% of the cases. The seductions occurred at much earlier ages than had been previously assumed, with 81% occurring before puberty and an astonishing 42% with children under the age of seven. (326)

"As high as these rates of abuse seem," says deMause, "they represent only a portion of the actual occurrences of sexual molestation because those interviewed do not include populations that have been shown to have extremely high rates of molestation, such as criminals, prostitutes, juveniles in shelters, people with psychotic disorders, etc.; but also because only conscious memories were counted, and the earliest seductions of children are almost never remembered except during psychotherapy. Adjusting statistically for what is known about these additional factors, I have concluded," says deMause, "that the real sexual abuse rate for America is 60% for girls and 45% for boys, about half of these directly incestuous."

NEW GUINEA: Boys in New Guinea cultures today are so traumatized by the early erotic experiences of neglect and assaults on their bodies that they need to prove their masculinity when they grow up and become fierce warriors and cannibals, with a third of them dying in raids and wars. In fact, says deMause, "I have found that rather than the incest taboo being universal, as anthropologists claim, it is incest itself that has been universal for most children in most cultures in most times. A childhood free from sexual abuse is in fact a very recent historical achievement, limited to a few fortunate children in a few modern nations." (326)

LATIN AMERICA: In Latin America, studies show a great deal of family sexual activity and widespread pederasty as part of macho masculine activity, though reliable statistics of incidence are not yet available. (326)

PUERTO RICO: In Puerto Rico, Oscar Lewis found danger of seduction by stepfathers and sexual rivalry between sisters as well as between mother and daughters. Male children are being erotically stimulated by their mothers and by other members of the family. E.N. Padilla reported parents and others regularly masturbating their infants and Romon Frendandez-Marina discovered that Puerto Rican fathers often masturbate their boys to show off their maleness to friends. (326)

MEXICO: In Mexico, J.M. Carrier reported that a large number of Mexican men have sexual relations with nephews, cousins, or neighbors who are between the ages of 6 and 9. (326)

EUROPE: European countries are about two decades behind the U.S. in interview techniques, and since they still use written questionnaires, they are only able to report sexual abuse rates of less than one percent. Most European researchers do not attempt to examine statistical frequency of sexual abuse, though some, such as a series of studies on Scandinavian incest, report considerable public acceptance of incest in some rural areas. (326)

Even though there are no reliable statistics for most European countries, a recent series of books, articles, and telephone hotline services have begun to uncover widespread sexual molestation. A recent BBC Child Watch program asked its female listeners, a large though biased sample group, if they remembered having experienced sexual molestation. Of the 2,530 responses, 83% remembered someone touching their genitals and 62% of the full sample group recalled actual intercourse.

GERMANY: The most thorough European study to date is a recent, unpublished German survey by the **Iinstitut fuer Kindheit.** For the first time, someone dared to ask the children themselves about their sexual experiences. Lloyd deMause reports that he has been told that these researchers found an 80% childhood sexual molestation rate among Berlin school children. The exact details of this study will certainly be revealing. It may be that direct questioning of children rather than relying on retrospective memory may produce even higher actual incidence rates of sexual molestation than our 60% and 45% estimates for the United States. Official estimates of German children sexually abused and raped each year now number over 300,000 and sexual abuse hot lines are becoming more widespread. (236)

The **SOS-infanzia** hotlines in Germany, which were initially very much supported by the public, have begun to reveal widespread pedophile networks, baby prostitution, Boy and Girl Scout leader molestation, as well as the widespread sexual abuse of children living in famine areas, with a particular emphasis on the pederasty of boys. (326)

Obviously, despite the achievement of some empathic, understanding parents of today, most of humankind still has a long way to go to get past the severe abuse of children and give them the love and respect they deserve. The presence of wide spread, severe child abuse and neglect in world history makes even the most horrific descriptions found in present-day clinical and child advocacy reports seem limited in comparison. It is no wonder that historians have chosen to hide, deny and whitewash the truth of child sexual abuse, in order to avoid confronting the parental holocaust that has been the central cause of violence and misery throughout history.

"No matter what anxieties a person has," says Lloyd deMause, "there are always children around for adults to use in relieving tension. The evolution of childhood experiences going from incest to love, and from abuse to compassion, and understanding has been a slow, uneven path, but one whose progressive direction is, I think, unmistakable."

What could possibly be the feelings inside a mother or father when they begin to meditate on the devastating truth that their precious child has somehow fallen victim to such a hideous crime? Can anyone even imagine the feelings of helplessness, guilt, anger, and sorrow?

It is our hope that each person who reads this book will gain the necessary knowledge with which to protect children and teach them their right to live and grow untouched by anyone with ill intent in their heart and mind.

The poem below was conceived out of the pain and suffering of a father of two young boys who were sexually molested by their youth pastor.

TO MY BELOVED SONS

Where is that look of a child's innocence
I used to see in your eyes?
And where is that look of confidence
that had no need of telling lies?

Who has tried taking your soul away
and caused many to cast you out?

Who has stolen your youth today
and enslaved you to fear and doubt?

How did it all happen without my knowing;
how much was I to blame?
How did I miss all your pain that was growing
and your feelings of suffering and shame?

When was the moment that I should have guessed
that something was very wrong?
When were the times that I should have pressed
instead of accepting your story for so long?

Now that the time for blaming has passed,
it's time we begin life anew,
And build our lives on the things that last
like the love I have for both of you.

~ Dad

NOTE: In 1982, the parents of these two young boys reported the youth pastor who molested their children and several other little boys. No one else was willing to press charges. Being the only ones to do so, they were asked to leave their church. Later, when the neighbors read about the incident in the newspapers, picket signs were placed in their front yard that read: We don't want your little perverts in our neighborhood.

When the mother of these boys read *The Friendly Enemy,* she begged me to get this information out to everyone saying, "If only I had read this book, I may have been able to prevent this nightmare from taking place." One month later, she died; they say, from a broken heart.

The author of the following heart-wrenching reflective, sorrowful poem is a woman who was sexually molested as a child. She wrote this to her four children, all of whom were sexually molested by a family friend.

THE CHILD INSIDE

This child inside me felt it was wrong, dirty, and ugly—a child of shame. Thirty years this inward child, now a mother, made a pact to never let this happen to her children whom she holds so dear.

Keeping the secret inside her made her blind to the demon as it attacked her very own children she so carefully tried to protect.

As she took the blame upon herself, the child she once was began to emerge. The shame! The guilt! The horror!

"How could this happen? Why was I so blind? Oh, God!" she cries. "Oh, their pain!" She feels her children's pain; pain so deep in the heart it hurts.

She can literally clutch the pain; hold it in her hands, her pain, and the pain of her children, raising it to God with pleadings of help. "Oh, God, please fix their hearts, the deep dark pain. It hurts so badly," she cries, as she feels it hurting once again. "Oh, God, help me."

God answers her and enters her presence as she, in so much pain, falls exhaustedly into His arms.

As the child inside surfaces, she gives everything to Him. For the child inside, innocence was violated and swept away.

Then the shameful secret. The child inside had to lock it away—deep down in a heart of severe pain, like a criminal, instead of the victim. The pain intensifies, will it ever leave? Not until it is released. She is angry now! She will not allow these feelings to happen to her children. They will not be violated any more and carry this demon as she did.

The child inside her cries out, desperate for help. But the cries are so often swept away and the images of the monsters, the molesters, only increase.

The time to fix it is now; the time to stop it is now! To fix it we must face it; facing it disgraces it, and then demolishes it.

Love always Mom

SOURCES

(1) Lonnie Bristow, M.D., President, American Medical Association, November 1995, raptorware.com

(2) Sorensen & Snow, 1991, raptorware.com

(3) Crimes Against Children Research Center projections based on estimates from, Child Maltreatment (1990-2000).Washington, DC: U.S. Department of Health and Human Services, Children's Bureau, ndaa.org/pdf/ncpca_statistics.pdf

(4) National Center for Juvenile Justice, July 2000, U.S. Department of Justice, Office of Justice Programs, childluresprevention.com/research/molester.asp

(5) National Institute of Mental Health, Department of Justice reports

(6) American Humane, Besharov, D. J., 1994. Responding to Child Sexual Abuse: The Need for a Balanced Approach. In R .E. Behrman (Ed.), The Future of Children (Vols. 3–4, pp. 135–155). Los Altos, CA: The Center for the Future of Children, The David and Lucile Packard Foundation

(7) Occult and Violent Ritual Crime Research Center, Deviant Behavior Research Center.url

(8) The Columbia Electronic Encyclopedia, Sixth Edition

(9) Lolita, Merriam-Webster's 11th Collegiate Dictionary

(10) Bernard 1975, 1982; Lautmann, 1994

(11) Long-Term Consequences of Childhood Sexual Abuse by Gender of Victim. Volume 28, Issue 5; The American Journal of Preventive Medicine, June 2005

(12) CCPCA 1992, raptorware.com/facts/offendermyths

(13) Americanhumane.org/site/PageServer?pagename=nr_fact_sheets_childsexabuseAmerican

(14) American Humane, Trocme & Wolfe, 2001p.13, therapistfinder.net/Child-Abuse/Sexual-Abuse-Incest-Statistics.html

(15) Hazelwood 4, Dark Dreams: A Legendary FBI Profiler Examines Homicide and the Criminal Mind, St. Martins True Crime Library Series, October 2002

(16) Burgess & GrothLonnie, Bristow, M.D., President, American Medical Association, November 1995, raptorware.com

(17) Kinsey-Report, Lautmann, Brongersma, Groth, November 2006

(18) The Occult and Violent Ritual Crimes Research Center, signatureprofilingassociates.com/sexualoffender

(19) Abel, G. G., Mittleman, M. S., & Becker, J. V. 1985, Sex offenders: Results of assessment and recommendations for treatment. In M. H. Ben-Aron, S. J. Hucker, & C. D. Webster (Eds.), Clinical criminology: The Assessment and Treatment of Criminal Behavior (pp. 207-220). Toronto, Canada: M & M Graphics, answers.com/topic/pedophilia#wp-_note-15

(20) Burgess & Groth, Lonnie, Bristow, M.D., President, American Medical Association, November 1995 raptorware.com

(21) Groth, AN, Oliveri, F 1989. Understanding sexual abuse behavior and differentiating among sexual abusers. In S. Sgroi (Ed.), Vulnerable Populations, (Vol. 2, pp. 309-327). Lexington, MA: Lexington Books, Jenny C, Roesler TA, Poyer KL 1994, child-abuse-effects.com/index.html

(22) The Abel and Harlow Stop Child Molestation Study, page 125, 2002

(23) The Abel and Harlow Stop Child Molestation Study, Alfred Kinsey, William Pomeroy, and Clyde Martin,
Sexual behavior in the Human Male, Philadelphia and London: W.B. Saunders Company, 1948: page 654

(24) Gene G. Abel and Candice A. Osborn, The Paraphilias, in Oxford Textbook of Psychiatry, Eds. M.G. Gelder, J.J. Lopez-Lbor and N.C. Andreason, Oxford University Press 2000

(25) Concerned Women for America, Homosexual Behavior & Pedophilia, By Frank V. York and Robert H. Knight, us2000.org/cfmc/Pedophilia.pdf

(26) Occult and Violent Ritual Crime Research Center Groth, A.N. 1978, Patterns of Sexual Assault Against Children and Adolescents, pp. 3-24 in A. Burgess, A.N. Groth, L. Hostrom & S. Sgroi (Eds.) Sexual Assault of Children and Adolescents. Lexington, MA: Lexington Books, Douglas et al 227-229, Griod 167 Hazelwood 1987, faculty.ncwc.edu/TOConnor/psy/psylect09.htm

(27) American Life League Provided, Chapter 137: Pornography and Its Connection to Child Molesters, uiowa.edu/policult/politick/Smithson/contents.htm

(28) The United Nations Children's Fund, di-ve.com/dive/portal/

(29) Julia Whealin, Ph.D. National Center for PTSD, raptorware.com/facts/offendermyths

(30) Ken Wooden, Sexual Assault of Young Children as Reported to Law Enforcement: Victim, Incident, and Offender Characteristics, by Howard N. Snyder, Ph.D.; National Center for Juvenile Justice, July 2000, U.S. Department of Justice, Office of Justice Programs, childluresprevention.com/research/molester.asp

(31) Focus Adolescent Services, therapistfinder.net/Child-Abuse/Sexual-Abuse-Incest-Statistics.html

(32) Bureau of Justice Statistics, U.S. Department of Justice, ojp.usdoj.gov/bjs

(33) American Psychological Association, PsyNet 2001, raptorware.com

(34) CCPCA, Lonnie Bristow, M.D., President, American Medical Association, November 1995, Gregory M. Weber, Grooming Children for Sexual Molestation, The Zero - The Official Website of Andrew Vachss: March 2, 2007, raptorware.com/facts/offendermyths, vachss.com/guest_dispatches/grier_weeks.html

(35) The Guildford Press, New York, 1986

(36) Timothy W. Maier, Suffer the Children, Insight on the News: November 24, 1997, p.11

(37) Personal interviews with sexually abused children, adults who were abused as children, child/adolescent psychiatrists and licensed counselors, 1983- 2003

(38) Tsai & Wagner 1984, raptorware.com/facts/offendermyths

(39) Finkelhor, et al., 1990 the Secret Chapter, Department of Justice. 2000, Juvenile Offenders and Victims: 1999 National Report, Washington, D.C.: U.S. Department of Justice, Office of Juvenile Justice and Delinquency Prevention (OJJDP), ncjrs.org/html/ojjdp/nationalreport99/toc.html U.S., raptorware.com/facts/offendermyths

(40) Johnson and Shrier, 1987, Canadian Children's Rights Council, crin.org/themes/

(41) Knopp and Lackey 1987

(42) Fritz, et al., 1981, Canadian Children's Rights Council, crin.org/themes/

(43) Fromuth and Burkhart, 1987, 1989; Seidner and Calhoun, 1984, Canadian Children's Rights Council, crin.org/themes/

(44) Bell, et al. 1981, Risin and Koss, 1987, Knopp, Lackey 1987, Canadian Children's Rights Council, crin.org/themes/

(45) Clark, Tani Leigh Firkins and Rebecca Ann Boicelli., Canadian Children's Rights Council, crin.org/themes/

(46) Pet/Mayer 1992 Rovich and Templer 1984, Groth, 1979, Briere and Smilianich, 1993, Canadian Children's Rights Council, crin.org/themes/,

(47) The American Journal of Preventive Medicine Long-Term Consequences of Childhood Sexual Abuse by Gender of Victim. Volume 28, Issue 5; The American Journal of Preventive Medicine. June 2005

(48) Kaufman et al., 1995, p. 30, 88%, Rudin, et al., 1995, p. 969, Canadian Children's Rights Council, crin.org/themes/

(49) Hunter et al., 1993; Mathews, Matthews and Speltz, 1989, Canadian Children's Rights Council, crin.org/themes/

(50) Lackey, 1987, Allen, 1990; Kaufman et al. 1995, Canadian Children's Rights Council, crin.org/themes/

(51) Hunter et al., 1993, Johnson, 1989; Knopp, Canadian Children's Rights Council, crin.org/themes/

(52) Linda Labelle, Focus Adolescent Services, focusas.com/Mail.html,

(53) Faller, 1987; Kaufman, et al., 1995; McCarty, 1986.Mayer, 1992, crin.org/themes/

(54) Rudin, et al.,1995, p.965, Canadian Children's Rights Council, crin.org/themes/

(55) Canadian Children's Rights Council, crin.org/themes/

(56) Rudin, et al., 1995, p. 969, Canadian Children's Rights Council, crin.org/themes/

(57) The Center for Sex Offender Management, Barbaree, Hudson and Seto, 1993, csom.org/pubs/mythsfacts.html

(58) The Center for Sex Offender Management, Sickmund, Snyder, Poe-Yamagata, 1997, Focus Adolescent Services, csom.org/pubs/mythsfacts.html, therapistfinder.net/Child-Abuse/Sexual-Abuse-Incest-Statistics.html

(59) Joyce F. Lakey, Kahn and Lafond 1988,concurred, findarticles.com/p/articles/

(60) Snyder, 2000, p. 8

(61) Cantell, 1995, p. 91, csom.org/pubs/mythstacts.html

(62) The Center for Sex Offender Management, Becker and Murphy, 1998, csom.org/pubs/mythsfacts.html

(63) The Center for Sex Offender Management, Hunter and Figueredo, in press, csom.org/pubs/mythsfacts.html

(64) Cavanagh Johnson, 1993, p. 74; Araji, 1997, csom.org/pubs/mythsfacts.html

(65) Lonnie Bristow, M.D., President, American Medical Association, November 1995, csom.org/pubs/mythsfacts.html, raptorware.com/facts/offendermyths

(66) Kikuchi, 1995, p. 111

(67) Joyce F. Lakey, Kahn and Lafond, 1988, concurred, Fehrenbach, et al., 1986; Johnson, 1988; Berliner, 1995, findarticles.com/p/articles/

(68) canadiancrc.com/female_sexual_predators_awareness.htm

(69) Johnson & Friend, 1995, p. 55, Reprinted with permission from Children's Services Practice Notes, vol. 7, no. 2, practicenotes.org or its equivalent

(70) Jessie M. Richards, MSW, personal interview, 2007

(71) The Center for Sex Offender Management, ssw.unc.edu/fcrp/cspn/vol7_no2.htm

(72) Ryan, 2000, practicenotes.org or its equivalent

(73) Patricia D. McClendon, MSSW candidate, November 23, 1991 report, Incest/Sexual Abuse of Children Blume, 1990, p. 4, Courtois, 1988, p. 12, clinicalsocialwork.com/incest.html

(74) Hayes, 1990, National Center for Victims of Crime, ncvc.org/ncvc/main

(75) Wiehe, 1998, p. 21, Darlene Barriere, Violence & Abuse Prevention Educator, Author: On My Own Terms, A Memoir, Available in PDF e-book format: child-abuse-effects.com/child-abuse-story.html

(76) Vanderbilt, 1992, ncvc.org/ncvc/main

(77) Matsakis, 1991, ncvc.org/ncvc/main

(78) Vanderbilt, 1992, ncvc.org/ncvc/main

(79) Gene G. Able M.D., Board-Certified psychiatrist, Clinical Professor of Psychiatry, Seminar GATSA (Georgia Association for the Treatment of Sexual Abusers), National Center for Victims of Crime, ncvc.org/ncvc/main

(80) Patricia D. McClendon, MSSW candidate, November 23, 1991 report, Incest/Sexual Abuse of Children, Weiner, 1962, Cormier, et. al.,1962, Molnar and Cameron, 1975, clinicalsocialwork.com/incest.html, Incest syndromes... linkinghub.elsevier.com/retrieve/pii/0272735881900040

(81) Patricia D. McClendon, MSSW candidate, November 23, 1991 report, Incest/Sexual Abuse of Children, Browning and Boatman, 1977, Finkelhor, 1979, p. 26, Sexually Victimized Children. The Free Press a division of Macmillan Publishing Co., Inc., New York, NY,clinicalsocialwork.com/incest.html

(82) Patricia D. McClendon, MSSW candidate, November 23, 1991 report, Incest/Sexual Abuse of Children, Calof, 1988, pgs. 3-4, Adult Survivors of Incest and Child Abuse, Part One: The Family Inside the Adult Child in Family Therapy Today, p. 1-5. Vol. No. 3, Issue No. 9, Van Nuys, CA: P. M., Inc., clinicalsocialwork.com/incest.html

(83) Patricia D. McClendon, MSSW candidate, November 23, 1991 report, Incest/Sexual Abuse of Children, Russell, 1986, p. 268, The Secret Trauma - Incest in the Lives of Girls and Women. New York, NY: Basic Books, Inc., clinicalsocialwork.com/incest.html

(84) Rape in America: A Report to the Nation, Arlington, VA: National Center for Victims of Crime and Crime Victims Research and Treatment Center. Vanderbilt, Heidi, 1992, February, "Incest: A Chilling Report" Lears, p. 49-77

(85) Matsakis, 1991, 2004 © National Center for Victims of Crime,.ncvc.org/ncvc/main

(86) Vanderbilt, 1992, 2004 © National Center for Victims of Crime, ncvc.org/ncvc/main

(87) Journal of the American Academy of Psychiatry and the Law Outline, Philip Firestone, PhD, Kristopher L. Dixon, BA, Kevin L. Nunes, PhD and John M. Bradford, MD, Williams LM, Finkelhor D: The Characteristics Of Incestuous Fathers: A Review Of Recent Studies, in Handbook of Sexual Assault: Issues, Theories, and Treatment of the Offender. Edited by Marshall WL, Laws DR, Barbaree HE. New York: Plenum Press, 1990, pp 231–55

(88) Hare RD: Journal of the American Academy of Psychiatry and the Law Outline, Philip Firestone, PhD, Kristopher L. Dixon, BA, Kevin L. Nunes, PhD and John M. Bradford, MD, Manual for the Revised Psychopathy Checklist. Toronto, Ontario, Canada: Multi-Health Systems, 1991, A Comparison of Incest Offenders Based on Victim Age, jaapl.org/cgi/content/full/33/2/223

(89) The DSFI: A Multi-Dimensional Measure Of Sexual Functioning, J Sex Marital Ther. 5:244–81, 1979 Medline

(90) Gibbens TCN, Soothill K, Way CK: Sibling And Parent-Child Incest Offenders, Br J Criminol 18:40–52, 1978

(91) Hanson KR, Slater S: Reactions To Motivational Accounts Of Child Molesters, J Child Sex Abuse 2:43–59, 1988, jaapl.org/cgi/content/full/33/2/223

(92) Matsakis, 1991, National Center for Victims of Crime, ncvc.org/ncvc/main

(93) U.S. Department of Justice, National Center for Juvenile Justice, Washington, D.C., ojp.usdoj.gov/bjs/pub/pdf/saycrle.pdf

(94) Department of Health and Human Services, Administration for Children and Families, Child Maltreatment, 1995, ojp.usdoj.gov/bjs/pub/pdf/saycrle.pdf

(95) Full Report of the Prevalence, Incidence, and Consequences of Violence Against Women: Findings from the National Violence Against Women Survey, (NCJRS) 2000, ncjrs.org/pdffiles1/nij/183781.pdf

(96) Stephen A. Wonderlich, M.D., et al, University of North Dakota School of Medicine and Health Sciences in Fargo, Journal of the American Academy of Child and Adolescent Psychiatry 2000; 391277-1283, Kenneth S. Kendler, M.D., et al, Medical College of Virginia Commonwealth University, Archives of General Psychiatry 2000; 57:953-959, khofer@medicine.nodak.edu

(97) Darlene Barriere, Rainy, Stevens-Simon and Kaplan, Blinn-Pike, et al., 2002, p. 1[9], An Analysis of an Intervention for Pregnant and Parenting Adolescents, Child and Adolescent Social Work Journal, child-abuse-effects.com/index.html

(98) Darlene Barriere, Ford, Schindler, & Medway, 2001, pp.25-44[8], School Professionals' Attributions Of Blame For Child Sexual Abuse, Journal of School Psychology, 39(1), child-abuse- effects.com/index.html

(99) Darlene Barriere, Societal Biases of Female Victims of Sexual Abuse, child-abuse-effects.com/index.html

(100) Darlene Barriere, Societal Biases of Female Victims of Sexual Abuse, Gibson & Leitenberg, 2000, pp. 1115-1125[5], Child Sexual Abuse Prevention Programs: Do They Decrease The Occurrence Of Child Sexual Abuse? Child Abuse and Neglect, 24(9), 1115-1125, child-abuse-effects.com/index.html

(101) Darlene Barriere, Holmes, W, Slap, G 1998, Sexual Abuse Of Boys: Definition, Prevalence, Correlates, Sequelae, And Management, Journal of the American Medical Association, 280:1855-1862, child-abuse-effects.com/index.html

(102) Lisak, D, Hopper, J, Song, P 1996, Factors In The Cycle Of Violence: Gender Rigidity and Emotional Constriction, Journal of Traumatic Stress, 9: 721-743, Finkelhor D, Hotaling G, Lewis IA, Smith C. 1990, Sexual Abuse In A National Survey of Adult Men and Women: Prevalence, Characteristics, and Risk Factors, Child Abuse and Neglect, 19:557-68 Darlene Barriere, child-abuse-effects.com/index.html

(103) Darlene Barriere, Lisak, D, Hopper, J, Song, P 1996, Factors in the Cycle of Violence: Gender Rigidity and Emotional Constriction, Journal of Traumatic Stress, 9: 721-743, child-abuse-effects.com/index.html

(104) NIS-funded by National Center on Child Abuse and Neglect, 1981 and 1988, child-abuse-effects.com/index.html

(105) US Dept. of Health and Human Resources, child-abuse-effects.com/index.html

(106) Watkins, B. & Bentovim, A.,1992, The Sexual Abuse of Male Children and Adolescents: A Review of Current Research, Journal of Clinical Psychology & Psychiatry, 33(10), 197-248, 1995 Andrews University, Berrien Springs, MI, sasian.org/papers/boysngirls.htm?ref=dopdolu.net

(107) MSNBC News, December 1998, Dr. William C. Holmes of the University of Pennsylvania School of Medicine, Darlene Barriere, prevent-abuse-now-.com/stats, child-abuse-effects.com/index.html

(108) Gartner, RB 1999, Betrayed as Boys: Psychodynamic Treatment of Sexually Abused Men, New York: Guilford Press, Darlene Barriere, child-abuse-effects.com/index.html

(109) Watkins, B. & Bentovim, A. 1992, The Sexual Abuse of Male Children and Adolescents: A Review of Current Research. Journal of Clinical Psychology & Psychiatry, 33(10), 197-248. 1995 Andrews University, Berrien Springs, MI, sasian.org/papers/boysngirls.htm?ref=dopdolu.net

(110) Ken Singer, LCSW, sasian.org/papers/char.htm, ken.singer@comcast.net

(111) Darlene Barriere, National Resource Center on Child Sexual Abuse, 1992. Adapted from The McCreary Centre Society, 1993, child-abuse-effects.com/sexual-abuse-victims-with-disability.html

(112) Clearinghouse on Family Violence, phac-aspc.gc.ca/ncfv-cnivf/familyviolence/html/nfntsdisabl_e.html

(113) cbsnews.com/stories/2006/10/18/fyi/main2102522.shtml?source=RSS&attr=_2102522

(114) Bcnedict and Susan Zuravin, Factors Associated With Child Maltreatment by Family Foster Care Providers, Baltimore: Johns Hopkins University School of Hygiene and Public Health, June 30, 1992, charts, pp. 28, 30, nccpr.org/newissues/1.html

(115) David Fanshel, et. al., Foster Children in a Life Course Perspective, New York: Columbia University Press, 1990, p. 90. How Are The Children Doing? Assessing Youth Outcomes in Family Foster Care, Seattle: Casey Family Program, 1998, nccpr.org/newissues/1.html

(116) Department of Health and Human Services, Administration on Children, Youth and Families 1999, Child Maltreatment 1997: Reports from the States to the National Child Abuse and Neglect Data System, Washington, D.C.: U.S. Government Printing Office, casanet.org/library/abuse/abuse-stats98.htm#_ednref10

(117) Kinship Care Specialist, Wisconsin Department of Health and Family Services, dhfs.wisconsin.gov/Children/Kinship/

(118) NSPCC, 1992; Bloom, 1992; Nunno and Rindfleisch, 1991, Finkelhor, Williams and Burns, 1988; Margolin, 1991, Roberts, 1986, p. 10, Andrew Kendrick, personal.strath.ac.uk/andrew.kendrick/tayfosas.htm

(119) Rosenthal, et al 1991, personal.strath.ac.uk/andrew.kendrick/tayfosas.htm

(120) personal.strath.ac.uk/andrew.kendrick/tayfosas.htm

(121) Jessie M. Richards MSW, Georgia Department of Juvenile Justice, Criminal Justice Specialist, a Certified Forensic counselor and a Human Services provider, authored many educational and training programs, personal interview 2001

(122) Children's Rights, Inc., Expert Research Report Finds Children Still Unsafe in Fulton and Dekalb Foster Care, Press release, November 5, 2004, nccpr.org/newissues/1.html

(123) Macaskill, 1991, p. 71, Roberts, 1986, 1989, and 1993, and Batty,1991, Macaskill, 1991, p. 86, personal.strath.ac.uk/andrew.kendrick/tayfosas.htm

(124) Personal communication, 1982, Russell, 1984, p. 267, Sexual Exploitation: Rape, Child Sexual Abuse and Workplace Harassment, Sage Publications, Newbury Park, personal.strath.ac.uk/andrew.kendrick/tayfosas.htm

(125) McFadden and Ryan, 1991, p. 215, Maclean, 1989; Rhodes, 1993; Robinson, 1991, personal.strath.ac.uk/andrew.kendrick/tayfosas.htm

(126) Carbino, 1992, pp. 502 - 504

(127) Carbino, 1992, p. 506, personal.strath.ac.uk/andrew.kendrick/tayfosas.htm

(128) William Moyer, Binghamton Press & Sun-Bulletin, May 5, 2007, nyclergyabuse.com/documents/Rochester/John%20Steger-9.pdf

(129) Katherine Van Wormer, MSSW, PhD, Family Safety – How Social Workers Help, About Priest/Clergy, Sexual Abuse, Trauma and Healing, helpstartshere.org/Default.aspx?PageID=1216

(130) CrusadersAgainstClergyAbuse.com and SnapNetwork.org

(131) RestorativeJustice.org

(132) Katherine Van Wormer, MSSW, PhD, Family Safety – How Social Workers Help, About Priest/Clergy Sexual Abuse, Trauma and Healing, Katherine van Wormer is a professor of social work at the University of Northern Iowa and the author of Human Behavior and the Social Environment, Micro Level, 2007, helpstartshere.org/Default.aspx?PageID=1216

(133) Barbara Blaine, Founder SNAP, snapnetwork.org/news/baptistindex.htm

(134) Reported by J. Michael Parker, Express-News, USA, 4th June 1998 Clare Pascoe, clergyabuseaustralia.org/stats.htm

(135) Clare Pascoe, clergyabuseaustralia.org/stats.htm

(136) SMH 20/2/2002, Clare Pascoe, clergyabuseaustralia.org/stats.htm

(137) Clare Pascoe, clergyabuseaustralia.org/stats.htm, geocities.com/Athens/Agora/2213/pedoph.html

(138) The Awareness Center, Inc., The Jewish Coalition Against Sexual Abuse/Assault, jewishsurvivors.blogspot.com/

(139) Donalda Shepardson, President/Founder, Creating Safer Havens, Donalda Shepardson, President/Founder, creatingsaferhavens.com/contact.html

(140) Cycle of Sexual Abuse: Research Inconclusive About Whether Child Victims Become Adult Abusers GFD-96-178, September 13, 1996, PDF GAO United States General Accounting Office, Washington, D.C. 20548, General Government Division B-272972, gao.gov/archive/1996/gg96178.pdf

(141) The Royal College of Psychiatrists, M. GLASSER (deceased), A study titled, Cycle of Child Sexual Abuse: Links Between Being a Victim and Becoming a Perpetrator, 2001

(142) The National Center for Victims of Crime in Washington, DC, Widom, 1992, National Institute of Justice, Cathy Spatz Widom, NIJ Research in Brief, March 1995, ncvc.org/ncvc/main.aspx?dbName=DocumentViewer&DocumentID=32315#7

(143) Seghorn, T. K., Prentky, R. A. & Boucher, R. J. 1987, Childhood Sexual Abuse in the Lives of Sexually Aggressive Offenders, Journal of the American Academy of Child and Adolescent Psychiatry, 26, 262-267

(144) The British Journal of Psychiatr: Invited Commentaries on the Cycle of Child Sexual Abuse—Links Between Being a Victim and Becoming a Perpetrator, by M Cannon –MRCPsych, 2001, bjp.rcpsych.org/cgi/content/full/179/6/495

(145) Prendergast, W. 1993, In The Merry-Go-Round of Sexual Abuse: Identifying and Treating Survivors (ed. W. Prendergast), New York: Haworth Press, ncvc.org/ncvc/main.aspx?dbName=DocumentViewer&DocumentID=32315#7

(146) (American Humane Association Children's Division, 1993, National Center for Victims of Crime, ncvc.org/ncvc/main.aspx?dbName=DocumentViewer&DocumentID=32315#7

(147) Whitlock & Gillman 1989, raptorware.com/facts/impact.html

(148) American Psychological Association, PsycNet 2001, apa.org/releases/sexabuse/

(149) Dr Bernadette Madrid Director, Child Protection Unit and Head, Section of Ambulatory Pediatrics, University of the Philippines Manila Philippine General Hospital Manila, Philippines. With inputs from: Ms Brandy McNeill, M.S. Certified Professional Counselor Community, and Family Services International Manila, Philippines

(150) Dr. Dianne Neumark-Sztainer, et al, University of Minneapolis, International Journal of Eating Disorders 2000; 28:249-258, aappolicy.aappublications.org/cgi/content/abstract/pediatrics;116/2/506

(151) Oldham, John M., and Michelle B. Riba (eds.) 1994, American Psychiatric Press Review of Psychiatry. American Psychiatric Press, Inc., Sexually Abused and Sexually Exploited Children and Youth, unescap.org/esid/hds/pubs/2208/M3.pdf

(152) MSNBC, Dr. William C. Holmes-University of Pennsylvania School of Medicine/News, December 1998, prevent-abuse-now.com/stats

(153) Victoria Polin, MA, ATR, LCPC and Gail Roy, MA, ATR, LCPC, E. Bass & L. Davis, 1988, The Courage to Heal: A Guide for Women Survivors of Child Sexual Abuse, New York: Harper & Row, theawarenesscenter.org/copingmechanisms.html,

(154) Center for Disease Control/ Seminar/GATSA Seminar 2001

(155) Dr Bernadette Madrid Director, Child Protection Unit and Head, Section of Ambulatory Pediatrics University of the Philippines Manila Philippine General Hospital Manila, Philippines., Groth 1979; Swanson & Biaggio 1985

(156) Courtois, C. A. & Watts, D. L.,1982, Counseling Adult Women Who Experienced Incest in Childhood or Adolescence, The Personnel and Guidance Journal, January, 275-279.

(157) Berlinger, L. & Barbieri, M. K., 1984, The Testimony of the Child Victim of Sexual Assault, Journal of Social Issues 40, (2), 125-137

(158) American Psychological Association, PsycNet 2001

(159) Gilbert, N. 1988, Teaching Children to Prevent Sexual Abuse, The Public Interest, 93, 3-15

(160) Sjöberg, R L; Lindblad, F, 2002, Delayed Disclosure and Disrupted Communication During Forensic Investigation of Child Sexual Abuse: A Study of 47 Corroborated Cases, Acta Paediatrica

(161) Tsai, M. & Wagner. N. N., 1978, Therapy Groups for Women Sexually Molested as Children, Archives of Sexual Behavior 1, 417-427

(162) Bureau of Justice Statistics 2000, Sexual Assault on Young Children as reported to Law Enforcement; US Department of Justice, Office of Justice programs, Washington DC, p.10, Page 3 Finkelhor, D., 1986, Sourcebook on Child Sexual Abuse; Sage, p.164-175, ojp.usdoj.gov/bjs

(163) Bureau of Justice Statistics 2000, Sexual Assault on Young Children as reported to Law Enforcement; US Department of Justice, Office of Justice programs, Washington DC, p.10, Finkelhor & Browne, 1986, American Psychological Association, PsycNet 2001, ojp.usdoj.gov/bjs

(164) Jessie M. Richards MSW, retired from the Department of Juvenile Justice for the State of Georgia with more than 30 years experience, holds a Masters of Social Work degree. She is a Criminal Justice Specialist, a Certified Forensic counselor, and a Human Services provider. Personal Interviews January-March 2000

(165) South Eastern Centre Against Sexual Assault, secasa.com.au/index.php/workers/17/48

(166) Elliot & Briere, 1994[1]; Sorenson & Snow, 1991[2]., 2000, Sexual Assault on Young Children as reported to Law Enforcement; US Department of Justice, Office of Justice programs, Washington DC, table one, p.2, ojp.usdoj.gov/bjs

(167) Sorenson and Snow, 1991[4], 2000, Sexual Assault on Young Children as reported to Law Enforcement; US Department of Justice, Office of Justice programs, Washington DC, table one, p.2, ojp.usdoj.gov/bjs

(168) Sexual Assault on Young Children as reported to Law Enforcement; US Department of Justice, Office of Justice programs, 2000, Washington DC, table one, p.2, ojp.usdoj.gov/bjs

(169) American Academy Of Pediatrics, Care of the Adolescent Sexual Assault Victim, Committee on Adolescence, with permission from Journal, Vol. 107, Page(s) 1476-1479, Copyright © 6 June 2001 by the AAP, aappolicy.aappublications.org/cgi/content/full/pediatrics;107/6/1476#B30B30

(170) Committee on Adolescence, 2000-2001, David W. Kaplan, MD,MPH, Chairperson American College of Obstetricians and Gynecologists Canadian Pediatric Society, Glen Pearson, MD, American Academy of Child and Adolescent Psychiatry

(171) The Journal of the American Dental Association (JADA), Chicago, September 16, 2005

(172) Personal interview with an adult victim of childhood sexual abuse, February 25, 2006

(173) ada.org/public/media/releases/0509_release03.asp

(174) American Psychological Association, PsycNet 2001

(175) Jody A. Gorran, Founder National Foundation to Prevent Child Sexual Abuse, Tsai and Wagner, 1978, fbifingerprintcheck.com/hiring.html

(176) Tsai, M. & Wagner. N. N., 1978, Therapy Groups for Women Sexually Molested as Children, Archives of Sexual Behavior 1, 417-427, Jody A. Gorran, Founder National Foundation to Prevent Child Sexual Abuse, fbifingerprintcheck.com/hiring.html

(177) The Personnel and Guidance Journal, January, 27, 1979, Jody A. Gorran, Founder National Foundation to Prevent Child Sexual Abuse, fbifingerprintcheck.com/hiring.htm

(178) Personal Interview, October 2003

(179) Finkelhor & Williams 1988, Nursery Crimes: Sexual Abuse In Day Care, Jody A. Gorran, Founder National Foundation to Prevent Child Sexual Abuse, fbifingerprintcheck.com/hiring.html

(180), Jody A. Gorran, Founder National Foundation to Prevent Child Sexual Abuse, Courtois & Watts, 1982; Tsai & Wagner, 1978, Courtois, C. A & Watts, D. L., 1982, Counseling Adult Women Who Experienced Incest in Childhood or Adolescence, The Personnel and Guidance Journal, January, 27, 1979, Tsai, M. & Wagner. N. N., 1978, Therapy Groups for Women Sexually Molested as Children, Archives of Sexual Behavior 1, 417-427, fbifingerprintcheck.com/hiring.html

(181) Maxine J. Stein, President/CEO, Stop It Now, stopitnow.com/comquest.html#Q11

(182) Shanghai Star, 2 May 2002, maruahsg.wordpress.com/2008/01/01/child-sex-and-prostitution-too-common-in-asean/

(183) Christine Dolan, The Global Coalition to End Human Trafficking Now

(184) Lutheran Immigration and Refugee Service, usccb.org/mrs/childtrafFAQ032406.pdf

(185) End Child Prostitution, Child Pornography, and Trafficking in Children for Sexual Purposes, Carol Smolenski, Founder, ecpat.net/eng/pdf/Trafficking_Report.pdf

(186) End Child Prostitution in Asian Tourism (ECPAT), The Commercial Sexual Exploitation of Children and the Work of ECPAT, Bangkok, 1996, National Commission for Women, Government of India: Societal Violence on Women and Children, Carol Smolenski, Founder, ecpatusa.org/child_prosti_us2.asp

(187) Lutheran Immigration and Refugee Service, Richard Estes and Neil Alan Weiner, The Commercial Sexual Exploitation of Children in the U.S., Canada, and Mexico, University of Pennsylvania School of Social Work, September 2001, usccb.org/mrs/childtrafFAQ032406.pdf

(188) O'Grady, R. Keynote Speech, World Congress Against Commercial Sexual Exploitation of Children. Stockholm, 1996, ecpatusa.org/child_prosti_us2.asp,

(189) O'Dea, P., Gender Exploitation and Violence: The Market in Women, Girls, and Sex in Nepal, A report for UNICEF, Kathmandu, 1993, ecpatusa.org/child_prosti_us2.asp

(190) Peter Piot, Executive Director, UNAIDS, End Child Prostitution, Child Pornography and Trafficking in Children for Sexual Purposes, thaiembdc.org/socials/childprs.htm

(191) CT Center for Prevention of Child Abuse, 1992

(192) Lim, L., The Sex Sector, International Labour Office, Geneva, 1998, O'Dea, P. Gender Exploitation and Violence: The market in Women, Girls, and Sex in Nepal, A report for UNICEF, Kathmandu, 1993, ecpatusa.org/child_prosti_us2.asp

(193) World Congress Against Commercial Sexual Exploitation of Children, Stockholm, 1996, ecpatusa.org/child_prosti_us2.asp

(194) Staebler, J. Tourism and Children in Prostitution, Paper submitted for the World Congress Against Commercial Sexual Exploitation of Children, Stockholm, 1996, End Child Prostitution in Asian Tourism (ECPAT), The Commercial Sexual Exploitation of Children and the Work of ECPAT,. Bangkok, 1996, ecpatusa.org/child_prosti_us2.asp

(195) Lim, L., The Sex Sector, International Labour Office, Geneva, 1998, ecpatusa.org/child_prosti_us2.asp

(196) Robinson, L., The Globalization of Female Child Prostitution: A Call for Reintegration and Recovery Measures via Article 39 of the United Nations Convention on the Rights of the Child, Indiana University School of Law, 1997, ecpatusa.org/child_prosti_us2.asp

(197) UNAIDS World AIDS Campaign with young people, Geneva, 1998, Belsey, M., Commercial Sexual Exploitation of Children: The Health and Psychosocial Dimensions, paper submitted by the World Health Organization for the World Congress Against Commercial Sexual Exploitation of Children, Stockholm,1996, ecpatusa.org/child_prosti_us2.asp

(198) Warburton, J. and de la Cruz, M., Prevention and Psycho-social Rehabilitation of Child Victims of Commercial Sexual Exploitation, paper submitted for the World Congress Against the Commercial Sexual Exploitation of Children, Stockholm, 1996, ecpatusa.org/child_prosti_us2.asp

(199) Piot, P., Address to the World Congress Against Commercial Sexual Exploitation of Children. Stockholm, 1996, 31. Pan American Health Organization (PAHO), AIDS: A Modern Epidemic, Washington, 1993, ecpatusa.org/child_prosti_us2.asp

(200) Population Services International, projects.psi.org/site/

(201) The International Organization for Adolescents, Alison Boak, President and Co-Founder, Katherine Kaufka, Executive Director, iofa.org/

(202) Press release, November 11, 2004, unicef.org/media/media_24067.html

(203) Shihata, I., The World Bank's Protection and Promotion of Human Rights, The World Bank. Washington, 1996, ecpatusa.org/child_prosti_us2.asp

(204) Muntarbhorn, V., International Perspectives and Child Prostitution in Asia, in US Department of Labor and Bureau of International Labor Affairs, Forced Labor: The Prostitution of Children, Washington, 1996, ecpatusa.org/child_prosti_us2.asp

(205) O'Briain, M., The International Legal Framework and Current National Legislative and Enforcement Responses, paper submitted for the World Congress Against Commercial Sexual Exploitation of Children, Stockholm, 1996, Fallon, P. and Tzannatos, Z., Child Labor: Issues and Directions for the World Bank, The World Bank, Washington, 1998, ecpatusa.org/child_prosti_us2.asp

(206) See World Congress Against Commercial Sexual Exploitation of Children, Stockholm, 1996, note 36, ecpatusa.org/child_prosti_us2.asp

(207) Calcetas-Santos, O., keynote speech, World Congress Against Commercial Sexual Exploitation of Children, Stockholm, 1996, Robinson, L. The Globalization of Female Child Prostitution: A Call for Reintegration and Recovery Measures via Article 39 of the United Nations Convention on the Rights of the Child, Indiana University School of Law, 1997, ecpatusa.org/child_prosti_us2.asp

(208) Funded by the Department of Health and Human Services/Office of Refugee Resettlement

(209) Sponsored by the Departments of Justice and Labor

(210) Public Communication Division, U.S. Department of State, Washington, DC 20520, Conference to Stop Child Trafficking: Modern-Day Slavery, Paula J. Dobriansky, Under Secretary of State for Global Affairs, Remarks to Trafficking in Persons Conference, June 1-3, 2003, state.gov/g/rls/rm/2003/21218.htm

(211) Lim, L.,The Sex Sector. International Labour Office, Geneva, 1998, World Congress Against Commercial Sexual Exploitation of Children, Stockholm, 1996, O'Briain, M., The International Legal Framework and Current National Legislative and Enforcement Responses, Muntarbhorn, V., ecpatusa.org/child_prosti_us2.

(212) National Coalition for the Protection of Children and Families guidestar.org/pqShowGsReport.do?partner=justgive&npoId=491957 about NCPCF

(213) Prof. Max Taylor, Combating Pedophile Information Networks in Europe, March 2003, mykidsafeinternet.com/internet-pornography-statistics.php

(214) Jessie M. Richards, MSW, personal interview, 2007

(215) Gow, Haven Bradford, Child Sex Abuse: America's Dirty Little Secret, MS Voices for Children, 3/2000, National Coalition for the Protection of Children and Families, nationalcoalition.org/resourcesservices/pornharm.html

(216) FBI studies, Det. Bill Dworin, Sexually Exploited Child Unit, LAPD, National Coalition for the Protection of Children and Families, guidestar.org/pqShowGsReport.do?partner=justgive&npoId=491957 about NCPCF

(217) Marshall, 1985

(218) Goldstein, Kant, and Hartman, 1973

(219) Lipkin & Carnes, 1970

(220) Dr. William Marshall, 1983

(221) Det. Bill Dworin, Sexually Exploited Child Unit, LAPD, National Coalition for the Protection of Children and Families, guidestar.org/pqShowGsReport.do?partner=justgive&npoId=491957 about NCPCF

(222) Reuters, 2003, My Kids Browser, mykidsbrowser.com/internet-pornography-statistics.php

(223) Dateline, January 2006, mykidsafeinternet.com/internet-pornography-statistics.php

(224) National Criminal Intelligence Service, 8/21/03, mykidsafeinternet.com/internet-pornography-statistics.php

(225) Donna Rice Hughes for Protect Kids, NJOV Study, 2007, Enough Is Enough, protectkids.com, enough.org/inside.php?id=2UXKJWRY8#

(226) Detective Chief Superintendent Keith Akerman, Telegraph.Co.UK, January 2002, mykidsafeinternet.com/internet-pornography-statistics.php

(227) Pew Study reported in JAMA, 2001, Pew Study reported in JAMA, 6/01, Online Victimization, NCMEC, June 2000, January 10, 2007, mykidsafeinternet.com/internet-pornography-statistics.php

(228) Online Victimization, NCMEC, June 2000, mykidsafeinternet.com/internet-pornography-statistics.php

(229) Internet Safety: Realistic Strategies & Messages for Kids Taking More and More Risks Online. December 21, 2005, Polly Klaas Foundation, February 17, 2006, pollyklaas.org/internet-safety/pkfsummary.pdf, mykidsafeinternet.com/internet-pornography-statistics.php

(230) mykidsafeinternet.com/internet-pornography-statistics.php

(231) Dr. Robert Weiss, Sexual Recovery Institute, Washington Times 1/26/2000, Donna Rice Hughes, protectkids.com/dangers/statsarchive.htm

(232) MSNBC/mit/Duquesne Study, Washington Times, 1/26/2000, Donna Rice Hughes, protectkids.com/dangers/statsarchive.htm

(233) N2H2, 9/23/03, Donna Rice Hughes, protectkids.com/dangers/statsarchive.htm

(234) Family Safe Media, January 10, 2006, familysafemedia.com/pornography_statistics.html, mykidsafeinternet.com/internet-pornography-statistics.php

(235) Child-Proofing on the Worldwide Web: A Survey of Adult Webservers, 2001, Jurimetrics, National Research Council Report, 2002, mykidsafeinternet.com/internet-pornography-statistics.php

(236) Nielsen/Net Ratings, Sept. 2003, mykidsafeinternet.com/internet-pornography-statistics.php, mykidsafeinternet.com/internet-pornography-statistics.php

(237) Family Safe Media, December 15, 2005, familysafemedia.com/pornography_statistics.html, mykidsafeinternet.com/internet-pornography-statistics.php

(238) IDC, a technology research firm, mykidsafeinternet.com/internet-pornography-statistics.php

(239) The Henry J. Kaiser Family Foundation Study, March 2005, Parents' Internet Monitoring: Study June 2005, Cox Communications, cox.com/TakeCharge/includes/docs/results.pdf

(240) Bryan-Low, Cassel and Pringle, David, Sex Cells: Wireless Operators Find That Racy Cellphone Video Drives Surge in Broadband Use, The Wall Street Journal, May 12, 2005, mykidsafeinternet.com/internet-pornography-statistics.php

(241) CampusKiss and Tell, University and College Sex Survey Released on February 14, 2006, February 17, 2006, campuskiss.com/default.aspx, mykidsafeinternet.com/internet-pornography-statistics.php, CampusKiss.com

(242) Internet Filter Review, blazinggrace.org/cms/bg/pornstats, safe families-blazing grace

(243) MSNBC/Stanford/Duquesne Study, 2000, Donna Rice Hughes, protectkids.com/dangers/statsarchive.htm

(244) Richardson, C.R., Resnick, P.J., Hansen, D.L., Derry, H.A., & Rideout, V.J., Does Pornography-Blocking Software Block Access to Health Information on the Internet, Journal of the American Medical Association, 2002, 288(22), (2887-2894), Parents' Internet Monitoring: Study, June 2005, Cox Communication,.cox.com/TakeCharge/includes/docs/results.pdf

(245) National Coalition for the Protection of Children and Families, guidestar.org/pqShowGsReport.do?partner=justgive&npoId=491957 about NCPCF

(246) Dangerous Access, 2001 Edition, David Burt, Donna Rice Hughes, protectkids.com/dangers/statsarchive.htm

(247) Donna Rice Hughes, Senate Hearing Testimony, 3/28/00, Donna Rice Hughes, protectkids.com/dangers/statsarchive.htm

(248) Protecting Kids Online, Editorial in The Washington Post, July 1, 2004, mykidsafeinternet.com/internet-pornography-statistics.php

(249) Arbitron New Media Study, October 1999, Donna Rice Hughes, protectkids.com/dangers/statsarchive.htm

(250) The Henry J. Kaiser Family Foundation Study, March 2005, Parents' Internet Monitoring: Study, June 2005, Cox Communications, cox.com/TakeCharge/includes/docs/results.pdf

(251) Telegraph.Co.UK, January 2002, Parents' Internet Monitoring: Study June 2005, Cox Communications, cox.com/TakeCharge/includes/docs/results.pdf

(252) Time/CNN Poll, 2000, Donna Rice Hughes, protectkids.com/dangers/statsarchive.htm

(253) WebSense, USA Today, 10/10-12/99

(254) Family PC Survey, 2000

(255) Yankelovich Partners Study, September 1999, Donna Rice Hughes, protectkids.com/dangers/statsarchive.htm

(256) Lenhart, Amanda and Madden, Mary,Teens, Privacy, and Online Social Networks, Pew Internet and American Life Project, April 18, 2007, pewinternet.org/pdf...privacy SNS Report Final.pdf

(257) Market Wire, November 6, 2006, i-SAFE Inc., December 12, 2006, marketwire.com/mw/

(258) Girl Scout Research Institute, 2002, mykidsafeinternet.com/internet-pornography-statistics.php

(259) London School of Economics, January 2002, Parents' Internet Monitoring Study, June 2005, Cox Communications

(260) Mitchell, K.J., Finkelhor, and D., Wolak, J., The Exposure of Youth to Unwanted Sexual Material on the Internet: A National Survey of Risk, Impact, and Prevention, Youth & Society, (34) 2003: 330-358,

Parents' Internet Monitoring: Study, June 2005, Cox Communications, cox.com/TakeCharge/includes/docs/results.pdf

(261) U.S. Customs Today, cbp.gov/xp/CustomsToday/2001/April/custoday_bluorchid.xml

(262) U.S. Customs Today, cbp.gov/xp/CustomsToday/2001/April/custoday_bluorchid.xml

(263) National Attitudinal Poll, Common Sense Media, June 7, 2006, a nonpartisan nonprofit dedicated to helping families improve their kids' media lives,commonsensemedia.org/news/press-releases.php?id=23

(264) Family, Friends & Community: Protecting Teens Online, Amanda Lenhart, March 17, 2005, Pew Internet & American Life Project, December 12, 2005, pewinternet.org/PPF/r/152/report_display.asp, mykidsafeinternet.com/internet-pornography-statistics.php, January 10, 2007

(265) cox.com/TakeCharge/includes/docs/results.pdf

(266) Cyveillance Study, March 1999, Donna Rice Hughes, protectkids.com/dangers/statsarchive.htm

(267) Parents' Internet Monitoring Study, June 2005, Cox Communications, cox.com/TakeCharge/includes/docs/results.pdf

(268) Cline, Pornography's Effects, 3-5, excerpted in part from Kids Online: Protecting Your Children In Cyberspace, by Donna Rice Hughes, Revell, September 1998, protectkids.com/effects/patternofaddiction.htm

(269) Victor B. Cline, Pornography and Sexual Addictions, Christian Counseling Today, no.4, 1996: 58, Cline, Pornography's Effects, 3-5, excerpted in part from Kids Online: Protecting Your Children In Cyberspace by Donna Rice Hughes, Revell, September 1998, protectkids.com/effects/patternofaddiction.htm

(270) Combating Pedophile Information Networks in Europe, March 2003, Det. Sgt. Paul Gillespie, Toronto Police Force, mykidsafeinternet.com/internet-pornography-statistics.php

(271) Donna Rice Hughes, protectkids.com/dangers/statsarchive.htm

(272) U.S. Customs Today, cbp.gov/xp/CustomsToday/2001/April/custoday_bluorchid.xml

(273) National Children's Homes report, mykidsafeinternet.com/internet-pornography-statistics.php

(274) Internet Sex Crimes Against Minors: The Response of Law Enforcement, Virginia, mykidsafeinternet.com/internet-pornography-statistics.php

(275) National Society for the Prevention of Cruelty to Children, 10/8/03, mykidsafeinternet.com/internet-pornography-statistics.php

(276) Red Herring Magazine, 1/18/02, My Kids Browser, mykidsbrowser.com/internet-pornography-statistics.php

(277) missingkids.com/missingkids/servlet/PageServlet?LanguageCountry=en_US&PageId=2451

(278) Wirthlin Survey, 2002, Parents' Internet Monitoring Study, June 2005, Cox Communications

(279) fcc.gov/cgb/consumerfacts/cipa.html

(280) Electronic Privacy Information Center, epic.org/free_speech/copa/tro_brief.html

(281) Federal Bureau of Investigation, fbi.gov

(282) Center for Sex Offender Management, csom.org/pubs/mythsfacts.html

(283) Dr. C. River Smith and Heidi J. Raynor, All About Counseling, online1998, allaboutcounseling.com

(284) Lieb, Quinsey, and Berliner, 1998

(285) Hall, 1995

(286) Hanson and Bussiere, 1998

(287) Psychology Today, psychologytoday.com/conditions/pedophilia.html

(288) University of Wisconsin, Board of Regentswhyfiles.org/154pedophile/2.html

(289) University of Wisconsin, Board of Regents, Paul Knuckman, a clinical psychologist, sex offender counselor at a Michigan prison, whyfiles.org/154pedophile/2.html

(290) Office of Legislative Research, Sandra Norman-Eady, Chief Attorney, February 21, 2006, 2006-R-0183, Castration Of Sex Offenders, legislative.library@cga.ct.gov, cga.ct.gov/2006/rpt/2006-R-0183.htm

(291) Fred Berlin-Lead, author of research, University of Wisconsin, Board of Regents, whyfiles.org/154pedophile/2.html

(292) Joyce F. Lakey, childresearch.net/RESOURCE/NEWS/1999/9903.HTM,

(293) Samuel Yochelson and Stanton Samenow, The Criminal Personality, criminology.fsu.edu/crimtheory/drafts/Yochelson_draft.doc

(294) Traditional Values Coalition, Diagnosis Statistical Manual, traditionalvalues.org

(295) Frank V. York and Robert H. Knight, Joe Woodward, Victims at Last, Alberta Report/Western Report, June 12, 1995, p. 28, Concerned Women for America, Homosexual Behavior & Pedophilia us2000.org/cfmc/Pedophilia.pdf

(296) Hilary White, LifeSiteNews.com, lifesite.net/ldn/2006/may/06053005.html

(297) Ken Wooden, parenting.ivillage.com/gs/gssafety/0,,qvv1,00.html

(298) Victims of Violence, victimsofviolence.on.ca/research322.html

(299) Federal Bureau of Investigationlosangeles.fbi.gov/pressrel/2006/la072606.htm

(300) WAA-Portions © Child Lures Prevention, and © Wikipedia, section21.m6.net/prf-activism.php

(301) FBI reports, National Institute for Mental Health, National Alert Registry, registeredoffenderslist.org/blog/sex-offenders/child-molestation-statistics/

(302) Bureau of Justice Statistics, February 1997, ojp.usdoj.gov/bjs/pub/pdf/soo.pdf

(303) rpc.senate.gov/_files/L49HR4427ChldprotBB072006.pdf

(304) 1 H. Rept. 109-218, at 22, 2 H. Rept. 109-218, at 22, 3 H. Rept. 109-218, at 22, 4 H. Rept., at 23, citing U.S. Dept. of Justice Office of Justice Programs—Bureau of Justice Statistics, Recidivism of Sex

Offenders Released from Prison in 1994, Nov. 2003, ojp.usdoj.gov/bjs/pub/pdf/rsorp94, rpc.senate.gov/_files/L49HR4427ChldprotBB072006.pdf

(305) Janis Wolak, Kimberly Mitchell, and David Finkelhor in Internet Sex Crimes against Minors: The Response of Law Enforcement, Alexandria, Virginia

(306) National Council of Juvenile and Family Court Judges, ncjfcj.org/content/blogcategory/84/111/

(307) Personal Interview, Lt. S. Kilgore, Paulding County, Georgia Sheriff's Department, December 5, 2007

(308) Mandated Reporters, Revised Edition September 2006, state.il.us/DCFS/docs/MANDATED2002.pdf

(309) Dale L. Koons, I.L.E.A. Certified Instructor in: Domestic Violence, Sexual Assault and Child Abuse, Court Certified Expert: Dynamics of Family Violence, Sexual Assault, Child Abuse, and Child Interviewing Techniques, members.iquest.net/~dkoons/technique.html

(310) Personal Interview, 12/5/07, Assistant District Attorney, Paulding County, Georgia

(311) fairness4families.org/Updates/sex_offender_legislation/Brief_Summary.html

(312) National Council of Juvenile and Family Court Judges, ncjfcj.org/content/blogcategory/84/111/

(313) David M. Heger, National Violence Against Women Prevention Research Center University of Missouri-St. Louis, Political Analyst, nvaw.org/policy/fedoffender.shtml

(314) Federal and International Law, amber-net.org/amberstatutes.htm

(315) International AMBER Alert, amber-net.org/amberstatutes.htm

(316) Reprinted with permission of the Center for Early Education and Development (CEED), College of Education and Human Development, University of Minnesota, 40 Education Sciences Building, 56 East River Road, Minneapolis, Minnesota, 55455-0223; phone: 612-625-2898; fax: 612-625-6619; e-mail: ceed@umn.edu, website:, W. Anthony Donohue, Ph.D., cehd.umn.edu/ceed/publications/briefsandreports/factfind/ff1989a.htm

(317) The Center for Behavioral Intervention in Beaverton, Oregon, also from the Colorado Bureau of Investigation's: Convicted Sex Offender Website, Author's personal experience in Sex Offender Treatment, beachildshero.com/abusetalk.htm

(318) Child & Family Canada, cfc-efc.ca/docs/vocfc/00000069.htm

(319) Barbara P. Homeier, MD, Preventing Abductions, Health Media Fellow, KidsHealth, Nemours Center for Children's Health Media, Alfred I. DuPont Hospital for Children, Wilmington, E., kidshealth.org/parent/positive/talk/abductions.html

(320) CoolNurse, coolnurse.com/date_rape.htm

(321) Kansas State University Women's Center, k-state.edu/womenscenter/Violencework

(322) Kenneth A. Hanfland, Robert D. Keppel, Joseph G. Weis, Case Management for Missing Children Homicide Investigation: Executive Summary. Olympia, Washington: Office of the Attorney General State of Washington and U.S. Department of Justice's Office of Juvenile Justice and Delinquency Prevention, May 1997, page 4, Case Management for Missing Children Homicide Investigation: findthekids.com/pdf/casemanag.pdf

(323) Professionals working with children, educators, LLDs, Child Psychologists, Crimes Against Children Officials, Department of Juvenile Justice Employee Trainers, Child Sexual Abuse Prevention Programmers, 1990-2007

(324) American Psychological Association, PsycNET 2001, Much of the information in this chapter is credited to Lloyd deMause, whose work is used in most college courses in psychohistory. For more information and to download all of his articles and books containing material on the sexual abuse of children visit his website psychohistory.com/

(325) Hubbard, 2003; p.79, wikipedia.org/wiki/Pederasty

(326) Lloyd deMause, The History of Child Abuse, psychohistory.com/

(327) Plato, Phaedrus; passim, Bruce L. Gerig, Homosexuality in the Ancient Near East, Beyond Egypt, In Homosexuality and The Bible, Supplement 11A, 2005 Plato, Phaedrus; Passim, en.wikipedia.org/wiki/Pederasty

(328) Hein van Dolen, Greek homosexuality, en.wikipedia.org/wiki/Pederasty

(329) Janet Afary & Kevin Anderson, Foucault and the Iranian Revolution: Gender and the Seductions of Islamism, University of Chicago Press, 2005, en.wikipedia.org/wiki/Pederasty

(330) Marshall Hodgson, The Venture of Islam, Chicago and London, 1974; 2:146, en.wikipedia.org/wiki/Pederasty

(331) en.wikipedia.org/wiki/Pederasty

(332) Childs,1980, p.6, en.wikipedia.org/wiki/Pederasty

(333) Holmberg, Langsdorff, Billing, Choris, Lisiansky and Marchand, en.wikipedia.org/wiki/Pederasty

(334) Bancroft, i.415 and authorities Palon, Crespi, Boscana, Motras, Torquemada, Duflot, and Fages. R. F. Burton, Terminal Essay, en.wikipedia.org/wiki/Pederasty

(335) J.G. von Hahn, Albanische Studien, 1854, p.166, en.wikipedia.org/wiki/Pederasty

(336) Proschan, Frank Syphilis, Opiomania, and Pederasty: Colonial, Constructions of Vietnamese and French Social Diseases' Journal of the History of Sexuality — Volume 11, Number 4, October 2002, pp. 610–636, en.wikipedia.org/wiki/Pederasty

(337) colorq.org/Articles/article.aspx?d=2004&x=ssmarriage, en.wikipedia.org/wiki/Pederasty

(338) Clement of Alexandria, Exhortation to the Greeks 2.28P, en.wikipedia.org/wiki/Pederasty

(339) Edward Gibbon, Decline and Fall of the Roman Empire, footnote on p. 76, vol. 1, en.wikipedia.org/wiki/pederast

CPSIA information can be obtained at www.ICGtesting.com
Printed in the USA
LVOW022248131011

250273LV00001B/3/P

9 780983 491026